Temporality and Film Analysis

Temporality and Film Analysis

Matilda Mroz

EDINBURGH
University Press

© Matilda Mroz, 2012, 2013

First published in hardback in 2012 by
Edinburgh University Press Ltd
22 George Square, Edinburgh EH8 9LF
www.euppublishing.com

This paperback edition 2013

Typeset in Monotype Ehrhardt by
Servis Filmsetting Ltd, Stockport, Cheshire

A CIP record for this book is available from the British Library

ISBN 978 0 7486 4346 2 (hardback)
ISBN 978 0 7486 8591 2 (paperback)
ISBN 978 0 7486 4347 9 (webready PDF)
ISBN 978 0 7486 6843 4 (epub)

The right of Matilda Mroz
to be identified as author of this work
has been asserted in accordance with
the Copyright, Designs and Patents Act 1988.

Contents

Acknowledgements vi

   Introduction 1
      Duration and Rhythm 2
      Resonance and Uncertainty 4
      Affect 5
      Sense and Texture 7
      L'Avventura, Mirror, Decalogue 8
1 Time, in Theory 13
      Moments in Film Theory 13
      Sensory and Affective Moments 24
      Moments and Duration 34
2 *L'Avventura*: Temporal Adventures 49
      Depth and Movement 53
      Looking and Imaging 62
      Temporalised Space 69
      Pace and Rhythm 76
      L'Avventura Today 82
3 *Mirror*: Traces and Transfiguration 90
      Time and the Long-take 92
      Memory and Narration 99
      Reflections on the Camera 104
      Texture and the Senses 107
      Aesthetic Transfiguration 111
      Audiophilia 121
      Mirrors and Crystals 125
4 Signs and Meaning in the *Decalogue* 137
      Significance: Omens, Objects and Patterns 140
      Temporality, Narrative, and Affect 168

   Epilogue 188

Bibliography 192
Index 201

Acknowledgements

This book has benefited from the wisdom of a number of people. David Trotter and Emma Wilson have been sources of inspiration from the very beginning of this project, as well as providing an extraordinary level of support at every stage. I am very grateful for their kindness, generosity and brilliance. Catherine Grant has never hesitated to offer encouragement and excellent suggestions, which I have greatly appreciated. I am grateful to all the people who have contributed to the book's development by reading extracts and offering their thoughts, including Zyg Baranski, Piotr Cieplak, Ewa Mazierska, Hannah Mowat, Alex Naylor, and David Sorfa. Several institutions provided financial support and a stimulating environment in which this project could take shape: Trinity College, Cambridge (with particular thanks to Joel Cabrita), The Cambridge Commonwealth Trust, Darwin College, Cambridge, The British Academy (for their generous award of a Postdoctoral Fellowship), the Faculty of English and the Department of Slavonic Studies at the University of Cambridge (with particular thanks to Emma Widdis and Simon Franklin), and the Warsaw Filmoteka. My colleagues within these institutions have provided me with invaluable opportunities and I remain in their debt. I am very grateful to my colleagues at the University of Greenwich, who have been nothing but patient, understanding and generous during the final stages of writing. I would like to thank Edinburgh University Press, particularly Gillian Leslie. Finally, I would like to thank David Woodman and my family in Australia, Kenya and Poland, for their continual encouragement and kindness. This book is dedicated to my parents, Grace and Peter Mroz, who have provided constant and invaluable support, advice and, when I needed it, diversion.

Introduction

Film theory, revolving as it does around a time-based medium, might be seen to be eminently suited to the development of discussion around temporal flow and change in relation to its particular objects. Temporality has consistently posed problems for critical theory, however. As Elizabeth Grosz has written,

> time is perhaps the most enigmatic, the most paradoxical, elusive and 'unreal' of any form of material existence . . . time is neither fully 'present', a thing in itself, nor is it a pure abstraction, a metaphysical assumption that can be ignored in everyday practice.[1]

Overwhelming us with its 'pervasive force', she continues, 'we prefer that it evaporates into what we can comprehend or more directly control', into, that is, discrete units of analysis that can be compared to one another, like shots on a film strip. According to Sarah Cardwell, dominant paradigms in film theory have in the past excluded temporal matters from discussion:

> the predominance of semiotics and the related notion of film as a 'language' or representational system comparable with that of verbal language guided scholars away from phenomenological and ontological questions (such as those concerning film's unique 'temporality') that are considered 'medium specific' or 'medium essentialist.'[2]

Although semiotic theories of cinema are no longer dominant, temporality continues to be a problematic area of film theory. As I outline in Chapter 1, 'Time, in Theory', writing on film has frequently privileged particular moments that can be extracted from the flow of a film's time; the temporal continuum of film emerges in much film analysis, explicitly or implicitly, as a threatening force. At times, film theory discusses cinematic images as though they were static and still, placed side by side in a series.

John Mullarkey has written that 'if film has a power . . . it is not by mirroring something static, but by being a part of something moving'.[3] This book aims to delineate a film analysis that will consider *both* moments in cinema which are significant for the purposes of criticism, and the way in which such moments might interrelate in temporal flux. Movement and fluidity is traced in three close viewings of specific films: Michelangelo Antonioni's *L'Avventura* (1960), Andrei Tarkovsky's *Mirror* (1975), and the ten short films that make up Krzysztof Kieślowski's *Decalogue* series (1988–9).[4] Rather than an overarching framework that dictates what temporality in film analysis should do, each of these films has guided particular conceptualisations of a variety of ways in which time can be configured in relation to film analysis. Nevertheless, several concepts have emerged that, to various degrees, inform the analyses that follow: duration and rhythm, resonance and uncertainty, affect, sense and texture. I outline their significance for my analysis in this Introduction, saving more detailed discussion for Chapter 1.

Duration and Rhythm

There are many different ways to think about temporality in cinema. Mary-Ann Doane has distinguished between several types of filmic time. There is the 'temporality of the apparatus itself – linear, irreversible, mechanical'.[5] There is also 'the temporality of the diegesis, the way in which time is represented by the image, the varying invocations of present, past, future, historicity'. 'And finally', Doane continues, 'there is the temporality of reception', in which we are encouraged to 'honor the relentless temporality of the apparatus.'[6] Within these distinctions, however, we can find more categories and more complexities. DVD and video can be used to halt or reverse the linearity of a film, shattering the ideal of a unified temporality of reception. Memory, too, affects the temporality of reception as viewers respond to images partly through interweaving their own past experiences with the viewing present. Films can contest the irreversibility of time through flashbacks or temporal disjunctions.[7] Diegetic temporality can be further analysed according to its varying temporal rhythms, created through editing patterns and camera movements.

An interest in temporal flux perhaps leads one inevitably towards Bergsonian thought, as articulated by Bergson himself, and taken up by contemporary writers such as Gilles Deleuze and Grosz. Bergson argued that duration, real time as it is lived, is not the same as clock time or calendar time. The latter is time presented as homogenous, spatialised, and measurable. As Yves Lomax writes, any talk of freezing or arresting the image assumes that the movement of time is made to continually stop at defined points that divide up the 'space' of, for example, a clock face.⁸ A vital aspect of duration in Bergson's thought is the distinction between differences in kind and differences in degree. Differences in kind are spatial differences such as distances between objects, and are more or less measurable. Differences in degree, however, which refer to psychic states, sensations and affects, cannot be simply measured or reduced in numerical terms. Our conscious states are not placed alongside one another spatially, but rather modulate through time, changing continuously through duration.⁹ Affective and psychical states are not like self-contained objects in space; they blend into one another in a process of transition. 'If we artificially arrest this indiscernible transition', writes Grosz, 'we can understand states as separate entities, linked by succession, but we lose whatever it is that flows in change, we lose duration itself.'¹⁰

For Bergson, duration is made up of variegated rhythms which interpenetrate in time rather than succeeding one another in space. Bergson frequently employed a musical analogy to explain duration. In *Time and Free Will*, for example, he discussed interpenetration in relation to 'the notes of a tune, melting, so to speak, into one another'.¹¹ In this book I argue that concepts surrounding duration can be useful for film analysis. In some sense, of course, cinematic time is subject to measure: a film, projected at the appropriate rate, lasts a measurable amount of time. A scene or a shot may last seconds or minutes. This kind of time is calculable. If, however, states of consciousness and affect are in a continual process of fusion and interpenetration, like the notes of a melody, if duration is made up of variegated rhythms, then we can also see the passing of time in film as made up interpenetrating processes and a multiplicity of rhythms. As Donato Totaro has argued, the idea of interpenetration can inform a practical type of film analysis that considers 'how two formal qualities work together (interpenetrate) to affect narrative or thematic time'.¹² We can question, that is, how various temporal strands interweave in the duration of a film, such as a voice-over with an image, a long-take with a piece of music, or a thematic link with a sensory evocation. In *L'Avventura*, for example, the rhythm of the music frequently refuses to match the movements of the characters or of editing patterns, creating a dissonance that echoes particular disjunctions in the narrative. In *Mirror*, voice-overs have a fluid relationship with the images, at times seeming to reflect and comment upon what is in the frame, and at other moments seeming to be ignorant of the images, as though two temporal rhythms (of voice and image) were being interwoven.

Although I draw on Bergson at various points throughout this book, my intention is not to apply Bergsonian thought to cinema, nor to present a philosophical explication of temporality and duration. Rather, I see Bergson's theories and their interpretation by contemporary writers as a way to engage with questions of filmic temporality when analysing specific films. What I take from Bergson is a particular formulation of time that I believe has resonance with the passing of time in cinema. As Totaro has argued, Bergsonian duration may be a useful tool for a film analysis that is interested in tracing the 'multiple temporal dimensions' of film, regardless of whether one accepts all tenets of Bergson's philosophy. Rather than engaging philosophically with Bergsonian thought concerning matter and image, the intellect and intuition, in this study I limit myself to particular ideas arising from the concept of duration that can productively be put into dialogue with the films I analyse.

Resonance and Uncertainty

The films under discussion can be seen as canonical works of the 'art' cinema, and have attracted particular configurations of meaning and symbolism, as well as particular descriptions of their aesthetic elements, such as framing, mise-en-scène, cinematography and editing. *L'Avventura*'s images, for example, are consistently described as static, fixed compositions that can be decoded to uncover the meanings that Antonioni intended, through a detached and distanced viewing process. The film's compositions are frequently examined in a way that lifts film frames from temporal duration. By contrast, critical writing on *Mirror* highlights the presence of a sensory intimacy and the passing of time through the long-take. Both of these aspects, however, tend to be discussed as a religious or spiritual experience, evoking the transcendent, which moves away from texture and time per se. Interpretations of the *Decalogue* series have focused upon symbolism and the relationship between the Ten Commandments, which inspired the series, and the individual films. While these are hardly invalid interpretations, they tend to be repeated rather than reworked and redeveloped. By utilising ideas around temporality, I hope to reinvigorate the customary critical profiles of these works. My analyses present particular conjunctions of meaning and uncertainty or indeterminacy around each film, arguing that the operation of temporality in cinema can put meaning into flux, unsettling the theoretical frameworks that we may want to attach to them. Meaning in cinema is not fixed but is continually in a process of development, change and dissolution. My analyses aim to be attentive to the ways in which meaning may develop through time, and to those stretches of time which evoke uncertainty rather than significance.

In *Cinema and Modernism*, David Trotter asks the following question:

'does cinema . . . deal in *meanings* at all'? He continues, 'Deborah Thomas remarks of a detail of décor in a scene in Capra's *It's a Wonderful Life* (1945) that although the detail does not "mean" or "symbolise" anything, it *resonates*.'[13] My analyses of the films attempt to draw out moments of resonance, moments that pulsate with a significance that nevertheless remains opaque. Trotter has suggested the existence of a 'hermeneutic threshold' that viewers may be unable to cross over into definite meaning or symbolization.[14] There are images, moments and events that we may fail to press into the service of meaning, moments where meaning is resisted, even as interpretation seems to be encouraged. In relation to the films of D. W. Griffith, Trotter writes, 'might there not be a sense generated by or in the photographic image which yet falls short of intelligibility?' – a 'surplus intensity . . . by which we are made to see, not meaning and value, but their opposite, or limit'.[15] At the other end of the spectrum of the 'addiction' to meaning, is, writes Trotter, 'a counter-narrative' which is concerned with material presence that is not reducible to meaning, or which is not 'used up in meaning'.[16] The continuum between tangibility and meaning emerges most clearly in relation to the *Decalogue* series, which continually encourages us to read its objects and events as signs of something 'other', while ultimately remaining indeterminate and mute, stubbornly material rather than strictly legible.

Affect

The idea of resonance dovetails with the concept of affect. As Brian Massumi writes, affect is intensity, something that moves beyond meaning, indeed, something that disrupts it. Affective sounds, moments or images suspend linear temporality and do not necessarily fit into narrative progression; affect is what might be called 'passion', 'incipient action and expression'.[17] This intensity of affect is a 'state of suspense, potentially of disruption'.[18] According to Massumi, affect 'escapes confinement' in 'formed, qualified, situated perceptions and cognitions'.[19] Massumi's writing on affect is suggestive for the films under discussion in this book, which frequently elide explanatory narrative development, while resonating with uncertain and often unlocalisable intensities.

In art, affect can refer to the effect of language, objects or images on the viewer or reader. Affects are liberated from organising systems of representation, such that, as Claire Colebrook writes, a poem can create the affect of 'fear' without 'an object feared, a reason, or a person who is afraid'.[20] Colebrook explains that intensities are not just particular qualities, such as redness, 'they are the becoming of qualities: say, the burning and wavering infra-red light that we eventually *see* as red'.[21] She continues that, in the influential writings of Deleuze,

> it is precisely because cinema composes images through time that it can present affects and intensities. It can disjoin the usual sequence of images – our usually ordered world with its expected flow of events – and allow us to perceive affects without their standard order and meaning.[22]

My discussion of *L'Avventura, Mirror* and the *Decalogue* series highlight the ways in which affect is disengaged from the customary constraints of spatial coherence and temporal chronology. This may occur in moments where the camera moves away from diegetic characters and associations with human perception, to itself perform movements through time and space. These are moments when attention is no longer focused on what functions specifically for the narrative, but on images and objects that instead may resonate with affective force.

The consistent emphasis upon affect's temporal dimension makes writing on affect particularly relevant to my study. As Massumi has written, while affect can be seen to be in some sense 'punctual', even described as a moment of shock, 'it is also continuous, like a background perception that accompanie[s] every event, however quotidian'.[23] As Siegworth and Gregg write, 'affect arises in the midst of *in-between-ness* . . . affect is an impingement or extrusion of a momentary or sometimes more sustained state of relation *as well as* the passage (and the duration of passage) of forces or intensities'.[24] Registering affect is a matter of registering intensities that have a temporal progression, an 'incremental shimmer'. Affect is fundamentally related to flux and change, a 'process underway, not position taken'.[25] Between-ness emerges as an important idea in my analysis of the *Decalogue* in particular. Critical writing on the *Decalogue* tends to attribute symbolic attachments to particular images. While I discuss the possible operations of symbolism, my interest also lies in bringing out those moments *in between* those that seem to be significant for the narrative, symbolically meaningful, or part of a system of repetitions and variations: that is, those moments which do not seem particularly concerned with meaning at all, or which escape definite meanings, but are, instead, affective.

According to Siegworth and Gregg, 'there is no single, generalizable theory of affect', but rather 'infinitely multiple iterations' that are as diverse as 'their own highly practical encounters with bodies, affects, words'.[26] This does not mean that we are thus thrust into some kind of 'conceptual free-fall', as Siegworth and Gregg put it, but it does blend and blur easy compartmentalisms.[27] Writing on affect provides an important vocabulary to talk about moments which are intense without necessarily being significant to narrative and theme, or constitutive of identification with characters. The idea of affect aids us in identifying and describing moments that resonate with a force that cannot necessarily be defined. Throughout this book, I suggest that affective responses can be evoked through the aesthetic processes of the films, through cinematic imaging. I use the term imag*ing* to imply a process and duration of development.

Sense and Texture

After what Massumi has referred to as the 'waning of grand narratives', there is a growing feeling in media and art theory that the senses are central to an understanding of our culture.[28] As semiotic and psychoanalytic theories of cinema have come to be seen as inadequate to expressing its powerfully affective nature, the question of how to write about experiences of viewing film has gained increasing relevance. Corporeal responses to cinema are gathering more and more theoretical force. Rather than seeing film viewers as passive receptacles of the illusory ideologies of a dominant apparatus, contemporary theorists are increasingly emphasising the importance of explaining how the viewer can have 'real' sensual and affective responses, how, as Vivian Sobchack writes, 'It is possible for human bodies to be, in fact, really "touched" and "moved" by the movies.'[29] In Sobchack's argument, theoretical writing in the past propagated a gap between 'our actual experience of the cinema and the theory that we academic film scholars construct to explain it – or perhaps, more aptly, to explain it away'.[30] One of the ways to remedy this seems to be to ground theoretical writing in the sensual responses of the theorist. Sobchack's avowed project in *Carnal Thoughts*, for example, is to ground her analysis 'in the flesh', or rather, 'in *my* flesh'.[31]

One of the most influential concepts that have emerged out of this recent focus on sensory viewing has been Laura Marks's distinction between optic and haptic images, drawing upon the work of art historian Alois Riegl.[32] According to Riegl, optical images historically arose from the distinction of figure from ground, making possible the illusion of space and the identification of figures not as concrete elements on a surface but as figures in space. Optical perception thus privileges the representational power of the image, allowing the spectator to organise themselves as a masterful subject. Haptic perception, by contrast, privileges material presence in a variety of ways. It may, for example, offer a close-up image that resolves itself into figuration slowly, if at all; or direct 'grazing' camera movements over the surface of an image; or generate an image of such detail that 'it evades a distanced view, instead pulling the viewer in close'.[33] In a mode of looking Marks terms haptic visuality, 'the eyes themselves function like organs of touch'.[34]

In Chapter 1, I identify a spectrum of theoretical thought relating to embodied viewing and the sensory appeal of cinema, as well as some questions that arise concerning film's temporal development. In my own analyses, I draw upon such concepts where they seem to be most useful, and also point out the areas where they may fall short when examining particular films. This approach is developed most in Chapter 3, on *Mirror*, where sensory immersion is to some extent presented as one of the film's themes, that is, as thematised. My analyses aim to be sensitive to the ways in which cinema can evoke powerful physical responses, and to how film images can resonate with materiality and hapticity, with texture and tactility. However, I also suggest that it is important to consider the wider temporal context in which such responses might be seen to arise. The way in which the sensory and touch is thematised in a film, brought to our attention through the actions of particular characters or even through camera movements, may in fact encourage viewers to become more receptive to haptic apprehension. Both *L'Avventura* and *Mirror* present particular ways of looking and experiencing the natural and built environment, through points-of-view and camera movements that depart from points-of-view, that may come to resonate with sensory experiences of the films. A Bergsonian notion relating to the interpenetration of psychical states may tell us something about the process of film viewing also. Film theory frequently divorces sensual apprehension and intellectual comprehension, as I outline in Chapter 1. In the duration of film viewing, however, we can argue that sense and thought intertwine.

L'Avventura, Mirror, Decalogue

Lesley Stern and George Kouvaros have extolled the benefits of description in film analysis; description aims to 'bring the film into imaginative being for the reader, so that she views it in the process of reading', as well as to offer 'persuasive interpretation based on attentiveness to the object, on detailed and accurate rendition'.[35] In the following chapters, descriptions of cinematic sequences aim to convey something of the temporal transformations of the films. In each analysis, certain sequences may be discussed more than once, to allow as many critical contexts and affective possibilities to resonate through them. I have also drawn upon a range of theoretical writing on cinema (and sometimes on art more generally). A variety of theoretical voices can be used to illuminate or emphasise particular aspects of the films that may not have had as much critical exposure as others. I agree with Mullarkey's opinion that 'it is the messiness of film, its resistance to singular theory, that makes it theoretically interesting'. Extolling a multi-critical and theoretical approach to cinema, he valorises the benefits of creating a 'montage of theories that refract each other simply by their being co-presented', a somewhat cinematic process of stitching together.[36] Having said this, my close focus upon time and the formal aspects of the films means that other contexts, such as the historical processes of producing and distributing the films, and their reception in their respective countries and internationally, are not as privileged. I trust, however, that these aspects have been well documented elsewhere.[37]

I hope that by placing the films side by side, they can be used to reflect on each other. The Epilogue to this book outlines more specifically how aspects of *L'Avventura*, *Mirror* and the *Decalogue* series can be seen to interrelate. In each analysis, temporality emerges in different ways. In Chapter 2, '*L'Avventura*: Temporal Adventures', I examine how the film presents a temporalised space thematically, as well as how landscapes shown in depth encourage a temporalised process of viewing. Depth in the film emerges as an aesthetic strategy, as well as thematising a particular process of disappearing into an unknowable space, which is the fate of *L'Avventura*'s Anna. The presentation of images in duration, in their modulation between depth and surface, destabilises efforts to abstract them from temporal flow. The film tends to extend those moments when the characters are performing everyday actions or have left the frame altogether, moments that have been termed 'temps morte' or dead times. I explore how these moments slow the pace of the film and contribute to its lingering rhythms. Contrary to what the term 'temps morte' may suggest, I argue that such moments encourage us to attend to the fluctuation of the images that pass before us, in a process of aesthetic pleasure.

Like *L'Avventura*, *Mirror* encourages a fascination with its own process of cinematic imaging, highlighted through camera movements, filters and disjunctive editing. Its movements through a series of episodes linked together through rhythm, thematic association, and patterning, reduces the importance of narrative and draws awareness to a heterogeneous temporality. As the film's narrator expresses his desire to re-enter the memories or dreams of his childhood, *Mirror* makes clear the fragility and creativity of memory, which can never access a 'pure' past. Temporality destabilises the corporeal and gives it an ephemeral dimension that is nevertheless powerfully affective. Chapter 3, '*Mirror*: Traces and Transfigurations', considers how a conceptualisation of time can be undertaken through the long-take and through editing. Montage sequences within the film, in which archival footage is edited together, tends to present a notion of time as a series of perceptual shocks; the long-take, on the other hand, evokes a thematic awareness of nostalgia while questioning the irretrievability of the past.

Chapter 4, 'Signs and Meaning in the *Decalogue*' engages more directly with questions of meaning, in relation to Kieślowski's *Decalogue* series. The series has encouraged a kind of exegesis, whereby critics attempt to ascertain the relationship between the films and the Commandments, but there are also larger questions at stake. A recurring concern that critics have found throughout Kieślowski's work, and in the *Decalogue* specifically, has been the question of whether there is a higher power coordinating our lives, or whether events are random and occur by chance. This is a question that I see as relevant as much for an analysis of the films as for the diegetic characters. The films, I argue, continually suggest the presence of an ordered system of meaning, through omens, significant objects, and patterns, while ultimately deferring a full explication of significance. Disjunctive chronologies and the slow unfolding of the films continually resist attempts to fasten meaning onto their images, resonating instead with uncertainty and indeterminacy.

In Chapter 1, I briefly outline how the momentary came to be privileged in writing about film, and how film moments have been configured in different ways, including in the discourses of photogenie and cinephilia. These latter are of particular interest to me because of their attempts to delineate the affective nature of film viewing, although the terminology that we associate with affect today is not used. I then turn to explore in more detail some of the concepts that I use in my analyses: sensation, affect, and duration.

Cinema's relationship to time is complex not only because of its temporal unfoldings – of narrative, theme, pattern – but also because of the multiple temporalities of film viewing and attendant possibilities, where each screening for each individual is unique. In every viewing, as Mullarkey has written, 'something new emerges: the film is seen at a different temporality, one belonging partly to it but also to the repetition imposed on it by reviewing and our own speeds of reception'.[38] Viewers can, for example, become accustomed to slowness in cinema such that films like *L'Avventura* seem relatively fast-paced. If in duration, 'each new moment is qualitatively different from the last', the same could be said of each screening.[39] In this book I can only offer my own analysis of the operation of temporality in particular films, which inevitably draws on my own viewing contexts and expectations. Nevertheless, I hope that tracing time through the narratives, images, and affects of the films in this book will add something new to our discussion of them.

Notes

1. Elizabeth Grosz, *The Nick of Time* (Durham and London: Duke University Press, 2004), pp. 4–5.
2. Sarah Cardwell, 'About Time: Theorising Adaptation, Temporality, and Tense', *Literature Film Quarterly* (2003), http://www.redorbit.com/news/science/6467/about_time_theorizing_adaptat n tsh.ndard order and mean ing.'lion_temporality_and_tense/.
3. John Mullarkey, *Philosophy and the Moving Image: Refractions of Reality* (Basingstoke: Palgrave Macmillan, 2010), p. xvii.
4. *L'Avventura*, film, directed by Michelangelo Antonioni. Italy/France: Cino del Duca Produzioni, 1960. *Mirror*, film, directed by Andrei Tarkovsky. USSR: Mosfilm, 1975. *Decalogue*, film/TV series, directed by Krzysztof Kieślowski. Poland: Zespół Filmowy Tor, 1989.
5. Mary Ann Doane, *The Emergence of Cinematic Time* (Cambridge: Harvard University Press, 2002), p. 30.
6. Ibid., p. 30.
7. Ibid., p. 30.
8. Yves Lomax, 'Thinking Stillness', in David Green and Joanna Lowry (eds), *Stillness and Time: Photography and the Moving Image* (Brighton: Photoworks, 2006), p. 56.
9. Grosz, *Nick of Time*, pp. 158–9.
10. Ibid., p. 195.
11. Henri Bergson, 'The Idea of Duration', in Keith Ansell Pearson and John Mullarkey (eds), *Henri Bergson: Key Writings* (New York and London: Continuum, 2005), p. 60.
12. Donato Totaro, 'Time, Bergson, and the Cinematographical Mechanism', *Offscreen* (11 January 2001), http://www.horschamp.qc.ca/new_offscreen/Bergson_film.html
13. David Trotter, *Cinema and Modernism* (Malden and Oxford: Blackwell, 2007), p. 61.
14. Ibid., p. 55.
15. Ibid., p. 51.
16. Ibid., pp. 62 and 66.
17. Brian Massumi, *Parables for the Virtual: Movement, Affect, Sensation* (Durham: Duke University Press, 2002), p. 30.
18. Ibid., p. 26.
19. Ibid., p. 35.
20. Claire Colebrook, *Gilles Deleuze* (London: Routledge, 2002), pp. 22–3.
21. Ibid., p. 39.
22. Ibid., p. 39.

23. Massumi, *Parables for the Virtual*, p. 36.
24. Melissa Gregg and Gregory J. Seigworth, 'An Inventory of Shimmers', Gregg and Seigworth (eds), *The Affect Theory Reader* (Durham and London: Duke University Press, 2010), p. 1.
25. Ibid., p. 11.
26. Ibid., p. 4.
27. Ibid., p. 4.
28. Massumi, p. 27.
29. Vivian Sobchack, *Carnal Thoughts* (Berkeley: University of California Press, 2004), p. 59.
30. Ibid., p. 53.
31. Ibid., p. 61.
32. Laura U. Marks, *The Skin of the Film* (Durham: Duke University Press, 2000), pp. 162–4.
33. Ibid., p. 163.
34. Ibid., p. 162.
35. Lesley Stern and George Kouvaros, 'Descriptive Acts: Introduction', in Lesley Stern and George Kouvaros (eds), *Falling For You: Essays on Cinema and Performance* (Sydney: Power Publications, 1999), p. 9.
36. Mullarkey, *Moving Image*, p. 207.
37. For more socio-historical readings, I would direct the reader to the following: Geoffrey Nowell-Smith, *L'Avventura* (London: BFI Publishing, 1997), Natasha Synessios, *Mirror* (London: I. B. Tauris, 2001), and Marek Haltof, *The Cinema of Krzysztof Kieślowski: Variations of Destiny and Chance* (London and New York: Wallflower Press, 2004).
38. Mullarkey, *Moving Image*, p. 170.
39. John Mullarkey, *Bergson and Philosophy* (Notre Dame: University of Notre Dame Press, 2000), p. 9.

CHAPTER 1

Time, in Theory

The question of how best to conceptualise the cinematic medium has been an ever-present concern throughout the history of film criticism. Early film theory often struggled to express the powerful emotion that cinema provokes, revealing a fascination with its nature as at once corporeal and ephemeral, emanating materiality as well as ghostly traces. As Lesley Stern has written, the filmic capacity to render the phenomenal world, or to enact what Kracauer called 'a process of materialisation', was thought to be equalled only by the film's capacity to 'unhinge the solidity and materiality of things'.[1] This seemed to perpetuate an endless cycle of attempts at definition. The discourses of *photogénie* and cinephilia became based upon the overflow of writing that emerged from the attempts to comprehend the contradictory affects of the medium. The nature of cinematic time and movement was debated at length in early writing on film, but became less visible in psychoanalytic and semiotic theories of cinema. This chapter initially presents a selection of writing on film that reveals particular attitudes towards cinematic time; a selection that is admittedly brief and partial, but is intended to provide some indication of time's presence in film theory. I then consider the temporal configurations that emerge in theories of the senses and embodied viewing, before returning to the notion of duration.

Moments in Film Theory

The inception of cinema in the 1890s coincided approximately with the emergence of new ways of thinking about time. The development of capitalist modernity necessitated the institution of an absolute temporal precision, a rigorous temporality embodied in clock time and synchronised timetables. Doane has explained that time came to be seen as homogenous, uniform and divisible into measurable units. This development was accompanied by an 'unrelenting search for [time's] representation in visual terms' that exceeded the capacities of natural perception.[2] The rationalisation of time, argues Doane, 'generated epistemological and philosophical anxieties exemplified by the work of Henri Bergson, in his adamant reassertion of temporal continuity in the concept of durée'.[3] At the same time, modern temporality was increasingly seen as an overwhelming flow of disjunctive impressions, as 'assault, acceleration, speed'.[4] Doane has explained further that the advent of mechanical reproduction 'inaugurated a discursive thematics of excess and oversaturation that is still with us. The sheer quantity of images and sounds is perceived as the threat of overwhelming or suffocating the subject'.[5] Time was no longer thought of as a 'benign phenomena most easily grasped by the notion of flow', but was instead seen as a 'troublesome and anxiety-producing entity'.[6] The overpowering nature of temporal experience in modernity can clearly be seen in Georg Simmel's 1903 text, 'The Metropolis and Mental Life', in which he describes his experience of modern city life as 'the rapid crowding of changing images, the sharp discontinuity in the grasp of a single glance, and the unexpectedness of onrushing impressions'.[7]

Contemporary writers formulated anxieties around both this overwhelming flow of disjunctive perceptions and around rationalised time. The latter, according to Doane, was seen to restrict the 'vicissitudes of the affective' and the 'subjective play' of desire and pleasure.[8] From this context, the contingent moment emerged as something that escaped rationalisation, being 'beyond or resistant to meaning'.[9] At the beginning of the twentieth century, chance and contingency were assigned important ideological roles, appearing to offer a reservoir of 'free play' irreducible to 'systematic structuring'. Contingency 'proffers to the subject the appearance of absolute freedom, immediacy, directness'.[10] Such moments hold the promise of singularity and uniqueness: 'the wind blowing at [that] moment in a certain direction, a foot having landed in the mud at precisely this place, the camera's shutter opening at a given time'.[11] Contingency seemed to present a time that was unpredictable and heterogeneous, and thus harboured the possibility of newness and difference.[12]

Contingent moments also, however, carried with them a certain threat, an alliance with 'meaninglessness, even nonsense'.[13] Contingency was thus highly ambiguous, presenting on the one hand a freedom from rationalisation, and on the other a dangerous abyss of randomness. The threat of contingency seemed partially allayed if the contingent moment was made somehow graspable and representable. New technologies of representation were consistently allied with contingency and the ability to 'seize' the ephemeral. 'The significance of the cinema, in this context', writes Doane, 'lies in its apparent capacity to perfectly *represent* the contingent, to provide the pure record of time.'[14] Providing the possibility of recording any event, photographic media appeared to guarantee the representability of the contingencies of modernity.[15] As Rachel Moore writes, 'the nature of one's daily experience and labour was so fragmented and confounding that the camera, which could function in a likewise fragmented fashion, was a good tool for its representation'.[16] The indexical nature of the photographic process ensured its 'privileged relation to chance and the contingent, whose lure would be the escape from the grasp of rationalisation and its system'.[17] As a medium of indexicality that can create an imprint of a unique moment, cinema was allied with the contingent as a 'pure indication, pure assurance of existence'.[18]

In the early twentieth century, then, cinema seemed to offer the capacity to represent contingent moments and make them repeatable, to somehow 'fix' the ephemeral. In presenting time as continuous, however, cinema potentially threatened to plunge the film viewer back into an overpowering temporal continuum. In his famous article on mechanical reproduction, Walter Benjamin, for example, made a revealing distinction between painting and cinema. The still frame of the painting, according to Benjamin, invites the spectator to adopt a position of contemplative 'absorption' toward an always distant object. The cinema, on the other hand, was posited as an agent of distraction; the flux of the film was seen to overwhelm the spectator. As Benjamin writes, quoting Georges Duhamel: 'no sooner has [the viewer's] eye grasped a scene than it is already changed. It cannot be arrested ... "I can no longer think what I want to think. My thoughts have been replaced by moving images."'[19] As Michael Taussig has written, Benjamin thus distinguishes between an experience of contemplation provided by painting, and the distraction of cinema's temporal flow.[20] Distraction, as Taussig explains, 'refers to a very different apperceptive mode, the type of flitting and barely conscious peripheral-vision perception unleashed with great vigor by modern life'.[21]

Benjamin also assigned distinctly threatening properties to the particular *moments* of the overwhelming flow of the film. He reinterpreted contingent moments as shock or trauma that never reach the depths of consciousness or experience, which could confer a stable meaning upon them; they are thus 'unassimilable in experience'.[22] Through allying itself with montage, cinema epitomised the ability of mechanically reproduced art to enact shock: 'montage functions for Benjamin not so much to confer order or meaning but to rapidly accumulate and juxtapose contingencies'.[23] Given that the examples used in his theoretical formulations came from Dadaist cinema, it is unsurprising that Benjamin associated the moment of sensation with a certain violence, with the possibility that cinema can become 'an instrument of ballistics. It hit the spectator like a bullet, it happened to him, thus acquiring a tactile quality.' Cinema, wrote Benjamin, 'assail[s]' the spectator.[24]

The 'tactile quality' that Benjamin attributes to cinema can be seen in relation to classical modernism's tendency to conjoin the machinic and the corporeal or sensory. Classical modernism represented a shift from idealist theories of aesthetic experience to materialist ones, as well as forging an ever closer relationship between the sensual and the technological.[25] Modernism, writes Danius, was 'an index of a general gravitation toward a conception of aesthetic experience based in a notion of the immanence of the body, a body inhabited by temporality and therefore also finite'.[26] Several contemporary writers have focused on this haptic element of Benjamin's writing. Miriam Hansen has argued that while Benjamin's concept of shock may be synonymous with the distracted mode of experience in modernity, it also entails a tactile element that can be recuperated as an activation or reclaiming of collective experience.[27] Susan Buck-Morss similarly argues that Benjamin's use of the word 'aesthetics' stages a return to its sensual, pre-linguistic origin, stemming from the body.[28] According to her analysis, Benjamin demands that art undo the alienation of the corporeal sensorium, 'to *restore the instinctual power of the human bodily senses for the sake of humanity's self-preservation*, and to do this, not by avoiding the new technologies, but by *passing through* them'.[29] According to Taussig, there is a 'certain tactility growing out of distracted vision'.[30] Benjamin's argument that what the camera revealed was not an optical reproduction of reality but an 'optical unconscious', a reality unavailable to the naked eye, was founded upon a 'tactile optics'. According to Taussig, in Benjamin's formulation of film viewing, the optical can dissolve into touch, suggestive of a certain thickness and density in the revelation of the 'physiognomic aspect of visual worlds'.[31]

One can also point to a certain clustering of the moment or instant from a film with the corporeal, rather than strictly meaningful, in the writing of Jean Epstein. According to Malcolm Turvey, Epstein's description of the spectator's phenomenal experience of cinema differs in important respects from the production of the spectator as a 'transcendental subject': 'for Epstein the effects of camera mobility on the spectator are unambiguously located in the *corporeal* density of the spectator's body'.[32] The terms Epstein used to specify sensations describe the visceral impact of powerful forces acting on the body. The physical nature of sensation is a central component of his 'prototypical spectator's perceptual experience of the cinema'.[33] Epstein, Turvey continues, often equates cinema's intense pleasures with bodily penetration, comparing the affect of close-ups with 'needles' and 'a sort of need', as the body is pulled and pushed as a 'projectile'.[34] In contrast to a cinema of transcendence and ocularcentrism, Epstein 'attempts to propose and envisage for us a cinema of *immanence*': a cinema that is not above and beyond the physical world of matter and time, but embedded in it.[35] As Christian Keathley has also noted, Epstein envisaged a 'sensuous proximity' of the film to the world.[36]

The earliest films were themselves brief moments, extracted from the flow of time: a train arriving at a station, workers leaving a factory, a boat moving out to sea. As Tom Brown and James Walters write, 'in its earliest form, the cinema was a moment: the projection of a few seconds recorded and exhibited for audiences'.[37] As these lengthened and became more complex, early writing on film grasped moments, or brief series of moments, from the flow of a film's duration. Moments in film writing were linked frequently to an absence of, or perhaps freedom from, meaning or signification, aligned instead with something almost physical. The most privileged moment of cinema in early writing, that of the close-up, was, as Doane points out, allied with a 'possession, possessiveness, the desire to "get hold of an object"'.[38] For Epstein, 'the close-up modifies the drama by the impact of proximity. Pain is within reach. If I stretch out my arm I touch you, and that is intimacy . . . it's not even true that there is air between us; I consume it. It is in me like a sacrament.'[39] The discourse on the close-up, writes Doane, 'seems to exemplify a desire to stop the film, to grab hold of something that can be taken away, to transfer the relentless temporality of the narrative's unfolding to a more manageable temporality of contemplation'.[40] Writing about this moment appeared to allow the theorist to grasp something concrete from the flow of the film, to garner something from the unstoppable march of images.

A series of moments in a film could provoke an encounter with *photogénie*, a revelatory and emotive instant that expressed the specificity of cinema for several early film writers. *Photogénie* was not, however, a phenomenon of continuity. As Epstein writes, *photogénie* is measured in seconds:

> if it is too long, I don't find continuous pleasure in it. Intermittent paroxysms affect me like needles do. Until now, I have never seen an entire minute of *photogénie* . . . the photogenic is like a spark that appears in fits and starts.[41]

The close-up privileged by *photogénie* became an isolatable entity which 'can be taken and held within memory'.[42] Extracting a moment from a film seemed to offer the potential to allay the threat of an overpowering temporal continuum. Discourses of *photogénie* have been subject to some derision by film theorists. Willemen, for example, accuses early writers of mysticism and elitism. *Photogénie*, he argues, is mobilised as counter to 'film theory' proper and suggests that the 'insistence on a quasi-mystical concept of the cinematic experience as beyond verbal discourse resurfaces today as part of a campaign to . . . [free] film critics from the heavy burden of rationality'.[43] Willemen is adamant that moments of cinephilia and *photogénie* are not aesthetic experiences, but rather psychological ones. As Keathley writes, Willemen 'not only rejects the idea that cinephilic moments can be equated with aesthetic experiences but also argues that they are specifically opposed to them'.[44]

To accuse the descriptions of *photogénie* as neglecting the aesthetic, however, is rather unsatisfactory. The endless debates on what constitutes 'cinematic specificity' can be seen as an expression of a desire to isolate precisely the aesthetic dimensions of film. While early theorists differed on what constituted the essence of cinema, the common point of agreement, as Robert Stam makes clear, was that cinema was an art.[45] What is often valorised in early theory is an aesthetic emotion emerging from, or a fascination with, cinematic technique itself. As Richard Abel has written, the early French critics who propagated *photogénie* engaged with a spectrum of *aesthetic* positions.[46] The 'lure of rhythmic specificity led to a fascination with technique for its own sake'.[47] A consistent link between the aesthetic and the emotional was also made: Germaine Dulac, for example, argued that cinema 'must try to find its emotion through the artistic movement of lines and forms'.[48] Marcel Gromaire also proposed that 'moving form' is the 'essential logic' of the film, provoking an 'aesthetic emotion'.[49]

The moment of *photogénie*, and other revelatory moments delineated by early film theorists, was often thought of as one that transforms the objects on screen. As Abel writes, *photogénie*, as the term was initially used by Louis Delluc, assumed that the 'real' was the basis of film representation, but also that it was transformed by the camera and screen, 'which, without eliminating that "realness", changed it into something radically new'.[50] *Photogénie* described the effect of making spectators see ordinary things as they had never been seen before. As Louis Aragon wrote, for example, 'on the screen, objects that were a few moments ago sticks of furniture or books of cloakroom tickets are transformed to the point where they take on menacing or enigmatic meanings'.[51] Similarly, Fernand Leger claimed that 'the cinematographic revolution is *to make us see everything that has been merely noticed*': project an object on screen and the audience reacts as though they had 'discovered' the object.[52] According to Jean Cocteau, we believe that we are seeing objects on the screen 'for the first time'.[53]

The still photograph was what Doane has called the 'crucial substrate' and the historical condition for the emergence of cinematic time.[54] The cinema, as Doane writes, is in many ways indebted to the nineteenth-century drive to fragment and analyse time and movement: 'the logic of photography inevitably inhabits that of cinema. The photographic instant becomes the basis for the representability of time.'[55] A valorisation of the momentary in *photogénie* should not, however, be confused with a glorification of the *static* photographic image. One of the ways in which the cinematic transformation of objects was seen to occur was through the quality of *movement*. Cinema was often specifically contrasted to the relatively more 'static' arts of sculpture and painting, which, as Epstein wrote, were 'paralyzed in marble or tied to canvas'; the cinema, on the other hand, 'is all movement'.[56] In 1918, Aragon criticised the cinema for remaining 'a succession of photographs. The essential "cinegraphic" is not the beautiful shot.'[57] The 'birth of a sixth art', as the title of Ricciotto Canudo's essay proclaimed film to be, was fundamentally based on movement that was specific to cinema, a 'plastic art in motion'.[58] Moments of *photogénie* frequently inspired lengthy descriptions. Despite arguing that *photogénie* was only intermittent, Epstein's descriptions, for example, seem to attempt to do justice to the development of movement through time. It takes him an entire paragraph to describe this formation of a smile, which clearly develops as a temporal process: 'a head suddenly appears on screen and drama, now face to face, seems to address me personally and swells with an extraordinary intensity . . . everything is movement, imbalance, crisis'.[59] Motionless close-ups, he wrote, 'sacrifice their essence, which is movement'.[60] As Elie Faure also argued, 'stop the most beautiful film you know, make of it at any moment an inert photograph, and you will not obtain even a memory of the emotion that it gave you as a moving picture'.[61]

The impassioned discourse of cinephilia that emerged in the 1940s and 1950s, propagated largely by the *Cahiers du Cinéma* critics, can be seen as echoing some aspects of *photogénie*. Cinephilia fetishised fragments of a film, often the fleeting moments where marginal or unintentional details were glimpsed. These moments, as Willemen writes, were 'experienced by the cinephile who beholds them as nothing less than an epiphany, a revelation'.[62] According to Willemen, the early writings of, for example, François Truffaut and Jean-Luc Godard can be seen as highly impressionistic responses to films as epiphanic. Cinephilic moments sparked the 'energy and the desire to write, to find formulations to convey something about the intensity of that spark', and to simultaneously grasp them from the flow of the film's duration.[63] Willemen compares cinephilic writing to a 'collector's activity', an attempt to preserve and store something out of the evanescent and fleeting experience that is the film in its duration.[64] The configuration of the moment, the corporeal, and the a-signifying that surfaced in writing on *photogénie* is also frequently present in writings on cinephilia. As Keathley emphasises, 'an encounter with a cinephilic moment is not just a visual experience, but also a more broadly sensuous one . . . linked in critical writing to the haptic, the tactile, and the bodily'.[65] The cinephilic moment, he continues, is one that 'resists co-optation by meaning'; this most intense moment of cinematic experience 'seems to draw its intensity partly from the fact that it cannot be reduced or tamed by interpretation'.[66]

Bergsonian notions of duration were not exactly alien to film critics in the first half of the twentieth century. In 1918, for example, Marcel L'Herbier noted that 'if it is true that . . . Bergsonism can be summarized as a desire to merge with the "flux" . . . is not Bergsonism . . . in all its propensity if not its essence, precisely analogous to current cinegraphie?'[67] In his 1952 *Theory of Film*, Béla Balázs compared the modulation of facial expression in a close-up to Bergson's analysis of melody. A melody is composed of single notes that follow each other in time, but the melody that they create, the relation of the notes to each other, lies outside of this time. Balázs writes, 'the melody is not born gradually in the course of time but is already in existence as a complete entity as soon as the first note is played. How else would we know that a melody is begun?' In facial expression, similarly, 'the single features . . . appear in space; but the significance of their relationship to one another is not a phenomenon pertaining to space'.[68] The particular moments of a facial close-up can be extracted, but the significance of facial expression in the close-up can emerge only in duration. It was not until Deleuze's *Cinema* books, however, that interest in the relationship between Bergsonism and the cinema became prominent.[69]

Writing on *photogénie* and cinephilia frequently revolved around attempts to comprehend the powerfully affective nature of cinema. With the introduction of semiotics and psychoanalysis in the 1960s, there seemed to be a conscious attempt to control and fix cinema's ungraspability by instituting a 'scientific' and rigorous mode of film analysis. The film's illusory nature was emphasised over its corporeal aspect, but the critic could avoid being 'deceived' by cinema's illusions by maintaining an explicit distance from the 'text' of the film. As Metz wrote, the writer must learn to carry their love of cinema 'inside one still so that it is in a place that is accessible to self-analysis, but carry it there as a distinct instance which does not over-infiltrate the rest of the ego with the thousand paralyzing bonds of a tender unconditionality'.[70] As Tim Groves has suggested, these remarks betray an anxiety about affect and its ability to disrupt the autonomy and control of the writer; cinema's affective dimension must be isolated and repressed.[71]

Semiotic and structuralist theories frequently isolated moments from a film as determinable sites of meaning and signification, while temporal flow was often seen as threatening or destructive. When formulating his ideas about filmic language, for example, Roger Odin wrote that

> filmic images, which disappear as soon as they appear . . . have to be seized as they rush past, on the spur of the moment, and with no hope of ever retrieving them; they follow one another relentlessly, allowing us no rest, no chance to take control.[72]

Among these slightly breathless, short clauses, we may find a similar anxiety about cinematic temporality to that exhibited by Benjamin. As Deleuze has argued, linguistic conceptions of cinema, such as that posited by Metz, reduced the cinematographic image to an utterance: 'at the very point that the image is replaced by an utterance, the image is given a false appearance, and its most authentically visible characteristic, movement, is taken away from it'.[73] Deleuze's critique of Metz's semiology is not simply an argument for the 'visual' specificity of the film, but is fundamentally concerned with Metz's failure to take into account the operation of immanence and temporality, which is part of his critique of structuralism in general.[74] For Deleuze, cinematic images do not constitute a 'language' but rather a potentiality and a process.[75] Structuralism reduces the 'materiality' of different forms of expression to a universal framework, a system of linguistic signs, which is understood as fundamentally static and unchanging.[76]

Prominent post-war theorists frequently isolated or valorised qualities in cinema that revealed particular conjunctions of stillness and flow. Roland Barthes, for example, was explicit in his predilection for still moments over moving images. One of his major statements on cinema, 'The Third Meaning', is in fact an essay on film stills. Barthes locates three levels of meaning in the image, the informational level (what can be learned from settings and mise-en-scène), the symbolic level (which involves a highly developed semiotic analysis), and the third or 'obtuse' meaning, of which he writes, 'I do not know what its signified is, at least I am unable to give it a name.'[77] This meaning 'exceeds' the referential, and can be grasped only 'poetically', not intellectually.[78] It is a supplement that 'my intellection cannot succeed in absorbing, at once persistent and fleeting, smooth and elusive'.[79] This moment 'outplays meaning', appearing as 'an expenditure with no exchange'.[80] It is 'theoretically locatable but not describable'.[81] Barthes's article echoes the debates on cinematic specificity that characterised earlier critical writings on film in attempting to establish an essence of cinema:

> it is at the level of the third meaning, and at that level alone, that the 'filmic' finally emerges. The filmic is that in the film which cannot be described, the representation which cannot be represented. The filmic begins only where language and meta-language end.[82]

Barthes ultimately concludes, while recognising the paradox, that the 'filmic' cannot be located within the film itself, that is within the film 'in situation', 'in movement', 'in its natural state', but only in 'that major artifact, the still'.[83] He defends this conclusion by arguing that the essence of film lies not in its movement but in this 'third meaning', which nevertheless painting and photography lack because they do not have a diegetic horizon. The still, he argues, is not to be seen as an 'extraction' from the film, but rather the trace of a distribution of traits 'of which the film as experienced in its animated flow would give no more than one text among others'.[84] Although the 'meaning' of this obtuseness is ungraspable, it is nevertheless made available in the stilled image. The still 'throws off the constraint of filmic time', a time which, unlike reading time, is not 'free'.[85] According to Barthes, 'the still, by instituting a reading that is at once instantaneous and vertical, scorns logical time'.[86] As Durand argues, the still for Barthes is the 'ideal object, in the sense that it is at the same time free of the narrative or sequential imperative of the film', while retaining its obtuseness.[87] The similarity between the terms Barthes used to describe the punctum in photography and that used to describe the obtuse meaning in film is striking.[88] The punctum is also a detail that 'overwhelms the entirety of my reading'; 'this *something* has triggered me, has provoked a tiny shock'.[89] It is something which cannot be named, for 'what I can name cannot really prick me. The incapacity to name is a good symptom of disturbance.'[90]

Laura Mulvey's famous polemic delineating the scopophilic gaze also reveals a particular configuration of stillness and movement, in that the presence of the woman on screen 'tends to work against the development of a story line, to freeze the flow of action in moments of erotic contemplation'.[91] Mulvey's latest book, *Death 24x a Second*, undertakes a self-conscious adjustment of many aspects of this position. She specifically indicates how her 'engagement with the cinema of the past has been changed by passing time'.[92] This partly refers to her movement from developing a notion of a possessive spectator, who has 'a fetishistic investment in the extraction of a fragment of cinema from its context', to a 'pensive spectator', who 'extracts and [then] replaces a fragment with extra understanding back into its context'.[93] The fetishist is driven by a desire to hold and stop stylised and iconic images, such as those depicting film stars. The pensive spectator, on the other hand, when confronted with a moment of stillness within the moving image, reflects on the cinema, recreating the resonance of the still photograph. When the film returns to movement the reflections continue to inflect the film's sense of 'past-ness'.[94] According to Mulvey, 'not only can the "pensive" spectator experience the kind of reverie that Barthes associated with the photograph alone, but this reverie reaches out to the nature of cinema itself'.[95] The pensive spectator can thus blend together in contemplation two kinds of time, recognising 'the inseparability of stillness from movement and flow'.[96] They can 'rescue those aspects of the cinema' that Barthes felt were lacking in comparison to the photograph.[97]

Over the last few decades, theorists using cognitive analysis have presented other possibilities for thinking about film in its temporal development. As David Bordwell has emphasised, cognitivism is not a theory but a 'stance', a general appeal to processes of mental representation and rational agency.[98] As 'the activity of *theorising*' it is opposed to the 'grand theories' of semiotics and psychoanalysis, as indeed the title of Bordwell and Carroll's collection of essays, *Post-Theory*, suggests.[99] An important tenet of this mode of analysis is that it purports to study narrative as a process that takes place continuously throughout the film as the viewer selects, arranges, and concretises story material.[100] Bordwell explicitly criticises the spatial terminology used in semiotic and psychoanalytic film criticism, which suggests that the spectator is positioned or placed by the film. Such metaphors, he writes, 'lead us to conceive of the perceiver as backed into a corner by conventions of perspective, editing, narrative point-of-view, and psychic unity. A film . . . does not "position" anybody. A film cues the spectator to execute a definable variety of *operations*.'[101] 'Art-cinema narration', according to Bordwell, has easily recognisable 'schemata', which the spectator applies in their viewing of the film. Art cinema, he argues, cues us to see its images as part of a subjective realism or narrational commentary, and allows for a certain open-endedness and ambiguity in its narration.[102] Stylistic effects which are not reducible to meaning are termed 'parametric form'. As in Kristin Thompson's notion of 'excess', Bordwell argues that a film's stylistic system can create patterns '*distinct from the demands of the syuzhet system*', that is, from the construction of the narrative.[103] One such example is the 'graphic match', a non-narrative device where lines, shapes, colours, and movements are matched by a similar configuration in the next shot.[104]

Bordwell's analysis of the structures of narrative cues, art-cinema schemata and parametric form are theoretically rigorous, yet leave much to be desired when attempting to explicate the heterogeneity inherent in the various ways in which viewers may relate to films. As Daniel Frampton has written, in analysing art cinema or parametric narratives Bordwell seems to want only to rationalise them: 'radical cinema is reduced to *principles, systems*, all towards trying to bring artistic cinema into the *rational* fold of classical cinema'.[105] Bordwell's assumptions that a filmgoer will initially aim for the most rational interpretation of a film encourages the notion that the films are '*problems to be solved*'.[106] It is not surprising, therefore, that theorists who stress the embodied nature of film viewing have criticised Bordwell and other writers on cognitivism. Rutherford, for example, criticises Bordwell for his deflection of attention 'away from absorption in emotional pathos, and onto detached intellectual contemplation'.[107] In applying what Rutherford calls the 'Modernist Grid' onto films by Antonioni and Angelopoulos, which emphasises 'de-dramatisation', empty spaces and 'dead intervals', Bordwell's analysis yields 'nothing but an inventory of devices of visual style, conceived as akin to static pictorial design'.[108]

Bordwell's analysis of time in cinema is limited to categorising strategies of temporal construction 'within' the film, distinguishing between fabula, syuzhet, and screen duration, and defining ellipses and compressions of time.[109] In Bordwell's writing, each image seems to affix a meaning or cue to itself to be decoded in the moment of its appearing; the durational flow of the film thus seems to stutter. Cognitivist or formalist writings can categorise shots by their camera angles and framings, but give little sense of the movement between moments where film configures itself through a specific angle or as a particular frame. The durational process through a film, in this mode of analysis, becomes fragmented into well-defined moments of succession. It is perhaps indicative of this spatialisation of cinematic time that Bordwell's *Narration in the Fiction Film* includes many pages of stills in chronological succession to demonstrate the techniques used and their narrative significance. While this can be extremely useful for certain types of film analysis, it does not contribute enough to an understanding of the aesthetics, affect, concept and operation of duration.

Sensory and Affective Moments

In *Carnal Thoughts*, Sobchack writes of an experience she had while watching Jane Campion's *The Piano*, which opens with an image that is no more than an indefinable pinkish blur. This is soon revealed to be fingers laced across the heroine's eyes, or, rather, over the camera lens. Before visually recognising and comprehending this fact, however, Sobchack claims that '*my fingers knew what I was looking at . . . grasped* it with a nearly imperceptible tingle of attention and anticipation'.[110] Anne Rutherford describes how watching a particular series of images from Mizoguchi's *The Story of the Last Chrysanthemums* 'almost invariably' throws her 'suddenly onto another dimension . . . I experience the shot in my stomach, as if my stomach turns over'.[111] Similarly, Lesley Stern writes of watching a character from *Blade Runner* somersault: 'my stomach lurches . . . the momentum remains in your body as a charge, a whoosh, a sense of exhilaration'.[112] A close-up image of a sari makes Laura Marks feel that she has been 'using my vision as though it were the sense of touch; I have been brushing the (image of the) fabric with the skin of my eyes'.[113]

These privileged moments of sensation have emerged more and more frequently in critical writing as contemporary film theory has moved towards definitions of film viewing as embodied and sensory. The frequency with which the theorist's body has become the focus of critical writing is partly a culmination of a tendency of responses to art in the twentieth century, which saw a relocation of experience from the generalised, transcendental order associated with Kant and Hegel, to a location in 'a particular body, concrete, singular, and finite'.[114] The materiality of the body in the twentieth century, as Danius argues, became the privileged site of aesthetics, and perception became valued as an aesthetically gratifying activity in its own right.[115] In theories of embodied viewing, a return to early film theory, with its configuration of the momentary and the corporeal, is often staged in contradistinction to the semiotic and psychoanalytic discourses that dominated film theory from the 1960s. Although they do not exactly constitute a coherent or organised group, and there is much variation among theorists on specific points, the attempts to understand film viewing as embodied and haptic share a dissatisfaction with semiotic and psychoanalytic methods of film analysis. In this section, I outline some important characteristics of such theories and the questions that they raise when considered in relation to filmic temporality.

Sobchack's phenomenological account of film viewing, *The Address of the Eye*, which appeared in 1992 and was heavily influenced by Maurice Merleau-Ponty's philosophy, constituted a significant step in the break from the semiotic discourses that had dominated the field for several decades. The book's aim was to produce a rigorous 'thick and radical description' of the embodied situation of the viewer.[116] As Sobchack noted, when she wrote the book, the concept of a film 'experience' was a suspect term, as was existential phenomenology in general, which was seen as naive in making claims about direct experience at a moment when contemporary theory was emphasising its inaccessibility and focusing instead on the mediating structures of language. Sobchack attributes her dissatisfaction with semiotics and psychoanalysis to their distortion of cinematic experience through a definition of cinema as essentially deceptive, illusionary, and coercive.[117] The psychoanalytic model of the 'mirror stage', which was often seen as directly applicable to the experience of film viewing, was based on an alienation of vision from the body and a deceptive misrecognition of the self. The kind of theory in question is perhaps best summed up by the work of Metz. In *Psychoanalysis and Cinema*, Metz argued that film was partly like a mirror, providing only an effigy, 'inaccessible from the outset, in a primordial *elsewhere*'.[118] Cinema presents 'no longer the object itself', but 'a delegate it has sent me while itself withdrawing'.[119]

Metz bases his idea of the spectator on the (male) voyeur, who requires distance from the object of his vision and his own body. Catastrophic results would ensue were this interval to collapse:

> to fill in this distance would threaten to overwhelm the subject, to lead him to consume the object (the object which is now too close so that he cannot see it any more), to bring him to orgasm and the pleasure of his own body, hence to the exercise of other drives, mobilizing the sense of contact and hence putting an end to the scopic arrangement.[120]

In this passage, Metz rather succinctly describes the kind of viewing experience that is in fact celebrated in an 'erotics' of embodiment or haptic theory. Susan Sontag was already hoping for an 'erotics' of art in place of a 'hermeneutics' in the 1960s.[121] It is only relatively recently, however, that film theorists are thoroughly formulating this erotic relationship, while bypassing voyeurism and mastery, and recuperating fetishism. According to Marks, for example, film images can be 'erotic in that they construct an intersubjective relationship between beholder and image ... the viewer relinquishes her own sense of separateness from the image – not to know it, but to give herself up to her desire for it'.[122] Sobchack similarly argues that 'our sensations and responses pose an intolerable question to prevalent linguistic and psychoanalytic understandings of the cinema as grounded in conventional codes and cognitive patterning and grounded on absence, lack and illusion'.[123] The positing of vision as only a 'distance-sense' abstracts it from a full-bodied experience.[124] Steven Shaviro has also criticised film theory for its 'scientific' endeavour to separate itself from its object, in praise, condemnation or analysis, which is most often dispassionate. In most film theory, Shaviro argues, the desire to keep at a distance 'the voyeuristic excitations that are its object' has too completely gained control; film theory continues to equate passion, fascination and enjoyment with mystification.[125]

Against such notions of distance and passivity, embodied phenomenology and other theories of haptic cinema posit the viewer's body as an active participant in an intimate relationship with the film. As Sobchack argues, many theories of spectatorship focus on how we forget ourselves in another's vision of the world, neglecting the moments of rupture in the film experience, where we experience the other's vision as different to our own. We never, according to Sobchack, appropriate the film's images as 'our own'. No matter how much we give ourselves up to them, there is always some degree of resistance to our incorporation of or by them, 'indeed, there would be no "play" were there not this mutual resilience and resistance I feel, this back-and-forth exchange I experience, in the encounter between myself and a film'.[126] The experience is never lived as a monologic one: 'the film's vision and my own do not conflate, but meet in the sharing of a world and constitute an experience that is ... intersubjectively dialogical'.[127] With every film we engage, 'we experience moments of divergence and rupture and moments of convergence and rapture'.[128]

Sobchack's writing in *Carnal Thoughts* presents a more direct engagement with the sensory in cinema. When we see a film, Sobchack writes, we 'do not leave [our] capacity to touch or to smell or to taste at the door'.[129] The viewer, she argues, 'is not to be presumed isolated and detached from her own processes of visual production ... the spectator as viewer is not abstracted from the act of viewing – in current terms, "objectified" and "alienated"'.[130] Seeing is informed by other modes of perception and the other senses: it is synaesthetic, always within a 'sighted body' rather than merely in 'transcendental eyes'.[131] Through an embodied vision 'informed by the knowledge of the other senses, the subject "makes sense" of what it is to "see" a movie'.[132]

What I particularly value in Sobchack's analysis in *Address* is her sense of the many variations possible in viewing experiences. In *Carnal Thoughts*, however, Sobchack focuses less upon the moments of rupture that can occur between film and viewer, and more upon a completeness of sensory experience in moments of bodily communion between self and film. While we cannot actually touch, smell or taste at the cinema, she argues, we do have a partially fulfilled sensory experience that is 'intelligible and meaningful'. For Sobchack, our experience in the cinema involves not a reduction of our sensuous being but a form of *enhancement* of it. According to Sobchack, in watching a film we intend towards the world on screen. When our intention cannot find the object that solicits our sensual desire to literally touch, taste and smell, it will reverse its trajectory to a more accessible sensual object, our own bodies.

> Thus, 'on the rebound' from the screen – and without a reflective thought – I will reflexively turn toward my own carnal, sensual, and sensible being to touch myself touching, smell myself smelling, taste myself tasting, and, in sum, sense my own sensuality.[133]

Through this relationship of 'sensual and cross-modal activity', she continues, the subject can both touch and be touched by the screen, 'able to experience the movie as both here and there rather than clearly locating the site of cinematic experience as onscreen or offscreen'.[134]

Sobchack echoes, and is echoed by, several other writers in this collapsing of a distance between film and viewer. Rutherford, for example, bases her writings on a concept of 'mimetic innervation', where there is a 'palpable sensuous connection between the very body of the perceiver and the perceived'.[135] Rutherford also echoes Sobchack in arguing that the film spectator does not abandon 'the embodied ground of their experience (or perception) – embodiment is one of the important culturally or historically-inscribed dispositions that the spectator brings to the cinema'.[136] The fact that the camera mediates our experience does not, in Rutherford's view, imply that we surrender everyday experiences such as kinaesthetic pleasure.[137] In a similar vein, Shaviro argues that spectators do not 'identify' with the images on the screen, but are rather brought into intimate contact with them through mimetic 'contagion'.[138] In this process of sympathetic participation, the subject is captivated and 'made more fluid and indeterminate' through a 'tactile convergence'.[139] The haptic sense, as Jennifer Fisher further describes, 'renders the surfaces of the body porous, being perceived at once inside, on the skin's surface, and in external space'.[140]

The dissolution of boundaries between viewer and film responds directly to previous attributions of an invasive and overwhelming quality to cinematic machinery. Those who developed the apparatus theory of the 1960s tended to describe viewers as passive and disembodied. Jean-Louis Baudry, for example, posited a cinema viewer whose eye was 'no longer fettered to a body'.[141] While Christian Metz, however, emphasised the powerlessness of the viewer in front of the cinema screen, the language he uses has an interesting resonance with haptic theory. 'At every moment', he writes, 'I am in the film by my look's caress.'[142] While Metz qualifies this by alluding to the ghostly nature of this 'hovering' gaze, conceptualisations of the corporeal nature of film viewing have developed the notion that vision can function like an organ of touch. According to Sobchack, when we watch the 'expressive perception' of the film's vision, we speak back to it through the address of our own vision, 'using a visual language that is also tactile, that takes hold of and actively grasps the perceptual expression, the seeing, the direct experience' of the film.[143] Echoing this, Shaviro understands cinematic 'fascination' to occur

> when what you see, even though from a distance, seems to touch you with a grasping contact, when the matter of seeing is a sort of touch, when seeing is a *contact* at a distance . . . when what is seen imposes itself on your gaze, as though the gaze had been seized, touched, put in contact with appearance.[144]

Reconfiguring vision as an organ of touch is also inherent in Marks's notion of 'haptic visuality'.

Much of the writing on embodied film viewing, like that on *photogénie* and cinephilia, privileges a particular moment that, through its corporeal evocations, provokes the desire to describe and explain. Contemporary theoretical writing has admirably described these moments of immediate sensual reaction, moments of direct 'tactile shock', to use Sobchack's words.[145] Such writing, however, sometimes operates on a principle of isolation: of a unique moment from the flow of the film and of sensuous apprehension from a comprehended context. Although Sobchack acknowledges that the images of a film always exist in temporal flow, she makes clear in *Address* that she is interested in space rather than time: 'the cinema's own meaning originates not in time, but in space and movement'.[146] Movement, however, is not privileged as contributing to a cinematic aesthetic, but rather in so far as it dynamises abstract space as inhabitable.[147] Sobchack expresses an interest not in temporality but in situation: 'it is not time, but space – the significant space lived as and through the objective body-subject, the historical space of situation – that grounds the response to. . .the question of cinematic signification'.[148] Particular questions can thus be raised that relate to temporality in film analysis. For example, how does the sensory moment, experienced in the body, interrelate with thought and intellectual processes? What is the relationship between sensory awareness and comprehension of a film's themes and narratives as they unfold in time?

Perhaps the most emphatic answer to such questions can be found in Sobchack's *Carnal Thoughts*. For Sobchack, sensation is pre-reflective, such that we can experience filmic images '*without a thought*'.[149] She agrees with Shaviro that the elision of the body in 'making sense' in its own right is grounded in the idealist assumption that human experience is originally and fundamentally cognitive. This assumption reduces the question of perception to a question of knowledge, and equates sensation with the reflective consciousness of sensation.[150] Our ability to touch and be touched, 'to sometimes even smell and taste the world on screen', she argues, does not involve 'thinking' a translation of sight into smell and taste.[151] According to Sobchack, the body already means and signifies without the intervention of the intellect, and thus it is not necessary to 'explain away' the film experience. Her fingers' recognition of fingers on screen, or her sensual awareness of a character's clothing are already meaningful experiences in themselves. One of the consequences of Sobchack's emphasis upon a pre-reflective moment of sensation is that the way in which sensual apprehension and intellectual comprehension interweave through the duration of the film remains a theoretically underdeveloped issue in her analysis. Sobchack's writings suggest that her physical reactions constitute a closed circuit, already a thought as well as a sensation, and thus are not extended into time.

In so far as it is structured around a moment of perception, Sobchack's phenomenological framework might be seen as more appropriate to an understanding of an instant from a film than to the duration of time that passes through the image. Eliding duration runs the risk of rendering film images static, of lifting them out of temporal development by a mode of analysis more suited to still images. While Sobchack's demonstration that it is possible to have a form of sensual experience in the cinema without having to interpret and justify our responses is undoubtedly useful, the intellectual experience of a film and its sensual evocations are held in an uncertain relationship in her theoretical writing. Sobchack's examples, however, indicate that sensory responses may emerge from a comprehended context. The moments of sensual response that she privileges depend upon the display of human contact. When watching *The Piano*, she emphasises that the moment when Baines first touches Ada's flesh through a hole in her stocking caused her to feel an 'immediate tactile shock'. This shock, she writes, diffused her sense of touch such that she felt 'not only my "own" body but also Baines's body, Ada's body, and . . . the "film's body"'.[152] What is missing from such an analysis is the importance of the context and temporal placement of this scene, a recognition that part of the effectiveness of this particular moment is the knowledge of the illicitness of the first contact between the two main characters. There may be a more complex symbiosis between a spectator's understanding of a scene's thematic or narrative presentation and their sensual, affective response. When touch and hapticity are thematised, as in the example from *The Piano*, it may be that we need more theoretical explorations of how the senses work in conjunction with comprehension.

Other theorists, such as Rutherford, tend to take contemplation for granted rather than consider it in its development through duration and its interweaving with sensual response. Writing on Theo Angelopoulos's *Ulysses' Gaze*, Rutherford argues that describing the film as a 'cinema of contemplation' or 'meditation' cannot do justice to the 'multi-layered experience which *in-corporates* – makes corporeal or material – our experience'.[153] That one is left contemplating a film like *Ulysses' Gaze* is not, she argues 'in question, but one is also left with inarticulate sensation, traces of sounds, spaces, fragments, that permeate and linger in the corporeal memory. It is, above all, a cinema of embodied affect.'[154] While I agree with Rutherford's description of the lingering sensations that the film provokes, I would argue that what is in question is precisely the relationship between contemplation and sensual response in time.

In her writing, Marks has addressed the notion that the senses must be seen in a more contextual manner. She critiques Merleau-Ponty for treating sense experience as 'pre-discursive and, hence, as natural'. She argues that 'while much of sensory experience is pre-symbolic, it is still cultivated, that is, learned'.[155] The 'order of the sensible', according to Marks, is the 'sum of what is accessible to sense perception at a given historical and cultural moment . . . we can only feel in the ways we have learned it is possible to feel'.[156] Sobchack's specific isolation of a female character's 'taffetas and woollens'[157] to demonstrate an unproblematic and unbroken stream of intentionality back and forth from the screen suggests the extent to which the senses must be seen in the context of cultural influence. Marks's writing largely emphasises the importance of thematic contextualisation in a balanced relationship with embodiment: 'tactile epistemology involves thinking with your skin, or giving as much significance to the physical presence of an other as to the mental operations of symbolisation'.[158] In cinema, 'the iconic and symbolic coexist with the indexical: representation is inextricable from embodiment'.[159] Her project is derived from and applicable to a specific group of films that she terms 'intercultural cinema', which appeal to embodied knowledge and memory in the absence of other resources.[160] These films represent and thematise the appeal to the senses as well as cinematographically enact them.

For Marks, the particular moment of sensory awareness becomes expanded in memory. She draws upon a Bergsonian form of film spectatorship that involves an 'attentive recognition' of images. Perception takes place 'not simply in a phenomenological present but in an engagement with individual and cultural memory'. Rather than unproblematically 'completing' the image in his or her body, the viewer oscillates between seeing the object, recalling the images which it brings into memory, and comparing these with the object before them. Thus the viewer can 'create anew not only the object perceived but also the ever-widening systems with which it may be bound up'.[161] This is a participatory form of spectatorship that emphasises how we draw upon our own reserves of memory and association in viewing film. Marks, however, also has some reservations about Bergson's 'ability to partake in the fullness of experience', moving back and forth between perception and memory 'as though at some great phenomenological buffet table'. For Marks, this process can also be traumatic.[162]

Another question arises as to the relationship between the sensory moment and passing time. What happens to the sensory moment as it passes? Does sensation cease, or is it elongated? What happens, that is, to the sensory presents as they pass? For Rutherford, sensory moments are intensified through time, 'the spectator is not jolted into fleeting moments of awareness and sensation, and time here is not the passing of this intense, fleeting experience of the ephemeral moment, not its undoing, but the intensification of the experience through duration'.[163] On the other hand, we may see the passing of time in cinema, its continual transformation of material textures on screen, as working to destabilise sensation. Cinema can simultaneously evoke a sense of texture and withdraw it – not necessarily, as in Sobchack's writing, enhancing texture through its very absence. This conjunction of materiality and ephemerality has been eloquently formulated by Stern, who writes that 'the cinema evokes the solidity and tactility of things in the very moment of their passing, their ephemerality. In the cinema solid things turn into phantasms, touch turns into memory.'[164] Marks reverses this phrasing in some sense when she discusses how cinema can evoke the memory of touch, exhibiting, nevertheless, a similar sentiment to Stern: cinema can withdraw sense as powerfully as it can evoke it. The experience of looking may make us reflect how 'memory may be encoded in touch, sound, perhaps smell, more than in vision', but can also create a 'poignant awareness of the missing sense of touch'.[165]

There is an overlap between descriptions of affective and sensory moments in cinema. Consider, for example, the following sentence: 'I watch a scene in a film and my heart races, my eye flinches, and I begin to perspire. Before I even think or conceptualise there is an element of response that is prior to my decision.'[166] This sentence could be mistaken for something that Sobchack has written; in fact, it appears in Claire Colebrook's informative work on Gilles Deleuze. Colebrook's writing on the pre-reflective moment of affect echoes Sobchack's emphasis upon the pre-reflective aspect of sensation. The 'sensory' and the 'affective' are hardly unrelated concepts or experiences. Colebrook's list of possible sources of affective response, for example, has a sensory dimension: 'the light that causes our eye to flinch, the sound that makes us start, the image of violence which raises our body temperature'.[167]

There are, of course, significant points of divergence between Sobchack's sensation and Colebrook's Deleuzian affect. One of these is the former's emphasis upon the everyday situation of film viewing, and the latter's insistence on how cinematic affect implies a dislodging of everyday situation and vision. Following Deleuze, Colebrook argues that we tend to subordinate affects and perceptions to recognisable objects and repeatable habits. Everyday vision is termed 'extensive': 'extension maps or synthesises the world in terms of presupposed purposes and intensions', whereby we isolate in vision those things which are to function for us. Affect, on the other hand, is 'intensive . . . it is not objectifiable and quantifiable as a thing that we then perceive or of which we are conscious.' Art can function to disengage affects from their expected origins, and thus 'open us up to whole new possibilities of affect'.[168] Art does not represent the world, but creates new worlds, which dislodges affect in ways which do not occur in everyday life.

An affective moment is not, in theory at least, the same as an emotional one. Massumi has described emotion as a 'capture' of affect. Emotion involves a measure of 'socio-linguistic fixing', a subjective content that is defined as personal, but can be attributed to a source within narrative or to character identification. Affect, on the other hand, escapes such fixation. In affect, Massumi writes, 'something remains unactualised, inseparable from but unassimilable to any *particular*, functionally anchored perspective'.[169] It is an intensity that cannot necessarily be explained. In the duration of the film, however, affect and emotion may not be so easily distinguished from each other. As Elena del Rio has written, in practice affect and emotion 'remain rather fluidly connected'. While 'emotion' describes psychologically motivated expression, 'emotion nonetheless actualizes and concretises the way in which a body is something affected by, or affects, another body. Thus, I regard affect and emotion as connected and coterminous'.[170] In the process of film viewing, affect and emotion may be intertwined.

The same question that I posited in relation to the sensory can be asked again regarding affect: what is the relationship between affective resonance and thematic presentation, between, that is, affect and cognition? After all, Colebrook argues that affect is a sensibility not organised into meaning; while concepts give order and direction to meaning, affect is the power to interrupt order and synthesis.[171] Affect, however, is not entirely divorced from cognition. Affective responses involve both the sensory and the cognitive: 'sensation is never simple. It is always doubled by the feeling of having a feeling.'[172] Massumi conceives of this doubling as the echoing or resonation of affect in thought. In discussing the relationship between narrative and affect, del Rio has argued that a film's narrative and the 'affective-performative moments' that seem to escape from it are in a continual alteration of dominance,

> a continuous rising of one at the expense of the other in a relation of overlapping simultaneity rather than oppositionality. At each moment, the representational imperatives of narrative and the non-representational imperatives of the affective-performative displace each other without ever completely canceling each other out.[173]

Similarly, O'Sullivan writes that the conceptual function of art is not really separable from its affective function, and in fact both are involved in a 'circular causality': 'we might understand concepts as themselves the result of affects, just as they "cause" new affects to arise'.[174] In the tradition of Spinoza and Bergson, affect is seen by Massumi as an impingement of the body *'and at the same time the idea of the affection'*.[175] In affect, the self is not brought back into a stable situation of self-fulfilled sensation, as embodied phenomenology might posit, but rather seen as emergent or incipient: 'intensity is *incipience*, incipient action and expression'.[176]

Moments and Duration

Definitions, descriptions and theorisations of film moments can be found throughout the history of writing on film. Less has been written about temporal flow in cinema, rhythms in time, developments in duration, unfolding, flux and change. If Massumi is correct in asserting that, in critical theory in general, 'the slightness of ongoing qualitative change [has] paled in comparison to the grandness of periodic "rupture"'[177] then we may see film theory as reflecting this trend. Much film criticism and theory, to appropriate the words of Guerlac, thinks more in terms of product (static composition, what images mean) than process (fluid movements, the gradual congealing and dissolution of meaning).[178] This is not to say that film moments cannot play a part in a temporally-inflected film analysis. In a recent volume entitled *Film Moments*, editors Tom Brown and James Walters write of the

> immediacy inherent in the experience of watching ... the moment-by-moment process that forms patterns, structures, and meanings in our minds ... by staying

with moments from films and discussing them in detail, the interpretive critic returns to the process by which we initially form an understanding of film's significance and meaning: moment by moment.[179]

There is a great variety of types of moments in film and in writing on film: a moment of pure sensation, as in Sobchack's writing, or a moment which has a 'cue' attached to it, as in cognitive theory. A film moment can help to fix meanings, or release us from them. While I continue to discuss particular moments in the films of Antonioni, Tarkovsky and Kieślowski, I seek also to attend to their placement in temporal flow, exploring how change in time may affect a particular scene, edit, or framing. My interest lies in opening up certain film moments to the flow of time.

Duration, wrote Bergson, is 'a continuity which is really lived, but artificially decomposed for the greater convenience of customary knowledge'. That is, we have acquired the habit of 'substituting for the true duration lived by consciousness, an homogenous and independent Time'.[180] We tend to think of time in terms of space. A clock, for example, represents time as spatial and measurable; as Lim writes, 'a number line is grafted onto its radial face so that the *progress in space* of the clock hand, moving across its circular trajectory, coincides with the *passage of time*'. According to the clock, the past has elapsed and ceased to exist. However, clock time does not tell the truth of duration but creates an illusion of measurable, predictable time.[181] The spatialisation of time, as Lomax has written, 'portrays time – my life-time – as measurable and open to calculation, with which comes prediction'. The activity of prediction assumes procedures through which time in its future appearance is sought to be known, neutralised, and controlled before it happens. What the spatialisation of time offers 'is not only the notion of points in time that are measurable but also the presumption that the time to come can be calculated and controlled'.[182]

The spatialisation of time betrays the nature of duration as it is lived. As Grosz explains, time functions both as a 'singular, unified whole, as well as in specific fragments and multiplicitous proliferation'. Time, she continues, 'is braided, intertwined, a unity of strands layered over each other; unique, singular and individual, it nevertheless partakes of a more generic and overarching time, which makes possible relations of earlier and later . . .'.[183] For Bergson, duration involves a 'succession without distinction . . . a mutual penetration, an interconnexion and organization of elements, each one of which represents the whole, and cannot be distinguished or isolated from it except by abstract thought'.[184] What the concept of duration might be seen to bring to film theory, then, is the notion of temporal strands intertwining and braiding together in cinema, as well as the process of their unfolding and expanding.

According to Bergson, the present moment cannot be reduced to a 'mathematical instant', an indivisible limit that separates past from future: 'the real, concrete, live present – that of which I speak when I speak of my present perception – that present necessarily occupies a duration'.[185] What we call the 'present', he continues,

> has one foot in my past and another in my future. In my past, first, because 'the moment in which I am speaking is already far from me'; in my future, next, because this moment is impending over the future: it is to the future that I am tending . . .'[186]

Perception is thus always entwined with memory, and, as Grosz argues,

> is thus never completely embedded in the present, but always retains a reservoir of connections with the past as well as a close anticipation of the imminent future. The present is extended through memory into the past and through anticipation into the near future.[187]

Grosz asks the pertinent question of how we are to measure the boundaries of the present moment – of when, that is, the present ceases to be 'present'. We are in the habit of seeing the present as a self-contained and clear-cut instant, but the living present that we experience 'has its own duration; it has no minimal units, no instants or length, except those imposed retroactively through analysis'.[188] The present moment must be seen to include memories of previous 'presents' that continue to 'generate sensations and cannot, except arbitrarily, be cut off from the present'.[189]

In Bergson's thinking, duration does not constitute a single rhythm but rather forms a variegated experience: 'it is possible to imagine many different rhythms, which, slower or faster, measure the degree of tension or relaxation of different kinds of consciousness'. Bergson compares duration to a 'myriad-tinted spectrum', in which 'insensible gradations' lead from one shade to another. 'A current of feeling which passed along the spectrum', he writes, 'assuming in turn the tint of its shades, would experience a series of gradual changes.'[190] While this might be helpful in giving an idea of duration 'in practice', Bergson remained unsatisfied with the comparisons he made in attempting to explicate it. The problem with the idea of the spectrum, he wrote, is that the successive shades are still juxtaposed, remaining external to one another. Pure duration, on the other hand, 'excludes all idea of juxtaposition, reciprocal externality and extension'.[191]

The way in which Bergsonian duration requires us to think beyond our dominant habits of representation, in which time is conceived in terms of space, was extremely significant for the development of Deleuze's thinking about cinema.[192] As Amy Herzog has written, 'the greatest achievement of the *Cinema* books is that they suggest a means of looking at film that explodes static views of the work that the work of art does'.[193] Of course, Deleuze had to first tackle the problem that Bergson associated cinema with mechanical, spatialised time rather than duration, seeing it as a kind of clockwork mechanism reducing time to the homogeneity of measurable space.[194] In the opening pages of *Cinema 1*, Deleuze reiterates Bergson's distinction between 'concrete duration' and 'abstract time'. Movement cannot be equated with positions in space or instants of time, with what are termed 'immobile sections'. Such positions or instants correspond to a notion of abstract time. Movement will always occur in a concrete duration, it cannot be divided or subdivided.[195] Bergson, Deleuze notes, associated abstract time with 'the cinematographic illusion'. Deleuze, however, argues that while cinema does present 'immobile' or 'instantaneous' sections (that is, images), it does not simply 'add' movement to an image, 'it immediately gives us a movement-image. It does give us a section, but a section which is mobile, not an immobile section + abstract movement'.[196] In fact, he continues, the 'mobile sections' presented in Bergson's *Matter and Memory* prefigure the temporal 'planes' of the cinema.[197] Deleuze thus uses Bergson to delineate instantaneous images or immobile sections, movement-images, or mobile sections of duration, and time-images that are 'beyond' movement itself.[198]

The time-image is discussed in depth in *Cinema 2*. Deleuze associates the moment of 'shock' in cinema with an indirect representation of time. In the pre-war cinema of the movement-image, he writes, time is subordinated to the montage that links images together. Eisenstein's dialectical montage epitomises this attempt to fix the image linguistically through its decomposition of a film into 'particularly well-determined moments'.[199] There is a shock between images or in the image itself; this shock 'is the very form of communication of movement in images'.[200] The indirect representation of time depends upon a movement that is 'normal' and centred, such that the viewer is 'able to recognise or perceive the moving body, and to assign movement'.[201] In Deleuze's analysis, in the post-war cinema, such stable centres of movement began to dissipate, and images came to be linked by false spatial continuities. The aberrations of movement, rather than 'halting' time, allowed it to surface directly, as anterior to movement, freed from its subordination to space. In the cinema of the time-image, temporality dislodges the linking of shots and emerges as a force distinct from movement and space. It is also through such aberrant editing practices, I argue, that indeterminate affect can be evoked in cinema.

Although Deleuze's *Cinema* books were not intended as a work on film spectatorship, they contain hints of impassioned viewing. For example, Deleuze writes that the 'optical and sound situation' of cinema can make us grasp 'something intolerable and unbearable', something too powerful, and 'sometimes also too beautiful': '*Stromboli*: a beauty which is too great for us, like too strong a pain'. He cites another example from *Les Carabiniers*: the 'girl militant' reciting slogans

> is so beautiful, of a beauty which is unbearable for her torturers who have to cover up her face with a handkerchief. And this handkerchief, lifted again by breath and whisper . . . itself becomes unbearable for us the viewers. In any event something has become too strong in the image.[202]

This unbearable beauty for the viewer might be seen to emerge with the breaking of the cliché and the upsetting of habitual perception. In habitual perception, as Bergson defined it, 'we do not perceive the thing or the image in its entirety, we always perceive less of it, we perceive only what we are interested in perceiving'.[203] Particular images can break this cliché, this pattern, allowing a different type of image (and a different form of affect) to emerge. Deleuze writes that the 'pure optical-sound image, the whole image without metaphor, brings out the thing in itself, literally, in its excess of horror or beauty'. Escaping from clichés, the image opens itself up to 'powerful and direct revelations'.[204]

In his *Cinema* books, Deleuze is said to think 'with' cinema, to place cinema and philosophy in dialogue with each other. His work is striking for the sheer number of films he uses to accomplish this. For this purpose, however, Deleuze often sacrifices close and detailed analyses of films as they proceed in duration, abstracting certain scenes that produce concepts, and generally conducting an analysis that binds the films together into their own philosophical systems. In my chapters on *L'Avventura* and *Mirror*, I demonstrate how his ideas on these specific films can be drawn upon for analysis, but also that we must move beyond his descriptions in order to draw greater attention to the way in which the films develop through time.

Writers other than Deleuze have also stepped forward to defend cinema from Bergson's accusations of spatialisation. For Lim, 'Bergson's cinema – as *reducible to the cinematographic apparatus* – is no longer our own', that is, no longer the 'mechanical novelty Bergson encountered in the medium's early years'.[205] For Paul Douglass, 'in its evocation of the flow of time, film has indeed approached Bergson's *durée*', although he warns against 'overturn[ing] Bergson's distrust of the camera'.[206] Totaro notes that 'when Bergson treats the cinematographical process as static frames independently aligned in succession he is falsifying film'.[207] Bergson also, however, insisted that as soon as we think or write of duration, we necessarily spatialise it, fixing temporal flow into successive moments and denying the continual modulation of time. Duration, according to Pearson, cannot be made the subject of logical treatment, owing to its character as a virtual multiplicity.[208] Duration can only be grasped through intuition, which Grosz defines as the 'close, intimate, internal comprehension of and immersion in the durational qualities of life'.[209] The intellect, on the other hand, produces snapshots, perspectives on the object, which incises it from a process of becoming.[210] According to Mullarkey, 'it is impossible to think about time without importing into it some of the features of homogenous space'.[211] This does not necessarily present an insurmountable barrier to thinking about temporality in cinema. We may not be able to reflect pure duration in writing, or define precisely what it is without spatialising time. However, we can work towards developing an analysis that will be sensitive to the ways in which various temporal strands and rhythms interweave in the duration of a film.

Two particular passages from Bergson's writing inform the analyses that follow. According to Guerlac, aesthetic pleasure for Bergson induces a rapid flow of ideas and sensations, explicated in *Time and Free Will* by the example of the pleasure that we take in the movements of a dancer, and in particular when 'the graceful movements obey a rhythm, and when music accompanies them'. Bergson writes that

> as we almost guess the pose the dancer will assume, the dancer seems to be obeying us when s/he actually strikes that pose. The regularity of the rhythm establishes a kind of communication between us, and the periodic returns of the beat are like so many invisible threads by means of which we make this imaginary marionette dance . . . the growing intensities of esthetic feeling really amount here to a variety of feelings. Each, already announced by the one that precedes it, becomes visible and then definitively eclipses the previous one.[212]

According to Bergson, throughout the duration of the dancer's movements we experience changing intensities or feelings, passages from one qualitative state to another. These feelings modulate through time, 'like the movements of the dancer, which anticipate one another as they flow forth in time'.[213]

Although Bergson does not mention mimeses or kinaesthesia, in its detailed and joyful attention to another's rhythmic movements this passage has an interesting resonance with the cinematic moments which contemporary film theorists such as Stern and Rutherford have isolated. For Stern, the bodily momentum of the actress who somersaults in *Blade*

Runner 'is transmitted and experienced in the auditorium as bodily sensation'.[214] 'It is breathtaking', she writes, 'the way the human body is suddenly charged, propelled by an apparently mysterious momentum into a virtuoso defiance of gravity.'[215] Rutherford's way of thinking about this emphasises, far more than Bergson, the sensory aspect of viewing (cinematic) movement. Aesthetics in cinema, she argues, implies a mobilisation of corporeality and the 'embodied responsiveness of the spectator'.[216] For Rutherford, the rhythms do not even have to be that of a human being. She describes a scene in *Story of the Last Chrysanthemums* in which the fluttering of multiple fans in a still frame conveys an explosive energy and activates a visceral response. Bergson, of course, was not writing about movement as mediated through cinematic form. In cinema, however, other kinds of temporal and energetic rhythms are created through changes in shots, rhythmic editing, and mobile cinematography, which may work to heighten the kinaesthetic sense of filmed movement. This is certainly the case for Rutherford, who writes that 'in so far as the mobile camera is implicated' in cinematic movement, it becomes a 'tool of choreography, not just representation or perception'.[217]

Another resonant passage for my analyses in this book can be found in Bergson's *Creative Evolution*, in which he famously delineates the durational rhythm of melting sugar. He writes:

> If I want to mix a glass of sugar and water, I must, willy nilly, wait until the sugar melts. This little fact is big with meaning. For there the time I have to wait is not that mathematical time which would apply equally well to the entire history of the material world, even if that history were spread out instantaneously in space. It coincides with my impatience, that is to say, with a certain portion of my own duration, which I cannot protract or contract as I like. It is no longer something thought, it is something lived.[218]

Mullarkey makes the following comments about this passage:

> this is always Bergson's temporal question . . . why aren't things instantaneous? . . . why is the universe temporal? Why do we have to wait for the sugar to dissolve? . . . these are questions born of affect, or enforced patience, born from the need to slow down for certain things and speed up for others.

This, Mullarkey continues, is 'as true of film as it is of life'.[219] Cinema can make us aware of rhythms of duration through images that are held for too long or not long enough. Mullarkey reads this passage from Bergson alongside a shot from Kieślowski's *Three Colours Blue*, in which the heroine, Julie, dips a sugar cube into a cup of coffee. For four and a half seconds, we see the sugar cube in close-up as the brown liquid soaks into it. Kieślowski was concerned that, should the shot last any longer, viewers would lose patience. Mullarkey writes that 'a sympathetic audience might be able to endure this extended duration too. Bergson would definitely think that it must.' Unless we fast-forward through a film's duration, we must share with the film a certain section of time.

Although I suggest various possibilities for viewing the films, and cite other critics' experiences of viewing and analysing them, it is clear that to speak of a homogenous process of film viewing is impossible. Whether a shot is held for 'too long' or 'not long enough' is dependent upon each viewer and each screening, the conditions of which will vary greatly. Mullarkey emphasises this also: 'what makes the moment stand out' is that it may be '*too long* against our expected norms,'[220] but what may be unexpected for some, may not be for others, and thus 'there is no one objective and infinite context other than the infinity of subjective finite contexts'.[221] What for one viewer might seem too long for another might offer a moment of elongated rapture. This issue comes to the fore in Chapter 2 on *L'Avventura*. For some of the original audience of the film, Antonioni's long-takes of everyday actions were simply too long when measured against the standards of the day. For others, the long-takes and dissolves that slowed down the pace of the films were some of the most affective aspects of the viewing experience.

Notes

1. Lesley Stern, 'Paths That Wind Through the Thicket of Things', *Critical Inquiry*, 28.1 (2001), p. 334.
2. Mary Ann Doane, *The Emergence of Cinematic Time* (Cambridge: Harvard University Press, 2002), p. 6.
3. Ibid., p. 9.
4. Ibid., pp. 4 and 33.
5. Ibid., p. 33.
6. Ibid., pp. 33–4.
7. Georg Simmel cited by Leo Charney, *Empty Moments: Cinema, Modernity and Drift* (Durham: Duke University Press, 1998), p. 74.
8. Doane, *Cinematic Time*, p. 11.
9. Ibid., p. 10.
10. Ibid., p. 11.
11. Mary Ann Doane, 'The Indexical and the Concept of Medium Specificity', *Differences*, 18.1 (2007), p. 133.
12. Doane, *Cinematic Time*, p. 11.
13. Ibid., p. 11.
14. Ibid., p. 22.
15. Ibid., p. 22.

16. Rachel Moore, *Savage Theory: Cinema As Modern Magic* (Durham: Duke University Press, 2000), p. 100.
17. Doane, *Cinematic Time*, p. 10.
18. Ibid., p. 94.
19. Walter Benjamin, 'The Work of Art in the Age of Mechanical Reproduction', in Gerald Mast, Marshall Cohen and Leo Braudy (eds), *Film Theory and Criticism* (Oxford: Oxford University Press, 1992), p. 678.
20. Michael Taussig, 'Tactility and Distraction', *Cultural Anthropology*, 6.2 (1991), p. 148.
21. Taussig, 'Tactility', p. 148.
22. Doane, *Cinematic Time*, p. 14.
23. Ibid., p. 15.
24. Benjamin, 'The Work of Art in the Age of Mechanical Reproduction', p. 678.
25. Sara Danius, *The Senses of Modernism* (Ithaca: Cornell University Press, 2002), p. 2.
26. Ibid., p. 194.
27. Miriam Hansen, 'Benjamin, Cinema and Experience: "The Blue Flower in the Land of Technology"', *New German Critique*, 40 (1987), p. 211.
28. Susan Buck-Morss, 'Aesthetics and Anaesthetics: Walter Benjamin's Artwork Essay Reconsidered', *October*, 62 (1992), p. 6.
29. Ibid., p. 5. Original italics.
30. Taussig, 'Tactility', p. 149.
31. Ibid., p. 149.
32. Malcolm Turvey, 'Jean Epstein's Cinema of Immanence: The Rehabilitation of the Corporeal Eye', *October*, 83 (1998), p. 34.
33. Ibid., p. 34.
34. Ibid., p. 34.
35. Ibid., p. 35.
36. Christian Keathley, *Cinephilia and History* (Bloomington: Indiana University Press, 2006), p. 100.
37. Tom Brown and James Walters, *Film Moments* (London: Palgrave Macmillan, 2010), p. xi.
38. Mary Ann Doane, 'The Close-Up: Scale and Detail in the Cinema', *Differences*, 14.3 (2003), p. 92.
39. Jean Epstein, 'Magnification and Other Writings', *October*, 3 (1977), p. 13.
40. Doane, 'Close-Up', p. 97.
41. Epstein, 'Magnification', p. 9.
42. Doane, 'Close-Up', p. 109.
43. Paul Willemen, *Looks and Frictions: Essays in Cultural Studies and Film Theory* (Bloomington: Indiana University Press, 1994), p. 124.
44. Keathley, *Cinephilia and History*, p. 60.
45. Robert Stam, *Film Theory: An Introduction* (Malden: Blackwell, 2000), p. 33.

46. Richard Abel, *French Film Theory and Criticism: A History/Anthology 1907–1939* (Princeton: Princeton University Press, 1988), p. xvi.
47. Ibid., p. 209.
48. Germaine Dulac, 'Aesthetics, Objects, Integral Cinegraphie' (1926), in Richard Abel (ed.), p. 397.
49. Marcel Gromaire, 'A Painter's Idea's About the Cinema' (1919), in Abel (ed.), pp. 176–7.
50. Abel, *French Film Theory and Criticism*, p. 110.
51. Louis Aragon, 'On Décor' (1918), in Richard Abel (ed.), *French Film Theory and Criticism: A History/Anthology 1907–1939* (Princeton: Princeton University Press, 1988), p. 166.
52. Fernand Leger, '*La Roue*: Its Plastic Quality' (1922), in Abel (ed.), p. 273.
53. Cocteau cited by Abel, p. 110.
54. Doane, *Cinematic Time*, p. 210.
55. Ibid., 209.
56. Epstein, 'Magnification', p. 10.
57. Aragon, 'On Décor', in Abel (ed.), p. 167.
58. Ricciotto Canudo, 'The Birth of a Sixth Art' (1911), in Abel (ed.), pp. 58–9.
59. Epstein, 'Magnification', p. 9.
60. Ibid., p. 9.
61. Élie Faure, 'The Art of Cineplastics' (1923), in Abel (ed.), p. 265.
62. Willemen, *Looks and Frictions*, p. 235.
63. Ibid., p. 235.
64. Ibid., p. 233.
65. Keathley, *Cinephilia and History*, p. 8.
66. Ibid., p. 9.
67. Marcel L'Herbier, 'Hermes and Silence', in Abel (ed.), p. 149.
68. Balázs, Béla, *Theory of Film: Character and Growth of a New Art*, trans. by Edith Bone (London: D. Dobson, 1952), pp. 61–2.
69. Gilles Deleuze, *Cinema 1* (London: Continuum, 2005), *Cinema 2* (London and New York: Continuum, 2005).
70. Christian Metz, *Psychoanalysis and Cinema* (London: Macmillan, 1983), p. 15.
71. Tim Groves, 'Cinema/Affect/Writing', *Senses of Cinema*, 2003, http://www.sensesofcinema.com/contents/03/25/writing_cinema_affect.html
72. Roger Odin, 'For a Semio-Pragmatics of Film', in Robert Stam and Tony Miller (eds), *Film and Theory: An Anthology* (Malden and Oxford: Blackwell, 2000), p. 55.
73. Deleuze, *Cinema 2*, p. 26.
74. D. N. Rodowick, *Gilles Deleuze's Time Machine* (Durham: Duke University Press, 1997), p. 40.
75. Deleuze, *Cinema 2*, pp. 27–8.
76. Rodowick, p. 40.

77. Roland Barthes, *Image, Music, Text*, trans. by Stephen Heath (London: Fontana, 1977), p. 53.
78. Ibid., p. 53.
79. Ibid., p. 54.
80. Ibid., p. 62.
81. Ibid., p. 65.
82. Ibid., p. 64.
83. Ibid., p. 65.
84. Ibid., p. 67.
85. Ibid., p. 67.
86. Ibid., p. 68.
87. Regis Durand, 'How to See (Photographically)', in Patrice Petro (ed.), *Fugitive Images: From Photography to Video* (Bloomington: Indiana University Press, 1995), pp. 142–3.
88. Derek Attridge, 'Roland Barthes's Obtuse, Sharp Meaning and the Responsibilities of Commentary', in Jean-Michel Rabaté (ed.), *Writing the Image After Roland Barthes* (Pennsylvania: University of Pennsylvania Press, 1997), pp. 78–9.
89. Roland Barthes, *Camera Lucida: Reflections on Photography*, trans. by Richard Howard (London: Cape, 1982), p. 49.
90. Ibid., p. 51.
91. Laura Mulvey, 'Visual Pleasure and Narrative Cinema', in Robert Stam and Tony Miller (eds), *Film and Theory: An Anthology* (Malden and Oxford: Blackwell, 2000), p. 488.
92. Laura Mulvey, *Death 24x a Second* (London: Reaktion, 2006), p. 7.
93. Ibid., p. 144.
94. Ibid., p. 186.
95. Ibid., p. 186.
96. Ibid., p. 186.
97. Ibid., p. 196.
98. David Bordwell and Noël Carroll, *Post-Theory: Reconstructing Film Studies* (Madison: University of Wisconsin Press, 1996), p. xvi.
99. Ibid., p. xiv.
100. David Bordwell, *Narration in the Fiction Film* (London: Routledge, 1995), p. xi.
101. Ibid., p. 29.
102. Bordwell, *Narration*, p. 205.
103. Ibid., p. 275; Kristin Thompson, *Eisenstein's* Ivan the Terrible*: A Neoformalist Analysis* (Princeton: Princeton University Press, 1981), p. 273.
104. Bordwell, *Narration*, p. 280.
105. Daniel Frampton, *Filmosophy* (London: Wallflower, 2006), p. 104.
106. Ibid., p. 109.
107. Anne Rutherford, 'Precarious Boundaries: Affect, Mise-en-scene and the Senses in Angelopoulos' Balkans Epic', *Senses of Cinema* (2002),

http://www.sensesofcinema.com/contents/04/31/angelopoulos_balkan_epic.html.
108. Ibid.
109. Bordwell, *Narration*, pp. 80–8.
110. Sobchack, *Carnal Thoughts*, p. 63.
111. Anne Rutherford, 'Cinema and Embodied Affect', *Senses of Cinema*, 2002, http://www.sensesofcinema.com/contents/03/25/embodied_affect.html.
112. Lesley Stern, 'I think, Sebastian, Therefore . . . I Somersault', *Paradoxa*, 3 (1997), http://www.lib.latrobe.edu.au/AHR/archive/Issue-November-1997/stern2.html
113. Laura U. Marks, *The Skin of the Film* (Durham: Duke University Press, 2000), p. 127.
114. Danius, p. 195.
115. Ibid., p. 196.
116. Vivian Sobchack, *The Address of the Eye: A Phenomenology of the Film Experience* (Princeton: Princeton University Press, 1992), p. xv.
117. Ibid., p. 17.
118. Metz, p. 61. See also Jean-Louis Baudry, 'Ideological Effects of the Basic Cinematographic Apparatus', in Mast et al. (eds), *Film Theory and Criticism*, p. 310.
119. Metz, p. 61.
120. Ibid., p. 60.
121. Susan Sontag, *Against Interpretation* (London: Eyre & Spottiswoode, 1967), p. 14.
122. Marks, *The Skin*, p. 183.
123. Sobchack, *Carnal Thoughts*, p. 59.
124. Ibid., pp. 59–60.
125. Steven Shaviro, *The Cinematic Body* (Minneapolis: University of Minnesota Press, 1993), pp. 14–15.
126. Sobchack, *Address*, p. 24.
127. Ibid., p. 24.
128. Ibid., p. 286.
129. Sobchack, *Carnal Thoughts*, p. 65.
130. Sobchack, *Address*, p. 129.
131. Ibid., p. 133.
132. Sobchack, *Carnal Thoughts*, p. 71.
133. Ibid., p. 77.
134. Ibid., p. 71.
135. Anne Rutherford, 'Precarious Boundaries'.
136. Rutherford, 'Cinema'.
137. Ibid.
138. Shaviro, p. 52.
139. Ibid., p. 53.

140. Jennifer Fisher, 'Relational Sense: Towards an Haptic Aesthetics', *Parachute*, 87 (1997).
141. Baudry, p. 307. See also Jean-Luc Comolli and Jean Narboni, 'Cinema/Ideology/Criticism', in Mast et al. (eds), *Film Theory and Criticism*, pp. 682–9.
142. Metz, p. 54.
143. Sobchack, *Address*, p. 9.
144. Blanchot cited by Shaviro, p. 47.
145. Sobchack, *Carnal Thoughts*, p. 66.
146. Sobchack, *Address*, p. 217.
147. Ibid., pp. 61–2.
148. Ibid., p. 31.
149. Sobchack, *Carnal Thoughts*, p. 65.
150. Ibid., p. 58.
151. Ibid., p. 65.
152. Ibid., p. 66.
153. Rutherford, 'Precarious Boundaries'.
154. Ibid.
155. Marks, *The Skin*, pp. 144–5.
156. Ibid., p. 31.
157. Sobchack, *Carnal Thoughts*, p. 78.
158. Marks, *The Skin*, p. 190.
159. Ibid., p. 142.
160. Ibid., p. xiii.
161. Bergson cited by Marks, p. 48.
162. Marks, *The Skin*, p. 64.
163. Rutherford, 'Precarious Boundaries'.
164. Stern, 'Paths', p. 354.
165. Marks, *The Skin*, p. 129.
166. Colebrook, *Gilles Deleuze*, p. 38.
167. Ibid., p. 39.
168. Ibid., p. 39.
169. Massumi, *Parables for the Virtual*, p. 35.
170. Elena del Río, *Deleuze and the Cinemas of Performance* (Edinburgh: Edinburgh University Press, 2008), p. 10.
171. Colebrook, *Gilles Deleuze*, p. 35.
172. Massumi, *Parables for the Virtual*, p. 13.
173. del Río, *Deleuze and the Cinemas of Performance*, p. 15.
174. Simon O'Sullivan, *Art Encounters Deleuze and Guattari* (New York: Palgrave Macmillan, 2006), p. 67.
175. Massumi, *Parables for the Virtual*, pp. 31–2.
176. Ibid., p. 30.
177. Massumi, *Parables for the Virtual*, p. 1.
178. Suzanne Guerlac, *Thinking in Time: An Introduction to Henri Bergson* (Ithaca and London: Cornell University Press, 2006), p. 77.

179. Brown and Walters, *Film Moments*, p. 2.
180. Henri Bergson, *Matter and Memory* (London: George Allen & Unwin, 1962), pp. 243 and 275.
181. Bliss Cua Lim, *Translating Time: Cinema, the Fantastic, and Temporal Critique* (Durham and London: Duke University Press, 2009), p. 10.
182. Yve Lomax, 'Thinking Stillness', in David Green and Joanna Lowry (ed.), *Stillness and Time: Photography and the Moving Image* (Brighton: Photoworks, 2006), p. 56.
183. Elizabeth Grosz, 'Thinking the New: Of Futures Yet Unthought', in Elizabeth Grosz (ed.), *Becomings: Explorations in Time, Memory and Futures* (Ithaca and London: Cornell University Press, 1999), p. 17.
184. Henri Bergson, 'The Idea of Duration', in Keith Ansell Pearson and John Mullarkey (eds), *Henri Bergson: Key Writings* (New York and London: Continuum, 2005), p. 60.
185. Bergson, *Matter and Memory*, p. 176.
186. Ibid., p. 177.
187. Grosz, *The Nick of Time*, p. 173.
188. Ibid., p. 176.
189. Ibid., pp. 176–7.
190. Henri Bergson, 'Duration and Intuition', in J. J. C. Smart (ed.), *Problems of Space and Time* (New York: Macmillan, 1976), pp. 140.
191. Ibid., 140.
192. Keith Ansell Pearson, *Philosophy and the Adventure of the Virtual* (London: Routledge, 2002), pp. 9–10.
193. Amy Herzog, 'Images of Thought and Acts of Creation: Deleuze, Bergson, and the Question of Cinema', *Invisible Culture* (2000), http://www.rochester.edu/in_visible_culture/issue3/herzog.htm
194. Lim, *Translating Time*, p. 11.
195. Deleuze, *Cinema 1*, p. 1.
196. Ibid., pp. 2–3.
197. Ibid., pp. 3–4.
198. Ibid., p. 12.
199. Deleuze, *Cinema 2*, p. 152.
200. Ibid., p. 153.
201. Ibid., p. 35.
202. Deleuze, *Cinema 2*, pp. 17–18.
203. Ibid., p. 19.
204. Ibid., p. 22.
205. Lim, *Translating Time*, p. 44.
206. Paul Douglass, 'Bergson and Cinema: Friends or Foes?', in John Mullarkey (ed.), *The New Bergson* (Manchester and New York: Manchester University Press, 2007), pp. 221 and 224.
207. Totaro, 'Time, Bergson'.
208. Pearson, *Philosophy and the Adventure of the Virtual*, p. 13.

209. Grosz, *Nick of Time*, p. 234.
210. Ibid., p. 235.
211. Mullarkey, *Bergson and Philosophy*, p. 19.
212. Guerlac, *Thinking in Time*, pp. 47–8.
213. Ibid., p. 50.
214. Stern, 'I think'.
215. Ibid.
216. Rutherford, 'Precarious Boundaries'.
217. Rutherford, 'Cinema'.
218. Henri Bergson, *Creative Evolution* (Palgrave Macmillan, 2007), pp. 6–7.
219. Mullarkey, *Moving Image*, pp. 165–6.
220. Ibid., p. 166.
221. Ibid., p. 166.

CHAPTER 2

L'Avventura: Temporal Adventures

When *L'Avventura* came out in 1960, cinema was undergoing a period of renewal. As Nowell-Smith explains, this was characterised by a rebellion against 'the false perfection of the studio film'. Film directors acquired a new visibility, as films increasingly displayed 'open-ended narratives, internal quotation, autobiographical references, first-person statements', while eschewing gloss and glamour.[1] Although most films released at this time kept to classical styles of composition and narrative form, cultural innovators such as Antonioni began to disrupt the coherence and continuity of space, time and narrative that cinema had previously worked to maintain.[2] The premiere of *L'Avventura* at the Cannes Film Festival in 1960 revealed, however, that the viewing habits of some spectators had not quite caught up with the radical changes that cinema was undergoing. The film was booed by the audience, while Antonioni and lead actress Monica Vitti fled in despair. Spectators seemed to have two related primary grievances. First, the film's ellipses and 'dead times', in which nothing is happening that appears to advance the narrative, ensured that the audience, to paraphrase Hamish Ford, saw what they expected to miss, and missed what they expected to see.[3] The slow temporality of the film provoked many negative affects, namely, boredom, frustration, and irritation. Second, the interpretive strategies that were commonly employed by film critics in the 1950s seemed to fail when set against the film's ambiguity and open-endedness.

In *L'Avventura*, Lea Massari, an actress well known to contemporary Italian audiences, plays Anna, a girl who disappears during a cruise taken by a group of wealthy Romans in Sicily. The film follows the relatively unknown Vitti, playing Anna's friend Claudia, and Anna's fiancé Sandro (Gabriele Ferzetti), who develop a love affair while meandering across the Sicilian countryside, ostensibly looking for Anna. Anna is last seen on the rocky, near-deserted island of Lisca Bianca, where the group have briefly stopped. Sandro and Claudia remain overnight on the island in a shepherd's hut in the hope that she will return. The next morning, Sandro unexpectedly kisses a shocked Claudia. With their plans disrupted by Anna's disappearance, the members of the cruise travel to a villa owned by their wealthy friends, the Montaldos; Claudia and Sandro, however, decide to look for Anna independently of each other. Sandro does attempt to remain with Claudia, but, confused and disturbed, she rejects him. They are eventually reunited when they both arrive in the town of Troina. They begin an affair and travel together to Noto on the basis of a reported sighting of Anna. Without any further news, they rejoin the other members of the cruise in Taormina, where Claudia catches Sandro with a prostitute, Gloria Perkins. Anna is never seen again.

What was more disturbing than the disappearance of Anna, who in the film's opening scenes seems to be established as the main character, was that the film did not appear concerned with finding her, leaving, as Brunette writes, 'a gaping hole in the film, an invisibility at its centre, which suggests an elsewhere, a nonplace, that remains forever unavailable to interpretation and that destroys the dream of full visibility', a dream that had been harboured by neo-realism.[4] While the radical deployments of temporal rhythms and the film's ambiguities of meaning angered some of the Cannes audience, *L'Avventura* was immediately recognised as a masterpiece by the jury panel, which awarded it a Special Jury Prize for 'a new movie language and the beauty of its images'. The film was eventually established as a classic of modern art cinema and for decades afterwards was regularly listed as one of *Sight and Sound*'s top ten films.[5]

Following the disastrous Cannes premiere, Antonioni was encouraged to release a statement 'explaining' the film, in which he stated that *L'Avventura*'s 'tragedy' emerged from a fundamental mismatch between our increasingly scientifically open-minded society and morally antiquated attitudes, which reveals itself most clearly in love relationships. Part of the statement read:

> Why do you think eroticism is so prevalent today in our literature, our theatrical shows, and elsewhere? It is a symptom of the emotional sickness of our time. But this preoccupation with the erotic would not become obsessive if Eros were healthy, that is, if it were kept within human proportions. But Eros is sick; man is uneasy, something is bothering him. And whenever something bothers him, man reacts, but he reacts badly, only on erotic impulse . . . the tragedy of *L'Avventura* stems directly from an erotic impulse of this kind – unhappy, miserable, futile.[6]

Much critical and theoretical writing on the film is based upon this statement. William Arrowsmith's chapter on *L'Avventura*, for example, revolves around the idea of the 'malaise of Eros' that supposedly plagues the film's characters.[7] The erotic disease, Arrowsmith notes, is most evident in Sandro's serial womanising and self-absorption. Arrowsmith likens Antonioni's treatment of the disease of Eros as a 'cool, clinical diagnosis . . . noting the ensemble of the symptoms – the phenomenology of the disease – not merely suggesting its ubiquitous operation'.[8] Peter Bondanella also draws on Antonioni's statement to illuminate the film: 'When sexuality fails as a means of communication and provides only physical relief, then, in Antonioni's terms, Eros is sick.'[9]

Critical writing on *L'Avventura* also tends to suggest that the film reflects the particular preoccupations of its time, such as alienation and the soullessness of modern bourgeois life. According to Bondanella, for example, Antonioni displayed an 'exceptional sensitivity to the philosophical currents of the times' by portraying 'modern neurotic, alienated, and guilt-ridden characters whose emotional lives are sterile – or at least poorly developed'. Bondanella likens Antonioni's presentation of 'existential boredom' to the writing of Alberto Moravia.[10] Connecting *L'Avventura* with three films that followed it, also featuring Vitti, *La Notte* (1961), *L'Eclisse* (1962), and *Il Deserto Rosso* (1964),[11] Seymour Chatman has similarly argued that the 'central thematic network' of this 'tetralogy' is 'the perilous state of our emotional life. Narcissism, egoism, self-absorption, ennui, distraction, neuroses, existential anxiety . . . these terms struggle to characterize a life lacking in purpose.'[12] Clara Orban echoes this in her analysis also, claiming that 'the women in Michelangelo Antonioni's films provide desperate proof of the alienation of the city . . . empty streets, stark urban landscapes, and thin, agitated, unhappy people represent the anxiety of modern city life'.[13]

While these readings are praiseworthy for their sensitivity to the films' historical contexts, interpretations focusing on the alienation and existential malaise of Antonioni's characters and their society have become rather repetitive. This chapter aims to suggest other ways in which the film can be described or analysed. Specifically, I hope to challenge a particular characteristic of interpretive frameworks around *L'Avventura*, namely, that the mise-en-scène is consistently seen as something to be decoded to find the appropriate clues or meanings that Antonioni 'intended'. Interpretations of Antonioni's films tend to allow for some ambiguity, but limit the scope of interpretation by a reliance upon the institutional and textual presence of the 'author'. James Stoller, for example, has written that Antonioni 'by not commenting, comments'.[14] According to Ian Cameron, who was writing in 1962, the release of *L'Avventura* created the impression that it was a film whose technique was so closely moulded to its author's intentions that it required the closest concentration for every second of its length.[15] Every gesture, he continues, 'has a precise significance and every technical device Antonioni can muster is used to help us see it'.[16] For Ned Rifkin, the 'essence' of Antonioni's visual language is 'the notion that dominant dramatic information can be delivered to the viewer through a visual mode of sign and symbol'.[17] Rifkin's argument that Antonioni's images form a kind of 'visual language' relies on the assertion that the image 'connotes a matrix of optical data which, when decoded, can be translated into meaning or a system of content'.[18] Ted Perry echoed this analysis in the 1990s, arguing that Antonioni 'fills every frame with his purposes. Density of expression is a truism in Antonioni's works ... everything is determined by the director to serve his artistic ends'.[19]

This chapter suggests that the relationship between image and meaning in *L'Avventura* is more fluid than the above statements indicate. As Brunette has written, critical interpretation of Antonioni's films seems to be

> only arrived at by means of a certain violent epistemological gesture of transcendence, a gesture that moves one quickly and painlessly from the supposedly 'superficial' (and certainly confusing) level of the film's particular, material details to a 'higher' more synoptic level where things can be made to cohere.[20]

A particularly interesting analysis of Antonioni's films in this respect was originally given by Roland Barthes in 1980, at a lecture in Bologna. Barthes spoke of a 'leakage' of meaning, 'which is not the same as its abolition', and a 'discomfiture of affect – which escapes the grip of meaning at the heart of the identity of events'.[21] Rather than particular meanings, Barthes finds a 'vibration': 'the object vibrates, to the detriment of dogma'.[22] Barthes here articulates one of the aspects of the film that my analysis will suggest, namely the way in which images may resonate or vibrate with affect, rather than necessarily or only put forward meanings to be interpreted. My main goal in this chapter, however, is to challenge the particular ways in which Antonioni's authorial signature is seen to manifest itself: in flattened, static compositions. Bondanella, for example, compares Antonioni to a still photographer, his shots marked 'as surely as though his signature were affixed to the celluloid'.[23] Brunette associates Antonioni with Manet, 'who, while remaining intensely naturalistic in style, also flattens the perspective of his canvas, thus purposely calling attention to the artificiality of the two-dimensional medium'.[24]

Such analyses tend to detach images from the temporal flow and movement of the film. My reading of *L'Avventura* questions whether stillness and flatness are the most adequate ways of characterising the film's images.

This chapter engages with questions of temporality as they relate to mise-en-scène, pace, and the film's spaces. In particular, I trace the movements of, and within, the images as they transform through time and are presented in depth. Structures of looking and imaging throughout the film, I argue, have the potential to encourage affective responses in viewers. The slow pace and lingering rhythms, where time ceases to be subject to strict narrative development and instead unfolds its own particular concerns, encourages an attentive awareness of the passage of time through the film.

Depth and Movement

In his monograph on Antonioni, Chatman expresses what he believes are the primary characteristics of Antonioni's images, flatness and stillness, by drawing upon art historian William Worringer to explain Antonioni's 'cool' mise-en-scène. Worringer, according to Chatman, distinguished between the two 'polar impulses' of art. The organic mode projects empathy and is deeply focused, so that 'our eyes delight in caressing the surfaces and depths' of an image, 'and hence in experiencing objects in the round'.[25] This 'flourishes in periods of psychological harmony'. The abstract mode signifies the point at which people feel discomfort at outside phenomena, a 'spiritual dread' of open spaces. 'The pure and regular geometry of abstract cartography then presents an attractive way of controlling, allaying and sublimating that anxiety.'[26] In applying this to Antonioni, Chatman writes that 'seeking whatever certainties it can find, all the camera is sure of is the regularity of plane geometry. In such moments, the screen ceases to be a window looking into deep space and becomes a nearby surface of uncertain expanse against which the characters are flattened.'[27] The rendering of a flat, surface composition is linked by Chatman to the inability of the characters to 'grasp' things, to have meaningful contact with their surroundings: 'the absence of contour and dimension makes imaginative as well as real touching difficult'.[28] The ways in which 'characters are frequently pinned to walls', writes Chatman, 'suggest moral or psychological entrapment, unbridgeable alienation', although Chatman does warn against an overly simplified symbolisation.[29] Chatman locates moments of graphic composition in *L'Avventura* that 'constitute a focused, intentional, and daring abstract painting right in the middle of a commercial feature film'.[30] Such frames are worth enlarging and exhibiting as independent works of art;

> they make us want to stop the film so we can gaze at greater leisure. The ongoing narrative is, I suppose, thereby impaired, but only if we insist on conventional ways

of watching films. In defence of Antonioni's style, one might argue that the movie audience can and should develop something of the art lover's capacity to appreciate beautiful visual composition for its own sake.[31]

While Chatman seems to have developed this art lover's desire to gaze upon still images, one could argue that an appreciation of cinematic movement and temporal flow is less well in evidence. Depth is by no means ignored by Chatman, but Antonioni's use of depth is compared to still images, the paintings of Giorgio de Chirico, rather than to moving images that unfold in time.[32] While I agree that touching and grasping are important, both for the film's themes and for an understanding of the mise-en-scène in ways that I outline below, my formulation of this in relation to *L'Avventura* is rather different. The emphasis upon flatness, surface and abstraction in writing on Antonioni tends to obscure the strategies of depth and the film's fluid mobility. In *L'Avventura*, very few scenes are arranged as flattened compositions. Instead, the film continually emphasises a process of *relativising* in depth; that is, foreground and background are continuously placed in positions of perspectival relativity. We can see this in operation in one of the film's key locations, Lisca Bianca, which is continually framed against other islands in the background. Locations such as the top of the church tower in Noto also seem to provide an ideal opportunity for depth perspectives to be distinguished: the town is built on sloping ground, and the architecture is terraced, presenting an extensive, multilayered space. The film thus seems to continually urge us to think about the relationship between foreground and background, presenting the possibility of glimpsed but impenetrable and thus unknown spaces. We are encouraged to consider depth compositionally and thematically, as an ungraspable space that Anna has disappeared into.

The downplaying of the film's movements through time can be seen in the emphasis upon how characters in Antonioni's films frequently seem to be framed in windows and doorways, something often associated with moments of self-reflexivity or an erotic objectification of women. For Forgacs, for example, framed or reflected shots of Antonioni's actresses, 'because they are not obviously subordinated or functional to narrative, become similar to still photographs', alluding to 'fashion photographs, pin-ups, and advertising'.[33] In the very opening sequence of *L'Avventura*, argues Brunette, the camera attempts to 'flatten [Anna] against the background', moving so that she appears to remain stationary, and thus turning her into 'an *objet d'art*, something to be looked at'.[34] However, if we look at this sequence paying greater attention to its movement and temporal progress, we can discover different ways of describing it. In the very first shot, Anna has already emerged from the villa and is walking towards the camera, which swivels to keep her in shot, moving as she moves, and then appears to back away from her as she comes towards it. In the background behind her is a hedge, a wall and trees, at differing depths, such that the landscape does not appear flat, but rather terraced and textured. Nor does Anna appear stationary; rather, she is immediately shown in decisive movement. It is true that she stands framed for a moment in a doorway, but if we reinsert this moment into the film's temporal context, what stands out about it is its diegetic import: Anna seems to be steeling herself to continue, perhaps in a reaction to the voice of her father, who is heard on the soundtrack at that point.

The first time we see her, then, Anna is crossing from one threshold to another, emerging from the depths of her home into another exterior, the walled garden, and then into another space, the open field in front of the house. As Rohdie has written, 'one of the effects of the scene ... is to upset perceptions: you believe something to be one thing only to find that it is quite another and this in turn is subject to a further revision and change of perspective as spaces enclose other spaces and become further modified'.[35] The way in which the scene draws out her movements in time allows for such revisions to be made.

The opening sequence of the film can be seen to introduce two important characteristics of the film's composition that will henceforth recur. First, the textured nature of *L'Avventura*'s backgrounds. Even if, for example, characters are framed against walls, these tend to be textured and detailed rather than blank. The wall that Claudia is framed against in the railway station waiting room is seen at a slight angle and visibly worn by time and use. When Sandro and Claudia are framed together against a wall in Noto, the ripped remnants of posters that had been pasted on it stand out from, and add a tactile element to, the background. This shot ends in a gentle dissolve which literally renders this surface fluid in movement. Decayed and dilapidated stone walls recur throughout the film, from the Roman square that Sandro's apartment overlooks, to the old stone tower in the film's final shot; geometry is thus textured rather than necessarily forming an abstract surface. Second, the opening introduces us to the way in which events, or micro-events, occur on thresholds or between spaces, such as the kiss between Sandro and Claudia that changes the direction of the narrative. On a threshold, characters are neither wholly in one space nor another, but in a state of limbo, an indeterminate state that also has temporal dimensions. There is a moment, for example, when Sandro imperfectly pulls the curtains together before getting into bed with Anna. In the space between the curtains, Claudia can be seen on the street below, a framing that anticipates a time when Claudia will 'replace' Anna as Sandro's lover. The characters are frequently seen *moving through* transitional spaces, rather than framed in static compositions, such as the several corridors (at the Montaldo villa, at Taormina) that Claudia runs through, and the train, also suggestive of an elongated corridor. Sometimes even the frame itself struggles to contain the bodies of the characters, who appear at the extreme edges of it, with some limbs in the frame and others out. Their body parts move in and out of the frame in a seemingly random flux. For example, when Claudia wakes up at sunset in the shepherd's hut on the island, she appears at the very edge of the visibility that the frame only pretends to contain.

Depth, movement and flux are also vital, but rather neglected, characteristics of *L'Avventura*'s close-ups. As I suggested in Chapter 1, a tendency to extricate a particular moment from a film in film theory in general can be seen most readily in the discourse on the close-up. As Doane has written, close-ups have been seen to invite a desire for a 'moment of possession in which the image is extracted, whatever the narrative rationalisation may be, from the flow of the story'.[36] The close-up 'detaches itself from the rest of the film to draw attention to one important thing'; it provides film's 'most fully developed form of the moment' and its 'closest analogy to the frame around the painting, to the frozen instant memorialised by the photograph'.[37] For Chatman, Antonioni's close-ups seem to function precisely in this way, being in his view an example of the 'flat, abstract style' used by the director. Antonioni's extreme and fragmented close-ups, however, seem to refuse this tendency to flatten and still motion, refusing extractability from the flow of time. Instead, long-held close-ups slow down the pace of the film and draw attention to microscopic changes of facial expression. Reinserting the close-ups within a temporal flow and acknowledging their movement in duration allows for a more variegated sense of *L'Avventura*'s images.

We can take a scene from near the beginning of the film as an example. Claudia and Anna have set out from Anna's home to meet Sandro at his apartment in Rome before the cruise. Getting out of her car, Anna attempts to explain to Claudia her dissatisfaction with Sandro, and even seems to be at the point of abandoning the planned cruise. When Sandro calls to her from the window, however, she enters his apartment, looking at him disdainfully. Without a word, she begins to undress and they move to the bed, leaving Claudia to wait outside. As they make love, Anna's face is presented in close-up, which falls in and out of the frame with the movement of her head. Her eyes largely remain fixed on a point beyond the frame. The camera's intense focus on her face seems to invite us to question her motives and behaviour. Her face may appear as a surface, but the extension of the image through time seems to draw attention to something beyond this surface. As Doane has argued in relation to early cinema, 'behind the perfect, seamless face, the unwavering stare, it is impossible not to project thought, emotion, although the face gives no indication of either'.[38] The shot appears to bring the face up close, providing what Doane calls 'an intense phenomenological experience of presence',[39] yet it also continually retracts this intimacy. As it develops through duration, the sequence performs precisely that which cannot be grasped or possessed. As Anna's face falls in and out of frame, a window in the background is revealed which, as it is out of focus, emerges as a blurred rectangle of light. This area becomes something deep within the image which is unavailable either to vision or to touch, something which forever falls away into depth. While the discourse on the close-up 'seems to exemplify a desire to stop the film, to grab hold of something that can be taken away',[40] this sequence not only presents Anna as a character who cannot be grasped (she will soon disappear), but also cinematically performs a refusal to abstract itself from temporality and from depth.

Antonioni frequently presents surfaces and depths within the same shot. When Claudia, passing time at the Montaldo villa and waiting for Sandro, hears a car arriving, she runs out on to the balcony to see who it is. The camera briefly follows her progress across the room, then stops just at the threshold of the glass door leading on to the balcony. This door splits the composition in half; on one side, we are presented with the flat, dark surface of the wall of the room, and on the other, the vast white balcony. Lines of perspective converge at the corner of the balcony, where Claudia stands looking out over the driveway. The dynamic oppositions in this composition activate a powerful resonance. The harsh lines of the balcony, for example, are juxtaposed with the softer, shadowed outlines of hills and trees in the distance. Claudia, furthermore, is never shown as a static figure, and the starkness of the balcony's lines and shades draws the movement of her body to the fore as she runs to and from the corner. The composition, again, is shown at a slight angle, such that even the flat surface in the foreground is granted perspective. This surface is also one that is heavily textured, consisting of a panelled, decorated wooden display cabinet with intricate sculpted figurines on top of it. The glass panel in the middle of the screen presents yet another 'terrace' of textured possibility. The composition encourages both what Marks has called optical visuality and haptic looking; the former perceiving 'distinct forms in deep space', the latter moving 'over the surface of the object . . . not to distinguish form so much as to discern texture'.[41] The presentation of optic and haptic modes simultaneously within one shot invites a fascinated look at the image. By being presented in a single shot rather than in succession, a movement is activated between the two modes.

Another significant series of close-ups in the film also activate an oscillation between tactile surface and ungraspable depth, between texture and incorporeality. After visiting a deserted Sicilian town in the search for Anna, a sudden cut shows us Claudia being held up in Sandro's arms, laughing into the sky. This slight perceptual shock carries a sense of uneasiness over into the duration of the sequence, as the lovers are shown kissing on the ground in close-up. Both Claudia and the camera seem to attempt to grasp something as closely as possible: Claudia repeats 'mine, mine, mine' while kissing Sandro, and the camera moves so close to their faces that sometimes only parts of their facial features are present on the screen. This sequence resonates powerfully with a kind of hapticity in which the surface of the screen appeals to the sense of touch. The textures of their hair, the grass, the lines on Sandro's face and their hands touching each other, resonate through the extreme close-ups. Touching and grasping are depicted, thematised, and enacted, performed by the camera. Because Claudia and Sandro are continually in movement, there is little sense of this being a static stilled image; instead, the sequence enacts a process in which these various textures come to the fore in duration. The affective power of the close-up seems to destabilise a sense of detached stillness. As Deleuze has written, the close-up image is 'difficult to define, because it is felt rather than conceived: it concerns what is new in the experience, what is fresh, fleeting and nevertheless eternal'.[42] The affect of the close-up contains an element of the temporal and the incorporeal: it enacts not an immediate bodily sensation or idea, but 'a possible sensation, feeling or idea' which extends in time.[43] According to Stern, furthermore, 'affect derives its force not merely from the immediacy of touch but from the capacity of the object to elude the voracious grasp of the moment (and the narrative), to reverberate beyond the frame, to generate ideas within a cultural landscape not circumscribed by the diegesis'.[44] The close-up can also draw attention to that from which it is extracted, alluding to what it has failed to capture. It is this tension between distance and closeness, intimacy and ungraspability that the close-ups perform in this sequence as they extend in time.

While not denying the critical consensus that many of the shots would function beautifully as photographs, it is important not to repress the way in which Antonioni's compositions are always in flux and movement, such that geometrical arrangements modulate in duration and tend to liquefy static lines. This modulation also serves to make the human figures, especially Claudia, stand out more powerfully in their expressive and fluid physicality. Where strong compositional lines are present, they often emphasise the soft outlines of the human figures through juxtaposition. In an early scene, for example, when Claudia is waiting for Anna and Sandro, we see a composition made up of the criss-crossing wooden beams of a ceiling, with the camera tilted upwards so that the angle of the ceiling recedes into the distance rather than forming a purely flat surface. Claudia's head, moving from side to side, gradually enters the frame, her face growing bigger until it almost fills the screen, and disrupts the geometrical construction of the mise-en-scène with her presence. As Jennifer Barker has argued in relation to Antonioni's films, the presence of the physical body may threaten non-compliance with, even subversion of, a film's organised systems of composition.[45] The force of these 'bodily irruptions', to use Barker's term, is also echoed diegetically: when prostitute Gloria Perkins arrives in a small Sicilian town, she causes a riot in which hundreds of men stream on to the streets and jostle for a look at her. Her naked flesh is shown beneath a tear in her skirt, as though the sensuousness of the body has ruptured the fabric. This scene seems to present a deliberately excessive eruption of bodily excitation, which is also frequently pushed to the fore compositionally.

While Antonioni's compositions are often compared to paintings, paintings themselves appear at several points in *L'Avventura*. They are frequently, however, set in opposition to, or at least distinguished from, the film's own temporal presentation of experience in depth. In Rome, Claudia wanders through an art gallery where two groups of visitors are examining two different paintings. An immediate diegetic relativity is established between them which echoes that established between the movement of cinema and the still frame of painting. The members of the first group are elegantly dressed and offer pretentious praise (in English) of the painting in front of them. The second group consists of Italian men who joke about the painter's brush with starvation. The scene is composed so that the two groups are on opposite sides of a wall, which we see only from the side (thus the paintings themselves are seen only obliquely). As Claudia walks between the two groups, the camera appears to track *through* this wall, performing the movement and temporal duration that sets it apart from stilled and flattened surfaces. Modernist painting is again introduced in a scene that takes place at the Montaldo villa. The studio of a young resident painter is full of geometrical compositions of nude women traced across blank backgrounds. As the painter pursues Giulia, one of the members of the cruise, the camera circles around this small space with graceful balletic movements, dynamising and activating it. Claudia, in the meantime, becomes absorbed by the landscape seen through the window, which presents a perfect vista of differently shaded hills in a perspective of depth. In this scene movements and modes of looking through time and space seem to be explicitly set apart from the kind of static and flattened compositions which so often serve as a comparison to Antonioni's frames.

When asked about the relationship between cinema and painting, Antonioni stated that

> while for the painter it is a matter of uncovering a static reality, or at most a rhythm that can be held in a single image, for a director the problem is to catch a reality which is never static, which is always moving towards and away from a moment of crystallization.[46]

This description of moving towards and away from crystallisation echoes a fluidity in cinema that I trace throughout this book in relation to meaning, symbol, and composition. With regards to Antonioni's images in particular, we can read the relationship between cinema and painting alongside Peucker's argument that, from the earliest days of cinema, films have often deliberately contrasted themselves to static painting through, for example, cinematic movement that attempts to 'outdo painting', or to 'bring it to life'.[47] We can see this in operation again in a scene in Taormina towards the end of the film. At a crowded hotel, a woman stands with her back to us looking at a painting. The scene is tightly framed so that we see only the back of her head. Sandro enters the frame in close-up, as the camera refocuses slightly to clarify the outline of his face. There begins a gracefully choreographed series of movements as Sandro and the woman, who is very similar to the woman in the painting, turn their heads towards and away from each other several times in turn. The static frame of the painting becomes the backdrop against which the movements of the characters and the subtle refocusing of the camera are activated.

Arguably, static compositions or isolated moments belong less to the experience of *L'Avventura* in its duration than to the way in which we are likely to remember it after viewing. That is, particular moments isolated in critical discourse and discussed as a stilled, static composition are more suited to our memory of the film than to our experience of it in duration. As Klinger has argued, films store themselves in memory most effectively in the form of affecting images. We often remember particular scenes and objects with more intensity than story details or narrative significance.[48] This seems to be especially true of close-ups. According to Doane, close-ups become 'one of our most potent memories of the cinema'.[49] As scenes from films become detached in memory, the duration of the film drops away. As Burgin writes, 'what was once a film in a movie theater . . . is now a kernel of psychical representations, a fleeting association of discrete elements ... the more the film is distanced in memory, the more the binding effect of the narrative is loosened. The sequence breaks apart.'[50]

It is significant, in this context, that cinephilia, the passionate engagement with film's privileged moments, has been seen as a 'collecting activity'. As Willemen writes, in cinephilic experience discrete objects and moments are serialised in the viewer's mind into collections: 'the moment of cinephilia has to do with the serialisation of moments of revelation'.[51] With the development of DVD technologies that allow the viewer to literally collect cinephilic moments, the experience of cinephilia has been transformed. Although Sontag proclaimed that the introduction of DVDs suggested that cinephilia was dead, Marijke de Valck and Malte Hagener have argued that it has reinvented itself with new technologies.[52] In their opinion, the term should not be restricted to its historical context as part of the discourse of *Cahiers du Cinéma*, but rather seen in the more general sense of a universal phenomenon in which the film experience invokes feelings of intense pleasure and rapture.[53] In writing of being able to literally still the moving image with DVD technology, Mulvey echoes the comparison of cinephilic moments with collected or found objects: 'like personal *objet trouvés*, such scenes can be played and replayed, on the threshold between cinephilia and fandom'.[54]

New practices of cinephilia have reinscribed the emphasis upon the momentary in film. DVD technologies have been seen to be more conducive to stopping the film than allowing it to continue uninterrupted. Mulvey, for example, develops the idea that the moment of stillness within the moving image creates a 'pensive spectator' who can reflect on the cinema, re-creating the resonance of the still photograph.[55] With the digital possibilities of the medium, the image itself can be frozen and subjected to a repetition or return that was not possible with earlier viewing conditions. As the 'new stillness is enhanced by the weight that the cinema's past has acquired with passing time,' Mulvey writes, 'its significance goes beyond the image itself towards the problem of time, its passing, and how it is represented or preserved'.[56] Indexing a film into chapters allows access to cinephilic moments, such that the films acquire a 'quasi-museum-like status'.[57]

What also needs to be acknowledged, however, is that being able to replay films such as *L'Avventura* also provides us with greater access to the film's temporal flow. The viewer is now presented with the possibility of embedding the affective moments that our memories serialise back into the temporal context from which they emerged. It thus opens up new possibilities for writing on temporality in film. There is a sense in which, as

Burgin writes, when we write of our memories of the film we betray them – either by taming them into symbolic meanings and interpretations, or by not recognising the affective networks that made them stand out in the first place.[58] Stern and Kouvaros begin the introduction to their book on cinema and performance with an anecdote that would ring true for many film critics: you see a scene which affects you, write about it, and then, upon re-watching it realise that your description of it is inaccurate.[59] The possibility of watching sequences repeatedly, then, 'opens up the possibility (and the challenge) of a more ostensive and demonstrative mode of description'.[60] In the duration of *L'Avventura*, images and textures are not easily extricable and flattened into an aestheticised surface, but rather resonate affectively through time and in movement. In memory, however, the duration of our experience, the temporal modulations that images, thoughts and affects undertake, may drop away. Being granted access to the film's duration through video and DVD can be seen as a way to reinsert these images into temporal flow.

Looking and Imaging

Critical writing on *L'Avventura* frequently mentions a coldness that seems to emanate from the film, and/or a distance inherent in our experience of it. According to Rifkin, for example, Antonioni maintains an emotional distance from his characters so that we do not feel their tragedies but rather observe them as representative of mankind's tragic condition.[61] 'Antonioni's "coldness"', he continues, 'involves a technique of objectifying people into "things".'[62] For Bert Cardullo, Antonioni's films tend to preclude 'simple emotional involvement on our part' in favour of a 'contemplative distance'.[63] In interview, Pierre Billard commented on the 'dark, cold mood' of Antonioni's films.[64] Viewing the film is sometimes assumed to be an anxious process of estrangement, suggested in Ford's comment that 'ontological violence . . . remains the central affective experience of a film like *L'Avventura*'.[65] Glen Norton suggests a similar relation of distance in the viewing experience of the film, writing, 'the difficulty of communication . . . mirrors the difficulty the viewer has in comprehending Antonioni's own cinematic language, a language which communicates the alienation and fragmentation of modern life'.[66] My view of the film differs from such assumptions, and emphasises two related characteristics: the way in which the editing might involve us intimately in the particular ways of seeing represented by the female lead, and the potentially affective process of cinematic imaging that the film's editing and cinematography perform.

It has been frequently noted in critical writing on *L'Avventura* that Claudia plays the part of witness; she is frequently shown simply observing, and we observe alongside her. As Nowell-Smith writes, 'Claudia observes, and her observation becomes the film's focus.'[67] In some critical writing, however, Claudia's look is subordinated to an auterist system of values. Claudia, writes Chatman, 'assume[s] the additional narrative task of mediating our vision', but is also given the function of 'freighting it with the unspoken values of the implied author'.[68] Commenting on the scene in which Claudia visits the art gallery, Brunette writes that: 'Antonioni is clearly instructing us in "proper" interpretive procedures.'[69] Claudia's looking prepares the audience to understand the film, 'these images are heavy, weighted, and seemingly full of clues . . . '; at this point, Brunette registers a tapering off of meaning, ' . . . but clues toward what solution?'[70]

It is interesting that, while presenting the centrality of Claudia to the film, actual identification with her is rarely acknowledged. This may in part be an extension of the fact that identification in general with the characters from Antonioni's films of this period is rarely considered a possible viewing experience. The barring of identification for many critics is not so much a question of characterisation but rather is inherent in the very structures of looking that the film presents. Rather than employing a classic point-of-view structure in which we see Claudia looking, and then what she is looking at, she tends to be included in the same frame as what she sees, frequently with her back to the camera, as though combining a shot/reverse-shot in one take. According to Cameron, while in certain respects our experience is paralleled with that of the characters, we are 'discouraged' from identifying with them through this structuring of our vision.

> We *are* shown what the characters see and learn what they learn, but without identifying with them, so that our appreciation of their feelings must be primarily intellectual. We are therefore more conscious than the characters of the meaning of their behavior (as we would not be if we started identifying with them). This places us in a position to correlate our observations of all the characters and reach the general conclusions which Antonioni expects us to draw.[71]

In relation to *L'Avventura*'s Claudia, I am not convinced that shots in which we see her observing only, or necessarily, encourage us to intellectualise her behaviour. Instead, the film creates a powerful sense of *being with* Claudia by both keeping her in view and creating a particular pace of observation. The film fluidly moves towards and away from her way of looking. While she looks, wandering through the art gallery or looking at the landscape out of a window, we partly share the duration of her look, and are thus drawn close to her experience of time. As Perez points out, 'this suspensive time, in no hurry to move ahead to the next thing, often gives us the sense of our sharing with the characters an unabridged interval in the passage of their lives'.[72] I agree with Perez that experiencing this time alongside the characters, particularly if it seems to be a moment inconsequential to any but themselves, may heighten 'the sense of our sharing a personal, private experience', something that may encourage an intimate sense of closeness to the characters.[73] The camera both gives her space and remains close to her through time.

If Claudia slows down to look at things in the diegetic world, the film will also slow down in presenting its images to viewers. Once again we can consider Claudia's movements in Rome. As she walks through the art gallery, the camera moves also, tracking her and keeping her in frame, but remaining on the other side of the wall. It both mimics her movement, and moves away from her way of looking. Three separate shots in which Claudia is seen looking are themselves preceded by a moment in which viewers simply look on to the film's spaces. That is, there is a pause before she appears on screen. For example, we are presented with the exterior of a building; Claudia is then shown walking into this shot and looking up at the window above her. A similar pattern is repeated in the next shot; the view of criss-crossing ceiling beams that I mentioned earlier. Again, she walks into this shot and is shown looking. Claudia is seen closing a door upon the corridor leading into Sandro's apartment building; a transitional space that is for now presented only as a future possibility, a threshold that is being indicated but that she is not yet crossing. In each of these three shots, the camera is already present at the location in which she will appear, waiting for her. The film slows its pace of observation as Claudia does. It pauses the narrative, as she pauses her movements, to observe, as though encouraging viewers to look at things in the way Claudia might. Following Claudia's impassioned plea to Sandro to leave her alone on the train, the film cuts to a view of the sea from the moving train, then back to Claudia as she emerges into the train's corridor. The film does not imply that this shot is from her perspective, but is, rather, structured as though to mimic the way in which she might look at the diegetic environment. Once again, we are presented with a relation of both closeness and distance: this is not Claudia's point of view, but the camera lingers on the coastal scene in the way that she has been seen lingering to look at the landscape.

The association between Claudia's looking and our own look at the film can only be taken so far, however, as *L'Avventura* frequently emphasises the difference between human vision and the aesthetic imaging process that cinema is capable of. As Colebrook has argued, art can disrupt our natural perception and 'free' affect from a world of coherent bodies, presenting itself as a power and process of becoming.[74] Cinema can present a mode of seeing that is not attached to the human eye, and can thus dislodge affects from their recognised and expected origins.[75] According to Colebrook, 'the material of the film, or elements of its aesthetic composition, is not something we see "through" to grasp reality, we see "seeing"'.[76] This can be an exhilarating experience. The film continually presents particular details or major aesthetic and narrative moments that even after several viewings seem paradoxically unexpected. In Deleuzian terms, we might think of the film as opposed to his definition of 'common sense' which 'organises the world according to fixed identities and stable spatial and temporal coordinates'.[77] Implicit in the notion of common sense is the model of thought as a form of recognition, a unified perspective and stable object: 'thought's goal in a world of recognition and representation is to eliminate problems and find solutions, to pass from non-knowledge to knowledge . . . a process with a definite beginning and ending'.[78] The 'dynamic unfolding of the world', however, 'is a process that escapes common sense and defies its set categories. That process is a ceaseless becoming in which things perpetually metamorphose into something else and thereby elude identification and specification.'[79] This seems to me an apt way of considering a film that continually disrupts a coherent presentation of time and space, encouraging us not to recognise the film's presentation of time and space as similar to the way we live it every day, but to see it as a new spatio-temporal configuration.

One of the ways in which aesthetic creativity is emphasised is through what Deleuze has termed 'aberrant' editing practices, shifts of perspective or scale which disrupt a cinematic construction based on natural perception, performing instead a creative imaging process. From a contemporary perspective, perhaps, *L'Avventura*'s aberrant editing practices are not as obvious or offensive as they may have seemed to some viewers upon the film's release. It is possible, rather, to speak of a continual process in which the film presents unusual framings and movements that seem to pull away from issues of characterisation or narrative, and human centres of vision. As Nowell-Smith has written, 'camera movements and editing are in a constant process of flux . . . events unfold from a series of camera positions, all of which uncover new details of a scene but none of which conforms to a stable narrative logic enabling the spectator to place events and assign them unequivocal meanings'.[80] Antonioni's sequences suggest new perceptual possibilities which Flaxman, following Deleuze, sees as part of the project of modern cinema: creating irregularities and heterogeneous durations. 'Such images', writes Flaxman, 'induce the imagination itself to take a trip', in a process in which the presentation of images disrupts conventional patterns and de-emphasises the meaningful or symbolic in favour of the affective.[81]

L'Avventura's editing simmers with creative energy, establishing editing patterns and then breaking them with surprising framings. When Claudia waits on a bench at a railway station on her way to the Montaldo villa, for example, she is approached by Sandro, who wants to remain with her. They have an emotionally tense exchange, in which their distraught expressions are illuminated and emphasised. The camera focuses first on Claudia before cutting to Sandro, who is visibly distressed at Claudia's insistence that he leave. The camera follows Sandro as he stands up, lingering on his expression for several seconds before he turns around abruptly to face Claudia. The film then cuts to Claudia, as though in a reverse shot following Sandro's perception. The framing of Claudia, however, differs significantly from that rendered previously: she is seen at the left-hand corner of the frame, occupying less than a quarter of it, while the rest is taken up by the wall of the station.

This unexpected framing disrupts the usual symmetry of the shot-reverse-shot structure in a moment of deviation and difference. The film's final sequence can also be seen in this manner. Claudia, having discovered Sandro with the prostitute Gloria Perkins, runs out of the hotel in Taormina to a deserted piazza. Sandro follows her there, sits on a bench, and begins to weep. The film cuts several times from close-ups to mid-shots. In the final such oscillation, Claudia's hand is seen in close-up, hovering around Sandro's head and eventually coming down to stroke his hair in time to the climax of the musical score. There is then a cut from this close-up to a long-shot, when the couple are suddenly shown in the foreground of an astonishing composition. Once again, the frame has been split in half: one side is taken up with the decaying stone wall of a house and its protruding balcony, the other shows a vast panorama of the sea with a snow-covered volcano in the distance. Brunette posits a self-reflexivity in this composition, which apparently unmasks the camera and strips it of its power.[82] The shot, he writes, has a 'stylised effect that is so self-reflexively powerful that it removes us forcibly (if only momentarily) from the story and reminds us that we are participating in a self-conscious work of art whose relation with reality is heavily conventionalised'.[83] I agree that this is a moment in which the film's aesthetic force surfaces powerfully, but not necessarily with the description of this moment in terms of self-reflexive unmasking, which conveys little of the affective resonance of the sequence. The aesthetic and the narrative elements are not necessarily divorced (such that we are 'removed' from the story); rather, the ambiguous ending of the film's narrative, the questions that remain over Claudia and Sandro's future, is given an even greater affective power through the aesthetic rendering of the moment.

L'Avventura invites a relation of fascination to its processes of cinematic imaging, which become visible rather than transparent; it is the cinematic techniques, as much as what they portray, that invite an affective reaction. In his commentary for the Criterion Collection DVD, Gene Youngblood, for example, enthuses over Antonioni's 'beautiful dissolves', especially that which literally wipes Anna off the screen for the last time.[84] This dissolve cinematically renders her disappearance as vague and indeterminate as it is narratively. Antonioni's dissolves render space and time fluid, as though continually escaping from critical desires to fasten rigid interpretations on to them.

In another example, a shot of Claudia standing under an archway at the Montaldo villa dissolves on to a shot of an unknown woman's face. The shape of the archway modulates through the dissolve into the shape of the face, which we soon learn belongs to the chemist's wife from Troina. According to Brunette, by beginning the scene with the wife's face in close-up before we know who she is, Antonioni 'mean[t] to articulate an emotion and suggest a theme even before placing the situation narratively'.[85] It is difficult to pin down, however, what this theme or emotion might be. The close-up, floating free from narrative fixation, presents itself to us before we can interpret it. Instead, we could see it as a moment of indeterminacy that demands our attention. Rohdie sees this moment as an example of a scene that simply compels and fascinates before it 'means' or 'narratively' functions.[86] The dissolve effects a transition between two spaces and scenes, and the unanchored close-up enacts a dissolution of narrative placement.

While the film's figures lend themselves to be 'placed in a scene, in a drama', they also, as Rohdie writes, 'come to have a life of their own, as images, and to become a source of fascination without the need for a narrative anchor'. Displaying his sensitivity to the flow of the film's duration, he also emphasises that, 'at the same time, and it is the reason for the fascination, the narrative and the figures are never completely lost, are poised to return and resume shape'.[87] In the scene above, we are soon directed back towards narrative concerns as Sandro questions the chemist about Anna's disappearance. In *L'Avventura*, affects may be evoked through cinematic rendering, but sometimes, it seems, thematic concerns are also 'poised to return'; affect and theme may emerge together.

This can be demonstrated with reference to a sequence in which Claudia and Sandro are shown leaving a deserted town near Noto. The camera observes them from an alleyway off a square, in which their car is parked. When the couple discover the town, the camera is already present, filming from the top of a building so that we see them entering the square from above. Sandro and Claudia are surprised and disturbed to find the town deserted, and wonder whether Anna could have passed through there. Claudia is distressed upon realising that what she thought was another town in the distance is in fact a cemetery, and asks Sandro if they can leave. Claudia and Sandro are framed in long-shot in the square; the camera watches from a passageway in shadow. As they enter the car and drive away, the camera tracks forward slowly for several seconds, moving towards the space they have vacated. The gliding movement of the camera departs from usual or 'natural' lines of vision; at these moments, as Durgnat has argued, 'the spectator becomes vaguely conscious of a certain uneasiness, or of exhilaration'.[88] The camera movement constitutes a moment of utter ambiguity, injecting uncertainty into the scene. It cannot be explained with reference to what the director intended, for Antonioni himself has stated that 'this is the most ambiguous shot in the whole film. I think it is impossible to explain. I don't know why I wanted it.'[89]

While it may not have an explanation, it certainly has a peculiar resonance which is elongated by the duration of the shot and its temporal placement within the narrative. By the time the camera begins its movement, both Anna and the idea of mortality are diegetically introduced (through the search and through the cemetery). The inexplicable presence of the camera and its gliding advance bring to mind the possibility of Anna's ghostly presence. This shot invites us to re-evaluate the camera placement at the beginning of the scene, reinforcing the sense that someone – not merely 'the camera' – was already present there, waiting for the characters to arrive. The sequence enacts an ambiguity that is not unlike the structure of the moment of anamorphosis as described by Slavoj Žižek. For Žižek, anamorphosis designates a small supplementary feature in the image that sticks out and does not make sense within the frame: 'the same situations, the same events that, till then, have been perceived as perfectly ordinary, acquire an air of strangeness'.[90] Such points of anamorphosis, which 'open up the abyss of the search for meaning', break open the ground of established, familiar signification, and plunge the viewer into the depths of a realm of total ambiguity.[91] While Žižek conceives of this moment as a 'point', however, it clearly has a temporal dimension; it activates the viewer's memory and requires a revision of what we have seen.

Significantly, Žižek does not see this as a moment of self-reflexive alienation from the film. Instead, the moment of anamorphosis undermines our position as 'neutral', 'objective' observers, implicating us in what we observe. Anamorphosis indicates the point at which the observer is already involved in the film, 'the point from which the picture itself looks back at us'.[92] Žižek's words echo Benjamin's, and Marks's, writing on the aura, specifically the characteristic that Marks identifies in objects or images that seem to 'look back at us'. Aura, she writes, 'is the sense an object gives that it can speak to us of the past, without ever letting us completely decipher it'.[93] While we are here dealing with a movement rather than an object, it is a movement that not only creatively performs a machinic departure from natural perception, but also alludes to the mystery of the film's past: the disappearance of Anna. The longer the shot is held, the more intense the uncertain affect of its movement grows. Deleuze may have had this sequence in mind in his general description of the film. In *L'Avventura*, he argues, the absent woman, Anna, 'causes an interminable gaze to weigh on the couple – which gives them the continual feeling of being spied on, and which explains the lack of coordination of their objective movements, when they flee whilst pretending to look for her'.[94] Placing the scene in its temporal context, then, suggests how the lurking of the camera and its process of imaging may intertwine with a more comprehensive and contextualised awareness. The image presents a certain modulation between a diegetic resonance and a cinematographic performance, an awareness of seeing 'through' the perception of the camera as well as of seeing 'imaging' itself.

In sum, then, there are several ways in which we might challenge the assumption that viewing the film involves a sense of alienation or coldness. Klinger has suggested that, rather than experiencing an emotional identification with a character in a film, viewers can affectively align themselves with a particular way of looking, perceiving and presenting the world. As I do, viewers may sense an affinity with the slow pace of observation that both Claudia and the film perform; to cite Klinger, viewers 'may find the allusion to the organisation of experience compelling'.[95] Groves has also noted that the affective rapport we may feel with a film is not necessarily dependent upon any object or character, rather, 'we are influenced by a kind of rhetoric through which we discover our identity in certain texts but not others', the success of which depends upon each viewer's 'suggestibility'.[96] It may be the creative, aesthetic performance of the film itself that draws viewers towards it.

Temporalised Space

Much of the critical writing on *L'Avventura*'s landscapes is focused upon an interpretation of the locations as metaphors, symbols or metonymies.

For Cameron, the island of Lisca Bianca is a 'symbol of barrenness'; for Rifkin it is a 'metaphor', though he does not specify for what. For Chatman, landscapes are objective correlatives which 'represent characters' states of mind'.[97] Schwarzer sees the volcano in *L'Avventura* as 'a symbol of humanity's connection to lasting meaning'.[98] This tendency toward symbolisation may stem partly from the sense that the images exceed whatever narrative purposes may hover around them; accounting for the appearance of certain spaces through narrative means is simply not enough to explain their affective power. According to Brunette, Italian writer Lorenzo Cuccu best summed up the idea that the source of the symbolic tendency 'lies in the overwhelming pressure that the director can put on visual images, [citing Cuccu] "the problematic and dynamic tension internal to an image that cannot be reduced to being a mere illustrative function of the story".'[99] However, symbolic interpretations tend to abstract space from its presentation in time, again suggesting images that are static and flattened, detached from depth, reconfigured in and through the interpretative process as a still frame.

L'Avventura's landscapes are also frequently presented in terms that stress their negative affects or associations. In Durgnat's view, for example, the film presents 'one broad, flat landscape after another [that] drags itself wearily up the long, slow haul to the horizon. Limp roads lead the eye to clutters of irrelevant shacks . . . the perspectives are a web of emptiness'.[100] Arrowsmith points to the immensity and violence of the spaces that the characters find themselves in. On Lisca Bianca, 'man' is 'dwarfed and humbled by the environing vastness . . . no longer centre stage but surrounded by a violence he cannot ignore, a mystery he cannot explain'.[101] Arrowsmith certainly has a point – the hints of violence in the landscape emerge in the shark that Anna pretends to see, the boulders that tumble down into the ocean, the twister at sea, and the ocean itself, with its rushing waves and threat of annihilation. For Deleuze, Antonioni's spaces are prime examples of the any-space-whatever, of disconnected space, 'the connection of the parts of space is not given, because it can come about only from the subjective point of view of a character who is, nevertheless, absent, or has even disappeared, not simply out of frame, but passed into the void'.[102] As the spaces lose their homogeneity and metrical relations, however, they can also become a 'pure locus of the possible' which is rich in potential affects. Viewers, furthermore, can personalise these spaces; anonymous spaces can become intimate for the viewer.

There are other ways of describing the spaces of *L'Avventura* than stressing their emptiness or violence. The spaces are also, for example, those of sensuous travel, of a continual revelation of new spaces to explore. This is presented on a thematic level throughout the film. The characters set out from Rome, viewing Sandro's apartment on the Tiber along the way, for a Mediterranean cruise amongst the small rocky islands marooned in a vast expanse of sea off Sicily. 'One pull to involvement in an Antonioni film', as Perez writes, 'is his keen documentary sense.[103] *L'Avventura* is no exception: Antonioni films dolphins playing in the water, and slowly manipulates the camera over immense rock formations and the vast expanse of the sea. Claudia and Sandro travel by train and by car across a rural area of Sicily, where tourism is continuously kept as a diegetic reminder. When the couple stop at a railway station, a poster advertising the Sicilian tourism industry is clearly visible in the background. In Noto, Sandro complains about the lack of respect shown to him as a 'tourist'. The police station Sandro visits is located in an ancient villa, and the camera explicitly draws attention to the frescoes which cover the walls, panning upwards and lingering on the textures of the marble. Claudia and Sandro's sightseeing tour in Noto culminates in the scaling of a church bell tower, which provides a panoramic view of the terraced architectural landscape. Claudia and Sandro are partly, and inescapably, tourists.

The shots taken from moving vehicles throughout the film explicitly make this touristic gaze available to viewers. Scenes in which the characters are driving or being driven are often filmed from within the car, as it moves towards a horizon which is presented as a depth opening in front of the viewer. There are also shots of the rocky island from the cruise boat (one of these moves up and down as though emphasising its physical situation), and from the window of the train, as the coastline unfolds alongside it. As Bruno writes, changes in shot heights, angles and speeds ensure that 'travel culture is written on the techniques of filmic observation'.[104] In this aesthetics of touristic practice, 'architectural space becomes framed for view and offers itself for consumption as traveled space'.[105] The diegetic and cinematographic presentation of a 'touristic gaze' invites a sort of relationship to the filmed landscape which is more intimate than has been allowed for in most interpretive or aesthetic criticism on Antonioni. Bruno can be placed on the opposite side of the spectrum from writers such as Cameron, Rifkin and Chatman, arguing for a consideration of space as a depth that viewers can imagine moving through. According to Bruno, a viewer can inscribe him (or her)self into a film by imagining themselves residing inside it, thus 'tangibly map[ping] oneself within it'.[106] There is, she argues, a 'mobile dynamics involved in the act of viewing films, even if the spectator is seemingly static. The (im)mobile spectator moves across an imaginary path, traversing multiple sites and times'.[107]

The space that the characters traverse throughout *L'Avventura* is one that is inflected with varying temporal associations. In the opening sequence, the dome of an old cathedral is shown on one side of the frame, and encroaching modern housing developments on the other. The opening dialogue between Anna and her father contains several different temporal statements, a continual battle to establish the supremacy of one time over another. For example, seeing Anna, her father states, 'I thought you were already on the high seas', to which Anna replies, 'Not yet.' Her father continues, 'Isn't it fashionable anymore to put on a sailor's cap with the name of the yacht?', to which Anna replies that it is no longer thus. Their journey to Sicily can also be construed as a journey into a place with different temporal characteristics, which was rather a stereotype at the time of the film's release.

In the 1950s and 1960s, Sicily was frequently seen in Italian culture and writing as a remnant of the primitive. The 'problem of the Mezzogiorno' in the 1960s was that southerners were seen to adhere to an essentially different conception of the world than northerners.[108] As journalist Oriana Fallaci quipped, 'The South. That's another planet.'[109] In the films of this era, then, the South became 'the ideal site in which to explore the changing manners and mores of a new society'. It provided an essential 'backwardness' and cultural distance from modernity.[110] This is continually and explicitly brought to our attention in the film through, for example, the over-emphasised, animalistic sexuality of the men, the town dweller in Noto who mispronounces and denounces the bikini, and the island's decrepit inhabitant and its buried ancient town. According to Arrowsmith, the movement away from the modern Roman housing developments, with which the film opens, to the Sicilian landscape, can be seen not only as a voyage toward the 'immensities of space', but also as 'a trip backward into time, into geologic time'.[111]

As in much Italian cinema, *L'Avventura* continually presents Italy as a country 'overloaded with traces of the past',[112] in the ancient pots rising up from the depths of Lisca Bianca, the police station with its marble and murals, and the architectural splendour of Noto. Layers of time are created in the image and announced through dialogue; Raimondo, for example, questions how man could ever have been an inhabitant of the seas, while Sandro bemoans the state of contemporary architecture in relation to the beautiful buildings of the past. The space of *L'Avventura* is one in which remnants of the past persist alongside the present. We can see this in relation to a Bergsonian notion of duration which, as Lim explains, implies the 'survival of the past', 'an ever-accumulating ontological memory that is wholly, automatically and ceaselessly preserved'.[113]

Lim links together Bergson and Chakrabarty in their 'insistence that older modes of being are never entirely surmounted'. The latter 'reveals that the charge of anachronism – the claim that something out of kilter with the present really belongs to a superseded past – is a gesture of temporal exclusion'.[114] The world of *L'Avventura* indeed seems to be one that refuses temporal exclusion, instead focusing on the coexistence of various temporal strata. Although writing in a different context, Andreas Huyssen sees the 'turn towards the residues of ancestral cultures and local traditions, the privileging of the non-synchronous and heterogeneous' as a reaction to the accelerated pace of modernity, 'an attempt to break out of the swirling empty space of the everyday present and to claim a sense of time and memory'.[115] This strikes me as an interesting gloss on both *L'Avventura*'s spatial journey from urban Rome to rural Sicily and on its slow temporal rhythms, as though reclaiming both a space and a time for close, unhurried observation. Tarkovsky's *Mirror*, as I argue in Chapter 3, performs a similar desire to slow down time and allow for the play of memory.

The use of depth in *L'Avventura* presents particular possibilities for describing the interrelation of space and time. It is useful at this point to consider Deleuze's writing on the effect of presenting space in depth. Images presented in depth are, according to Deleuze, fundamentally related to memory and time. Depth of field explores a 'region of past' *within* the frame rather than presenting a chronological succession of time through editing. This continuity of duration ensures that 'unbridled depth is of time and no longer of space'.[116] Time's subordination to movement is reversed, and temporality appears directly for itself. Depth in the image, then, becomes less a function of presenting a spatial realism, encouraging a sense of inhabitation, than of activating a 'function of remembering, of temporalisation: not exactly a recollection but an "invitation to recollect"'.[117] In Bazin's influential analysis pitting depth against montage, he argued that depth encourages a greater contribution on the part of the spectator to the meaning of the images unfolding before them. Thus needing to exercise personal choice when deciding what part of the frame to look at, 'it is from [the viewer's] attention and [their] will that the meaning of the image in part derives'.[118] Although most critics have given priority to Bazin's spatial configurations, Rosen emphasises that temporality is central to his concept of cinematic depth. Our eyes search out the points that interest us in an image composed in depth, 'introduc[ing] a sort of temporalisation on a second level by analysis of the space of a reality, itself evolving in time'.[119]

As Deleuze explains, the evocation of memory can be shown in the act of occurring: images are presented in depth when there is a need for the characters to recall. In this situation, searching overcomes the characters' ability to act; seeing takes the place of action. Rather than logically linked movements in space, characters enact anomalies of movement, 'a trampling, a to-and-fro'.[120] The sequence on Lisca Bianca in which the characters search for Anna can to some extent illustrate Deleuze's understanding of depth. Viewers do not see Anna leaving the island, either as the event occurs or through flashbacks. Instead, we watch the characters as they search for her, tracing her possible trajectories of movement. To appropriate Deleuze's words, the characters enact an 'actual effort of evocation'; they attempt to 'summon' her up, exploring 'virtual zones of past, to find, choose, and bring [her] back'.[121] As Deleuze writes, depth can thus become 'a function of remembering, a figure of temporalisation. It then gives rise to all kinds of adventures of the memory, which are not so much psychological accidents as misadventures of time, disturbances of its constitution'.[122]

These misadventures of time and memory are, however, primarily restricted by Deleuze to the experiences of the figures on screen rather than to possible viewing experiences. Deleuze entertains the possibility that when we read, look at a painting or watch a 'show', we ourselves weave between levels of temporality and thus 'extract a non-chronological time'.[123] Watching a film is, notably, not mentioned. Ultimately for Deleuze, it is the screen, not the viewer, that enacts these temporal adventures, 'the screen itself is the cerebral membrane where immediate and direct confrontations take place between the past and the future'.[124] The Lisca Bianca sequence, however, demonstrates how images in depth can also invite viewers to recollect. Shooting the scenes in depth ensures that all the characters are in focus in their relative positions on the island. As Anna and Sandro make a final effort to communicate, for example, the small figures of Giulia and Corrado are seen in sharp focus in the background, suggesting that what we have seen of their failed relationship may remain present to our minds as we watch the other couple.[125] During the search for Anna, the characters are once again presented in various configurations among the rocks, recalling scenes preceding the disappearance. While the characters search the space, however, viewers are invited to search their memories in time, encouraged to recall our last glimpse of Anna. As the landscape is presented in perfect depth, the possible past of her traversal of it may emerge in efforts of recollection. One could compare this scene to the ending of *L'Eclisse*. Throughout the film, Vittoria (Vitti) and Piero (Alain Delon) are seen in a variety of locations in Milan as their romance develops. Towards the end of the film, they arrange to meet the following day – however, only the camera turns up.

The film then displays several shots of the spaces where we had seen them previously, spaces that they are now absent from. Although depth is not as significant in this sequence, it shares with the Lisca Bianca scene an insistence upon involving viewers' memories. As Perez has written, 'We share with the camera a recollection of the lovers through a beholding of things associated with them, things that for the camera, for us, carry their memory and at the same time point up their absence.'[126]

Filmed landscapes are apprehended through duration, and our perceptions of them are dependent upon memory. Bergson has written that 'however brief we suppose any perception to be, it always occupies a certain duration, and involves consequently an effort of memory which prolongs one into another a plurality of moments'.[127] The landscape of Lisca Bianca is formed from an accumulation of images persisting in memory. As Jean-Clet Martin writes, 'every landscape is a virtual construction in relation to a memory able to stock piles of images in all their encroachments upon each other'.[128] Rather than facilitating this process, however, the landscape sequences are edited so as to disrupt a coherent sense of space. In the long sequence on the island, it is difficult to anchor the frequent pans over the rocks to individual characters. Shots of characters gazing on the landscape are sometimes followed by shots of rocks that they could be looking at, or by what may seem to be a completely different location; this shot may itself be followed by a view that shows us the same character moving across the landscape, or someone different, leaving us with little sense of where the rocks are in relation to them or to other features of the island. At times, characters are framed so that we do not see the land under their feet at all; they seem then, to be moving over an abyss.

A holistic landscape constructed out of all these fragments, a coherent setting that we may picture in our minds, is jeopardised. This does not necessarily mean, however, that we are kept at an aloof distance by the compositions; instead, viewers can be seen to be intimately involved in thickening perception with memory. According to Martin, landscape thus becomes 'something volatile that undoes itself with the rapidity of movement and the successive shifting of perspectives', allowing us to conceive of point of view as 'more on the side of "memory" than "matter"', that is, as extending in time rather than only occurring in space.[129] A possible effect of this effort of recollection is that the images of the landscape will resonate in memory long after the film itself has ended. The visual arrangement of the landscape in memory is a part of the temporal process of interacting with a film. Burgin has written that films may come to be deeply imbricated in our memories, until it can be difficult to tell a memory of a film from a memory of a 'real' experience.[130] For Rosenbaum, the landscapes of *L'Avventura* may 'haunt our memory like sites with highly personal associations from our own pasts'.[131] This description of *L'Avventura*'s impact is far removed from the frameworks of distance and alienation cited previously.

Pace and Rhythm

Antonioni began making films, initially documentaries, when neo-realism was flourishing in Italy. As Nowell-Smith points out, Antonioni had 'always stood aloof from neo-realism and even when he agreed with its methods or objectives (the preference for location shooting, for example), he did so for different reasons'.[132] What is striking about the way in which Antonioni's relationship to neo-realism is discussed is the frequent emphasis upon time as the differentiating factor. Antonioni stated that neo-realism 'attracted attention to the relationship existing between the character and surrounding reality ... now, however, when for better or worse reality has been normalised once again, it seems to me more interesting to examine what remains in the characters from their past experiences'.[133] Deleuze emphasises this temporal difference when describing Antonioni's movement away from neo-realism; Antonioni, he argues, replaces the neo-realist quest of movement 'with a specific weight of time operating inside characters and excavating them from within'.[134]

This stress on what remains from past experiences, the remnants and traces of the past, and how they work through the present, could be seen to shape the narrative structure as a whole. One could speculate that a more conventional narrative might begin by exploring Anna and Sandro's relationship. In the middle she may disappear and be searched for, and in the end she would be found, dead or alive. *L'Avventura*, however, gives the impression that everything important for Anna has already happened – what we see is what remains, a character struggling to come to terms with her experience, and then presumably deciding that she cannot continue on in the same way. Seen in this manner, the film starts too late and continues past the point at which it 'should' have ended. Claudia and Sandro are left to deal with the aftermath. Of course, this analogy can only go so far. Through this process of pastness operating within the characters, a new beginning is formed for a new relationship.

Both Deleuze and Rodowick describe the kind of temporality that operates through Antonioni's characters as one of waiting. According to Deleuze, the body 'contains the before and the after, tiredness and waiting ... even despair are the attitudes of the body ... the body as revealer of the deadline'.[135] For Rodowick, *L'Avventura*'s 'ironic title points to spaces where any decidable action or interpretation has evaporated, leaving characters who wait, who witness only the passing of time as duration'.[136] This kind of waiting can be glimpsed on the basic level of narrative. From its opening scenes, *L'Avventura* presents characters who are always waiting; Anna for Claudia at the film's beginning, Claudia for Anna and Sandro, Anna for Sandro to express something definite about their relationship, Claudia for Sandro when they are separated, and both Claudia and Sandro are in some sense waiting for Anna, or her body, to reappear. At the film's conclusion, Claudia waits for Sandro; too tired to go to dinner, she goes to bed instead, while Sandro frolics downstairs with Gloria. The duration of waiting appears excruciating to her, and she attempts to pass the time by spatialising it: looking at the clock face, counting the seconds, and writing down numbers on an open magazine. Lim's formulation of Bergsonian duration comes to mind: 'while we wait impatiently, we become (somewhat painfully) aware not only of our own duration but of the multiple durations outside our own'.[137] Like the philosopher waiting for sugar to melt, the time Claudia has to wait is not a mathematical, measured time, but coincides with her impatience; she must submerge her desire to rhythms that do not coincide with her own.[138] It is through such times of waiting that the operations of duration can come to the fore. As Elizabeth Grosz writes,

> duration is experienced most incontrovertibly in the phenomenon of waiting. Waiting is the subjective experience that perhaps best exemplifies the coexistence of a multiplicity of durations, durations both my own and outside of me, which may, by chance, coalesce to form a 'convenient' rhythm or coincidence, or may delay me and make me wait.[139]

From one perspective, the film also makes the viewer wait; for each sequence to integrate itself into a narrative, for the narrative to reach its expected conclusions, for causes to have effects. This sense of waiting for something to happen is connected to the phenomenon of so-called 'temps morte', or 'dead times'. The term is often associated with Antonioni's statement that he preferred his actors' performances when they had stopped acting, 'when everything has been said, when the scene appears to be finished, there is what comes afterwards. It seems to me important to show the character, back and front, just at that moment – a gesture or an attitude that illuminates all that has happened, and what results from it.'[140] However, the term is associated more generally with other types of apparently 'empty' moments: when the characters have left the frame or before they have entered it, or when there is nothing of narrative interest in the scene, yet the camera lingers on the space. As Nowell-Smith writes, this stretching out of the scenes provides 'a sense of indefinite time, rather than time defined by action'.[141]

These are moments in *L'Avventura* when the narrative and its drama seems to be pulling away. One such moment occurs after Sandro and Claudia's passionate conversation at the station, where she refuses to allow him to accompany her. On the platform, Sandro is shown looking after the train for a moment, before running after it. The camera remains where it was, registering in long-shot the fact that Sandro just makes the train. For a few seconds we watch the train, the characters, and the narrative centre pulling away from us, as we are left behind on the station platform, for a moment abandoned. There is then a cut to the interior of the train and the feeling is dispelled. It was partly these 'dead times' that the Cannes audience were reacting to with anger and impatience; according to Ford, a scene in which Claudia runs down the length of the hotel corridor in Taormina brought shouts of 'Cut, cut!'.[142]

As the name suggests, dead times have often been associated with a kind of attack on the viewer's centred subjectivity. Ford, for example, has written that *L'Avventura* causes anxiety not only through its narrative decentring, but also because of duration's 'destabilising of essence'. The slow movement of time, he writes, hollows out subjects and their agency, showing us a devastating temporal reality that radically challenges our thought, disabling action and escaping our desire for control. These moments 'inflict fissures onto the diegesis (perhaps even terminally), severing narrative control, killing our desired centering of human presence, destroying the subject's ontological confidence in itself – and, of course, coldly reminding us of our own enforced personal *telos*'.[143] Not only, however, does this seem rather a lot of responsibility for film sequences to carry, it is also misleading to equate a radical temporality with a negative affect, to define *L'Avventura*'s temporal progression in terms of violence, coldness, and severance. Although Ford does not make this explicit, his writing gives the sense that temporality can only be seen as a threatening force, echoing early writing on cinema and critical desires to escape from temporal flux.

From another perspective, however, viewers may not necessarily be waiting for something else to happen, but attending to the slow fluctuation of the image before them. One of the important consequences of the 'dead times' is that they allow us to pay attention to the modulations of the image through time. They may provoke an impatience or boredom in some viewers, and in others, a calm sense of patient observation, entirely at ease with allowing the temporal development of the images to progress at their own pace. As Chatman writes, we are encouraged to examine space away from the 'immediate exigencies of plot', allowing us time for sensing, if not fully understanding, its 'odd value'.[144] The 'dead times' create a particular pace for the film and give it its slow temporal rhythms. We are invited to pay attention to things that might ordinarily escape us. Movement and aesthetic awareness is something that emerges from, and takes place in, duration, precisely through these 'dead times'. With each long take, as Schliesser writes, 'we are quietly swept up by the soothing yet humbling force of this vision, encouraged to ponder the stillness and mystery of what would ordinarily pass as mundane'.[145] Allowing the viewer this time to notice and observe slows the pace of the film. As indicated previously, this also aligns the viewer with Claudia's way of looking. She, too, slows down to look at things, such as the landscape outside the painter's studio, and the rising sun on the island and in the resort at the film's ending.

Throughout the film, scenes of drama are balanced with moments of observation that move away from human concerns. For example, in the moment that I have already mentioned, after Claudia's passionate exclamations on the train with Sandro, the camera cuts to shots from the moving train, of rolling surf and sea, seen in glorious movement. When Claudia is weeping on the piazza at the film's ending, there is time for a shot, visually and aurally resonant, of the leaves of a tree rustling in the wind. As Rohdie has written, if the narrative can be seen to 'die' at all in such moments, then the duration of the film allows a new interest to take hold: in textures, the light and tone of things, compositional frames, and a 'shimmering' between figure and ground. As these transform through duration, they can provide the spectator with 'the most intense, exquisite joy'.[146] For viewers inclined to do so, the slow temporality allows for a pleasurable wallowing in the images and their transformations through time, their aesthetic compositions as well as the textures, landscapes, characters and objects depicted within the frame.

A languid pace is also created by the frequent use of slow dissolves in between scenes, such that even moments of action and movement, such as the journey from Rome to Sicily, seem slowed down. In this sequence, there is a dissolve from a shot of Claudia to an open stretch of road; we hear a roaring engine sound before a car bursts on to the road from off-screen and passes off-screen again. A cut shows us the car's occupants: Claudia, Anna, who is looking displeased with Sandro's dangerous driving, and the reckless Sandro. The film then fades to black, introducing a moment of pause before fading back on to a changed landscape: a wide vista of sea and sky with a volcanic island in the background. A small boat can be glimpsed in the foreground, its engine noise marking a continuance with the sound of the car heard beforehand. While these are moments of action and travel, the dissolves and fades inject a slowness into the journey; even the fact that the seascape is presented in long-shot, which does not indicate how fast the boat in the foreground is moving, adds to this effect.

Of course, *L'Avventura*'s rhythms are not always languid. As Perez notes, 'drawing things out and cutting them short is the distinctive Antonioni rhythm. Lingering and interruptive, suspensive and elliptical, a crisp deliberate pace, a restless, syncopated movement of unhurried attention.'[147] Straight cuts can propel us into the next scene, into an unexpected filmed space, such as the cut from the slowly moving camera in the deserted town visited by Sandro and Claudia, to the image of the couple in a field. As Biro has written, 'ellipsis can be a wonderful trigger to "jump" to new or amazing paths, bringing about freshness and astonishment, satisfying the spectator's hunger for enjoying surprise'.[148] The scene in the field introduces an interesting moment of temporal disjunction, as well as being a beautiful example of the more lingering temporal rhythms of the film. After the cut, Sandro and Claudia move away from the camera, which continues to register the stunning landscape – a rolling hill, a vast sea, a clear sky – for a moment, before cutting to a close-up of Sandro and Claudia as they kiss. Several close-ups are alternated for approximately two minutes. The hum of the waves can be heard throughout this close-up sequence, and at the final shot of Claudia's face its volume slightly increases. The sound is transposed onto the sound of a train, aurally covering over a visual cut which shows a train on the right-hand side of the screen in long-shot. The camera pans as it follows the progress of the train across the landscape, again revealing an expanse of grass and rock in the foreground, and the vast sea with Mount Etna visible in the background. There is then a cut showing Claudia and Sandro in mid-shot lying on the hillside. The sound of the train approaching is audible for several seconds before we see it passing at the top left of the screen.

There have been various approximations of what effect this sequence might have. According to Brunette, it presents a 'mini-alienation effect of the Brechtian variety'.[149] Brunette's explanation of the effect of this sequence as one of alienation depends upon the viewer ascribing the first passage of the train to the viewpoint of the couple, 'we motivate the shot by ascribing it, generally, to the point of view of Claudia and Sandro'.[150] When it passes them, then, it seems as though it is passing for a second time, and we have to retrospectively de-ascribe this shot. As much as I am interested in retrospective revisions, there are other ways of describing this sequence. I agree that the scenes may be disorientating. However, what these shots also perform is a loosening of temporal chronology, thus elongating the film's pace. In between each shot – of the kiss to the train, of the train to the couple – uncertain ellipses are taking place. The shot is disjunctive because the link between the train and the couple on the hillside seems to be temporally tight, thus when the shot of them lying down appears, I assume that the train has already passed. A train may have passed before the camera, however, but not yet before the couple. This temporal disjunction creates a sense that time has escaped, which resonates as the train moves off-screen. The disjunction in the edits echoes diegetic concerns: the train passing the couple is a signal for Sandro, who says: 'It is late', recognising that time has slipped away from them.

In the above example, the soundtrack is the source of both a continuity – from waves to train, which draws out a similar rhythm – and a discontinuity – the train, sounding closer this time and finally bursting through the visual image. It is important to note the possible effects that the use of music also has on the pace and rhythm of particular scenes, despite Antonioni's frequent pronouncements explaining his distaste for music in films: 'Every time I have music in films it means a terrible sacrifice for me. In my opinion, the image is not enriched but rather is interrupted, even, I'd dare to say, vulgarised.'[151] After the stirring, energetic rhythms of the credit sequence music, played on bass and mandolins, the first piece of music enters the soundtrack when the characters are looking for Anna on Lisca Bianca. After the dissolve that wipes Anna away, the sound of the sea seems to increase; a sound both exhilarating and threatening. The music itself begins as we see Claudia, with Corrado and Giulia following close behind, emerge into long-shot with the mass of the rocky island piled high before them. The music was to encompass several temporal associations; Antonioni asked his composer Giovanni Fusco for a jazz score if jazz had been written in classical Greece.[152] The double bass and wind instruments, and dissonant rhythms of the piece, add a sense of whimsy to the search, as though, at this point, the characters were not really taking it seriously.

The music does not particularly accord with the choreography of the movements of the characters entering and exiting the frame, nor does it match the cuts in the editing. It is as though several distinct temporal rhythms were being overlaid onto one another. The rhythm of the music and that of the frame seem to unsettle each other in turn. The dissonance also points to a gap, a mismatch, to something out of kilter in the narrative. Another somewhat dissonant use of music occurs just after Sandro and Claudia arrive at their hotel room in Taormina. Claudia begins to undress and kneels down to look in her suitcase. At a relatively low volume, the credit music from the opening of the film begins to play. It continues as Sandro helps Claudia into bed, tells her that he loves her (and, jokingly, that he doesn't). The re-playing of the credit music here has an odd effect, for it relates back to the beginning of the film, and encourages us to realise how much change the relentless passage of time has wrought.

The music also has an interesting effect on two scenes of waiting. In the first, Claudia is at the Montaldo villa, trying on rings and holding them up to the light. The music, consisting of the staccato sounds of the clarinet, flute, French horn and strings, gives the scene a restless, impatient feel.[153] This seems to accord with the type of waiting being experienced by Claudia; she is not simply passing time idly, she is waiting for something definite, namely Sandro. The temporal rhythm of the waiting is announced as different partly through the music. In Taormina, after Sandro has gone downstairs, Claudia is shown in bed; we first see a close-up of her hand against a white pillow. Similar music to that used in the island sequence recurs here, but with lower, even more ominous, tones. The music seems to match her frame of mind, heightening momentarily, for example, when she finds one of Sandro's shirts and presses it to her body. In this sequence, the continuity of the music helps to condense the hours of waiting that the sequence depicts. At the beginning of the sequence, the clock strikes one, soon after it strikes three, and then Claudia is seen emerging on to the balcony at dawn. Within the sequence, it is the editing that is discontinuous. Straight cuts interject into the action in a disjunctive way. For example, a shot shows Claudia beginning to lie down; cutting into this action, the next shot shows her lying on the bed; from a shot of her face while she is counting the time, a straight cut shows us the balcony door that she enters. The film suggests that the rhythms of waiting are both disjunctive, flitting from one activity that seems to 'fill' the time to a seemingly endless stretch of emptiness, and continuous, an elongated duration, suggested through the continuity of the music.

L'Avventura Today

L'Avventura is a film with the powerful potential to evoke affects, ranging from anger, frustration and boredom to adoration and exhilaration. Reviews and critical essays abound in personal statements of deep attraction to it. Youngblood explains that when he met Monica Vitti for the first time he told her that '*L'Avventura* changed my life'.[154] Nowell-Smith recalls his experience of seeing the film for the first time, 'for two and a half hours I sat spellbound in the cinema . . . no film before or since has ever made such an impression on me as *L'Avventura* did on that occasion'.[155] His reaction may have been 'extreme', he continues, 'but it was not – I soon discovered – untypical. I still meet people who remember it in much the same way.'[156]

The twenty-first-century context for viewing the film is naturally very different from the context of seeing the film upon its release. Nowell-Smith suggests that, while the film shocked audiences originally, 'the film now comes gift-wrapped. It can move but it can no longer shock'.[157] The viewer of *L'Avventura* today, he writes, is likely to be more prepared for seeing an art-house classic, perhaps at a film retrospective, as part of a film course, or through watching a specifically packaged DVD.[158] Some of the techniques of the film, such as the ellipses and slow rhythms, may be more familiar to viewers through the work of other filmmakers whose careers largely developed after 1960 (for example, Tarkovsky, Kieślowski, or Bela Tarr). On the other hand, viewing the film today may be imbued with a certain nostalgia for some of the films of the past; for their now rather quaint emphasis upon bourgeois modernity, for their gorgeous costumes, for their slow duration or affective compositions. Writing of the 'effect of new technologies on cinema that has now aged', Mulvey has written that there is a 'different kind of voyeurism at stake when the future looks back with greedy fascination at the past and details suddenly lose their marginal status and acquire the aura that passing time bequeaths to the most ordinary objects'.[159] Watching *L'Avventura* today might be seen to project a kind of gaze of re-enchantment upon its world. Ford suggests that an encounter with this film may be even stranger today than in 1960, despite Antonioni's enormous influence on other filmmakers: '*L'Avventura*'s own temporality as a text is now quite odd – reaching forward to us like science-fiction from an exotic "modernist" past, as we in our new century debate the transforming role the moving image has played in re-making time and space.'[160]

Nowell-Smith has concluded that the film cannot be entirely 'new' for viewers today. While it is obviously true that the historical context in which contemporary viewers watch the film is very different from that of the early 1960s, even with the caveat that viewing conditions vary greatly within any given period, every encounter with a film is, in some senses of the word, 'new', a new adventure. Here I directly echo Antonioni's statement that 'every day, every emotional encounter gives rise to a new adventure'.[161] It is perhaps a truism that, even on repeat screenings, viewers will respond differently to films as well as make new discoveries amongst their images and significances. *L'Avventura* seems particularly to encourage this through the ambiguity and richness of its images, and the continual creative innovativeness displayed in its cinematography and editing practices. Despite this, however, particular readings of the film that emphasise distance and alienation in the narrative and themes, and flatness and stillness in the mise-en-scène, continue to be repeated in critical writing. Through tracing the operation of time in narrative, composition, and editing, this chapter has suggested a different critical configuration, one which foregrounds intimacy, fluidity, and affect.

Notes

1. Geoffrey Nowell-Smith, *L'Avventura* (London: BFI Publishing, 1997), p. 11.
2. Pierre Sorlin, *European Cinemas, European Societies 1939–1990* (London: Routledge, 1991), p. 140.
3. Hamish Ford, 'Antonioni's *L'Avventura* and Deleuze's Time-image', *Senses of Cinema*, 28 (2003), http://www.sensesofcinema.com/contents/03/28/l_avventura_deleuze.html.
4. Peter Brunette, *The Films of Michelangelo Antonioni* (Cambridge: Cambridge University Press, 1998), p. 31.
5. In 1962 *L'Avventura* was in second place on the list; in 1972 at number 5; in 1982 at number 7; in 1992 it did not appear. Jonathan Rosenbaum, *Placing Movies* (Berkeley: University of California Press, 1995), p. 308.
6. Michelangelo Antonioni, 'Cannes Statement', in Seymour Chatman and Guido Fink (eds), *L'Avventura: Michelangelo Antonioni, Director* (New Brunswick, NJ and London: Rutgers Films in Print, 1989), pp. 178–9.
7. William Arrowsmith, *Antonioni: The Poet of Images* (Oxford: Oxford University Press, 1995), p. 31.
8. Ibid., p. 32.
9. Peter Bondanella, *Italian Cinema* (New York: F. Ungar Pub. Co., 1983), p. 212.
10. Ibid., p. 211.
11. *La Notte*, film, directed by Michelangelo Antonioni. Italy/France: Nepifilm, 1961. *L'Eclisse*, film, directed by Michelangelo Antonioni. Italy/France: Cineriz, 1962. *Il Deserto Rosso*, film, directed by Michelangelo Antonioni. Italy/France: Film Duemila, 1964.
12. Seymour Chatman, *Antonioni: or, the Surface of the World* (Berkeley: University of California Press, 1985), p. 55. See also Bondanella, p. 211.
13. Clara Orban, 'Antonioni's Women, Lost in the City', *Modern Language Studies*, 31.2 (2001), p. 11.
14. James Stoller, 'Antonioni's *La Notte*: Dissolution of Love', in Pierre Leprohon (ed.), *Michelangelo Antonioni: An Introduction* (New York: Simon & Schuster, 1963), p. 173.
15. Ian Cameron, 'Michelangelo Antonioni', *Film Quarterly*, 16.1 (1962), p. 1.

16. Ibid., p. 5.
17. Ned Rifkin, *Antonioni's Visual Language* (Michigan: UMI Research Press, 1982), p. 14.
18. Ibid., p. 15.
19. Ted Perry, 'Introduction', in William Arrowsmith, *Antonioni*, p. 11.
20. Brunette, *The Films*, p. 3.
21. Roland Barthes, 'Cher Antonioni', in Geoffrey Nowell-Smith, *L'Avventura* (London: BFI Publishing, 1997), p. 65.
22. Ibid., p. 66.
23. Bondanella, *Italian Cinema*, p. 213.
24. Brunette, *The Films*, p. 44.
25. Chatman, *Antonioni: or, the Surface of the World*, p. 118.
26. Ibid., p. 118.
27. Ibid., p. 119.
28. Ibid., p. 121.
29. Ibid., p. 119.
30. Ibid., p. 127.
31. Ibid., pp. 114–15.
32. Ibid., p. 115.
33. David Forgacs, 'Antonioni: Space, Place, Sexuality', in Myrto Konstantarakos (ed.), *Spaces in European Cinema* (Exeter: Intellect, 2000), p. 101.
34. Brunette, *The Films*, p. 44.
35. Sam Rohdie, *Antonioni* (London: BFI Publishing, 1990), p. 97.
36. Laura Mulvey, *Death 24 x a Second* (London: Reaktion, 2006), pp. 163–4.
37. Leo Charney, *Empty Moments: Cinema, Modernity and Drift* (Durham: Duke University Press, 1998), p. 45.
38. Mary Ann Doane, 'The Close-Up: Scale and Detail in the Cinema', *Differences*, 14.3 (2003), p. 104.
39. Ibid., p. 94.
40. Ibid., p. 97.
41. Laura U. Marks, *The Skin of the Film* (Durham: Duke University Press, 2000), p. 162.
42. Gilles Deleuze , *Cinema 1: The Movement Image* (London: Continuum, 2005), p. 100.
43. Ibid., p. 100.
44. Lesley Stern, 'Paths That Wind Through the Thicket of Things', *Critical Inquiry*, 28.1 (2001), p. 354.
45. Jennifer M. Barker, 'Bodily Irruptions: The Corporeal Assault on Ethnographic Narration', *Cinema Journal*, 34. 3 (1995), p. 58.
46. Cited in Bert Cardullo (ed.), *Michelangelo Antonioni: Interviews* (Jackson: University Press of Mississipi, 2008), pp. 153–4.
47. Brigitte Peucker, *Incorporating Images: Film and the Rival Arts* (Princeton: Princeton University Press, 1995), p. 62.

48. Barbara Klinger, 'The Art Film, Affect, and the Female Viewer: *The Piano* Revisited', *Screen*, 47.1 (2006), p. 21.
49. Doane, 'Close-Up', p. 108.
50. Victor Burgin, *The Remembered Film* (London: Reaktion, 2006), pp. 67–8.
51. Paul Willemen, *Looks and Frictions: Essays in Cultural Studies and Film Theory* (Bloomington: Indiana University Press, 1994), p. 233.
52. Marijke de Valck and Malte Hagener, 'Down with Cinephilia? Long Live Cinephilia? And Other Videosyncratic Pleasures', in Marijke de Valck and Malte Hagener (eds), *Cinephilia: Movies, Love and Memory* (Amsterdam: Amsterdam University Press, 2005), pp. 12–13.
53. Ibid., p. 11.
54. Mulvey, *Death*, p. 167.
55. Ibid., p. 186.
56. Ibid., p. 22.
57. Ibid., p. 27.
58. Burgin, *The Remembered Film*, p. 16.
59. Lesley Stern and George Kouvaros, 'Descriptive Acts: Introduction', in Lesley Stern and George Kouvaros (eds), *Falling For You: Essays on Cinema and Performance* (Sydney: Power Publications, 1999), p. 1.
60. Ibid., p. 17.
61. Rifkin, *Antonioni's Visual Language*, p. 7.
62. Ibid., p. 12.
63. Cardullo, *Michelangelo Antonioni*, p. xii.
64. Ibid., 64.
65. Ford, 'Antonioni's *L'Avventura*'.
66. Glen Norton, 'Antonioni's Modernist Language', [no date], http://www.geocities.com/Hollywood/3781/antonioni.html
67. Nowell-Smith, *L'Avventura*, p. 40.
68. Chatman, *Antonioni: or, the Surface of the World*, p. 93.
69. Brunette, p. 45.
70. Ibid.
71. Cameron, 'Michelangelo Antonioni', p. 23.
72. Gilberto Perez, *The Material Ghost: Films and Their Medium* (Baltimore: Johns Hopkins University Press, 1998), p. 370.
73. Ibid., p. 370.
74. Claire Colebrook, *Gilles Deleuze* (London: Routledge, 2002), pp. 39–40.
75. Ibid., p. 23.
76. Ibid., p. 32.
77. Deleuze cited by Ronald Bogue, *Deleuze's Way: Essays in Transverse Ethics and Aesthetics* (Hampshire: Ashgate, 2007), p. 55.
78. Ibid., p. 59.
79. Ibid., p. 55.
80. Nowell-Smith, *L'Avventura*', p. 46.
81. Gregory Flaxman, 'Cinema Year Zero', in Gregory Flaxman (ed.), *The*

Brain is the Screen: Deleuze and the Philosophy of Cinema (Minneapolis: The University of Minnesota Press, 2000), p. 104.
82. Brunette, *The Films*, p. 38.
83. Ibid., p. 39.
84. Gene Youngblood, Criterion Collection DVD Audio Commentary, *L'Avventura*, film, directed by Michelangelo Antonioni. Italy/France: Cino del Duca Produzioni, 1960.
85. Brunette, *The Films*, p. 33.
86. Rohdie, *Antonioni*, p. 66.
87. Ibid., p. 65.
88. Raymond Durgnat, *Films and Feelings* (London: Faber & Faber, 1967), p. 56.
89. Antonioni cited by Rifkin, p. 74.
90. Slavoj Žižek, *Looking Awry* (Massachusetts: The MIT Press, 1997), p. 88.
91. Ibid., p. 91.
92. Ibid., p. 91.
93. Marks, *Skin*, p. 81.
94. Deleuze, *Cinema 2*, p. 8.
95. Klinger, 'The Art Film', p. 36.
96. Tim Groves,'Entranced: Affective Mimesis and Cinematic Identification', *Screening the Past*, 20 (2006), http://www.latrobe.edu.au/screeningthepast/20/entranced.html.
97. Cameron, 'Michelangelo Antonioni', p. 11; Rifkin, *Antonioni's Visual Language*, p. 19, Chatman, *Antonioni: or, the Surface of the World*, p. 90.
98. Mitchell Schwarzer, 'The Consuming Landscape: Architecture in the Films of Michelangelo Antonioni', in Mark Lamster (ed.), *Architecture and Film* (New York: Princeton Architectural Press, 2000), p. 200.
99. Brunette, *The Films*, p. 14.
100. Raymond Durgnat, *Films and Feelings*, p. 109.
101. Arrowsmith, *Antonioni*, p. 35.
102. Deleuze, *Cinema 2*, p. 8.
103. Perez, *The Material Ghost*, p. 379.
104. Giuliana Bruno, *Atlas of Emotion: Journeys in Art, Architecture and Film* (New York: Verso, 2002), p. 62.
105. Ibid., p. 62.
106. Bruno, *Atlas of Emotion*, p. 36.
107. Ibid., p. 56.
108. Angelo Restivo, *The Cinema of Economic Miracles* (Durham: Duke University Press, 2002), p. 47.
109. Fallaci cited by Restivo, *The Cinema*, p. 47.
110. Restivo, *The Cinema*, p. 47.
111. Arrowsmith, *Antonioni*, p. 37.
112. Restivo, *The Cinema*, p. 5.

113. Bliss Cua Lim, *Translating Time: Cinema, the Fantastic, and Temporal Critique* (Durham and London: Duke University Press, 2009), p. 15.
114. Ibid., p. 15.
115. Andreas Huyssen, *Twilight Memories: Marking Time in a Culture of Amnesia* (New York and London: Routledge, 1995), p. 28.
116. Deleuze, *Cinema 2*, p. 105.
117. Ibid., p. 105.
118. Andre Bazin, *What is Cinema?* (Berkeley, Los Angeles and London: University of California Press, 2005), p. 36.
119. Philip Rosen, 'History of Image, Image of History: Subject and Ontology in Bazin', in Ivone Marguiles (ed.), *Rites of Realism: Essays in Corporeal Cinema* (Durham and London: Duke University Press, 2003), p. 55.
120. Deleuze, *Cinema 2*, p. 124.
121. Ibid., p. 107.
122. Ibid., p. 107.
123. Ibid., p. 119.
124. Ibid., p. 121.
125. Youngblood, Criterion Collection DVD Audio Commentary.
126. Perez, *The Material Ghost*, p. 392.
127. Bergson, *Matter and Memory*, p. 25.
128. Jean-Clet Martin, 'Of Images and Worlds: Toward A Geology of the Cinema', in Gregory Flaxman (ed.), *The Brain is the Screen: Deleuze and the Philosophy of Cinema* (Minneapolis: The University of Minnesota Press, 2000), p. 66.
129. Ibid, p. 64.
130. Burgin, *The Remembered Film*, p. 15.
131. Rosenbaum, *Placing Movies*, p. 313.
132. Nowell-Smith, *L'Avventura*', p. 15.
133. Cited by Bondanella, *Italian Cinema*, p. 108.
134. Deleuze, *Cinema 2*, pp. 22–3.
135. Ibid., p. 182.
136. Rodowick, *Gilles Deleuze's Time Machine*, p. 13.
137. Lim, *Translating Time*, p. 67.
138. To appropriate Grosz's words, *Nick of Time*, p. 198.
139. Ibid., p. 197.
140. Antonioni cited by Chatman, p. 126.
141. Nowell-Smith, *L'Avventura*', p. 27.
142. Ford, 'Antonioni's *L'Avventura*'.
143. Ibid.
144. Chatman, *Antonioni: or, the Surface of the World*, p. 125.
145. John Schliesser, 'Antonioni's Heideggerian Swerve', *Literature Film Quarterly*, 26.4 (1998), pp. 278–87 (p. 280).
146. Rohdie, *Antonioni*, p. 139.
147. Perez, *The Material Ghost*, p. 371.

148. Yvette Biro, *Turbulence and Flow in Film: The Rhythmic Design* (Bloomington: Indiana University Press, 2008), p. 76.
149. Brunette, *The Films*, p. 40.
150. Ibid., p. 40.
151. Antonioni cited in Cardullo, *Michelangelo Antonioni*, p. 141.
152. Nowell-Smith, *L'Avventura'*, p. 27.
153. Seymour Chatman and Guido Fink (eds), *L'Avventura: Michelangelo Antonioni, Director* (New Brunswick, NJ: Rutgers University Press, 1989), p. 105.
154. Youngblood, DVD Commentary.
155. Nowell-Smith, *L'Avventura'*, p. 9.
156. Ibid., p. 10.
157. Ibid., p. 9.
158. Ibid., p. 10.
159. Mulvey, *Death*, p. 192.
160. Ford, 'Antonioni's *L'Avventura*'.
161. Antonioni cited by Arrowsmith, p. 31.

CHAPTER 3

Mirror: Traces and Transfiguration

Andrei Tarkovsky's fourth feature film, *Mirror*, had a complex and difficult production history. The shooting script and film itself went through torturous changes, many of which were demanded by Goskino, the State Committee for Cinematography in the USSR.[1] The project developed over ten years, but was always fundamentally concerned with memory and the traces of passing time. *Mirror* was partly inspired by Tarkovsky's own childhood memories, of a time spent in the countryside during wartime evacuation, and by the poetry of his father, Arseniy Tarkovsky, which is recited in the film.[2] Many of the film's scenes take place in a dacha (country house) that was rebuilt to mirror the dacha where Tarkovsky had spent time as a child. Tarkovsky's family photographs were used to recreate not only the house but also the clothes, poses, objects and lighting in *Mirror*.

Unlike Antonioni, Tarkovsky has not inspired criticism based upon an aesthetic of the 'momentary', but rather upon the passing of time in the long-take. This has largely been encouraged, it seems, by his own writing on film in his theoretical work *Sculpting in Time*, where he privileges duration and rhythm in film. According to Tarkovsky,

> Rhythm in cinema is conveyed by the life of the object visibly recorded in the frame. Just as from the quivering of a reed you can tell what sort of current, what pressure there is in a river, in the same way we know the movement of time from the flow of the life-process reproduced in the shot.[3]

It is the 'distinctive time running through the shots', rather than the edited assembly of shots, which makes 'the rhythm of the picture'.[4] Although contested by his fellow editors, the director continually claimed that he edited *Mirror* not on the basis of concepts or readily definable intellectual 'meanings' but through the images' 'own intrinsic pattern'.[5] Tarkovsky re-edited the film over twenty times before the assembly of the shots and the rhythm of the work as a whole was acceptable to him.

Mirror interweaves different temporal strands, which can be broadly divided up into the film's 'present' of 1975, sometime during the Second World War, and the 1930s. A pre-credit sequence, which I discuss in more detail below, seems to be set in 1975, while in the first sequence after the credits, a narrative voice-over introduces the images to us as occurring during wartime. The voice-over thus suggests that the images could be a memory of the (as yet unseen) Narrator. Other images that follow are variably coloured, sepia and black and white; these images could be present, past, memory, fantasy, dream, or anything in between. Attempts to parcel the film's sequences into such categories are largely untenable. The film continually touches the boundaries of these definitions without ever resting entirely in one, like the continually mobile camera movements within the film that refuse to still.

Mirror features multiple temporal versions of the same characters. In the pre-war sequences, we see a young mother with her two children, Marina (a character based upon Tarkovsky's younger sister) and Alexei (the younger version of the narrator). These children are shown in their slightly older manifestations in the wartime sequence, along with the mother, Maria. In the 1975 scenes, Natalia is the narrator's wife and Ignat is his son, played by the same actor as the older child Alexei. An older version of Maria appears in all three time periods, played by Tarkovsky's own mother. The film weaves together archival footage with the footage filmed by Tarkovsky and Georgi Rerberg, the director of photography on the film. At one point, for example, Natalia is shown entertaining some Spanish guests; interspersed with these scenes is documentary footage from the Spanish Civil War. We are then shown stratosphere balloons and aviator Valeri Chkalov's return to Moscow after flying across the North Pole, footage apparently inserted to appease the authorities, who criticised the work for its lack of optimism and heroism.[6] Other footage shows Soviet soldiers crossing Lake Sivash in 1943, hauling a cannon.

Through its presentation of the heterogeneous nature of temporality and through the enactment of a slowed down time in the use of long-takes, the film can be seen to be concerned with the passing of time as duration. *Mirror* proceeds through a series of episodes or moments that are unlinked from linear time. This is not to say that they do not relate to one another, but rather that they do so through rhythm, pattern, and theme, rather than linear chronology or narrative structure. This chapter charts the heterogeneity of the film's temporal rhythms, spaces, and sound signatures, emphasising the film's fascination with the textured traces of passing time and time's destabilisation of coherent filmic space. While the film's Narrator attempts to re-experience the memories and dreams of his childhood, the film reveals the transfigurative nature of memory, which can never return us to a pure past. Transfiguration, I argue, is both thematised and enacted in the film. The images of natural textures and elements – water, trees, plants, wooden surfaces, fire, grass – are transfigured through filters, movements, slow motion and sound discrepancies. These images both appeal to the senses as well as invite an awareness of the aesthetic imaging process itself.

Time and the Long-Take

Much of the critical writing about Tarkovsky's long-takes, following Tarkovsky's own writing in *Sculpting*, privileges its experiential possibilities, that is, the way in which viewers can experience the passage of time through the shot's duration. Frequently, however, this experience is described as a spiritual or religious one. Between the experience of duration and its apparent ultimate spiritual significance, which may be accessible to spiritually receptive spectators, there seems to be a less theorised area to be considered: the relationship between the experience of time through the elongated long-takes, and the thematic presentation of the operation of temporality. Drawing upon the writing of Deleuze, this chapter traces some possibilities relating to how the film's thematic concerns about passing time develop through the film's duration.

In *Sculpting*, Tarkovsky claimed that he was opposed to the type of montage propagated by Sergei Eisenstein partly because it was too literary, and thus 'contradicts the very basis of the unique process whereby a film affects an audience'. According to Tarkovsky, montage deprives the person watching of that prerogative of film that distinguishes it from literature, 'namely, the opportunity to live through what is happening on the screen as if it were his own life, to take over, as deeply personal and his own, the experience imprinted in time upon the screen, relating his own life to what is being shown'.[7] Tarkovsky claims that he aimed to make films 'which carry no oratorical, propagandist speech, but are the occasion for a deeply intimate experience'.[8] Tarkovsky's stance against montage endeared him to Deleuze, whose writing on temporality and the time-image in many ways correlates closely with his own. Deleuze pays special attention to Tarkovsky's opposition to Eisensteinian montage and preference for the long-take in formulating his own distinction between the movement and time-images. Montage, as Deleuze emphasises, relies upon the experience of a series of momentary shocks. Concepts arise from the opposition of images in succession. Time is thus represented indirectly, as it arises out of the montage which links the movement-images together.

In the cinema of the time-image, conversely, the link between perceptions and actions is 'shattered from the inside', and spaces are no longer coordinated or filled.[9] Characters become 'caught' in pure optical and sound situations, as 'pure seers' who exist in the interval between perception and action.[10] Centres of movement dissipate and images are no longer logically centred in space, which allows time to surface directly. The time-image reveals what Deleuze understands to be the underlying basis of all cinema: rather than being a language system or a language, cinema is made up of 'a plastic mass, an "a-signifying and a-syntaxic material"', an utterable which gives rise to utterances, a state of process, becoming and possibility.[11]

Totaro has suggested that throughout the history of filmmaking and film criticism, editing has often been associated with expressing the rational and intellectual, and the moving camera seen to be more suited to 'intensifying the experiential'.[12] In privileging duration, Jon Beasley-Murray has argued that Deleuze seems to return to the problematic of film's reality and ontology, which was generated by Bazin.[13] In their opposition to a semiotic analysis of film and a conception of the ontology of the cinematic image, both Bazin and Deleuze offer 'an anti-representational analysis of the cinema ... the cinema viewer is maintained as part of an immanent functional (and corporeal) effect of the film's unfolding through time; the cinema *is* before it *means* or signifies'.[14] Long-takes are especially associated with an 'inhabitation' of the real duration of time, in which the bodily sensation of temporality is prioritised over its disjunctive narrative coding.[15] For both Bazin and Deleuze, according to Beasley-Murray, 'the specificity of cinema remains its unfolding of the image in the real time that becomes the lived time of thought and the body'.[16] Many of Tarkovsky's critics similarly oppose the experience of duration in cinema to a linguistic or interpretive drive. As Synessios writes, the almost imperceptible tracking of Tarkovsky's camera creates a sense of being drawn within the frame in a kinaesthetic movement: 'the mesmerising camera movements, together with the unusual events taking place within the frame, confound all attempts to interpret the image. The emphasis is on directly experiencing it and allowing it to affect a deeper layer of our consciousness.'[17] According to Petric, Tarkovsky attempts 'to evoke emotional, often highly visceral responses in the viewer, instead of triggering ideas meant to support a particular attitude toward history and society'.[18]

In Tarkovsky's writings, however, there is also a tendency for this experience of temporality to translate directly into a spiritual encounter. As Tarkovsky writes, how does time make itself felt in a shot? It becomes tangible when you sense something significant, truthful, going on beyond the events on the screen; when you realise, quite consciously, that what you see in the frame is not limited to its visual depiction, but is a pointer to something stretching out beyond the frame and to infinity.[19]

While temporality is here 'tangible' and lived through, it is also directed toward a transcendental, spiritual experience. Tarkovsky imagines the cinema-goer as 'seek[ing] to fill that spiritual vacuum which has formed as a result of the specific conditions of his modern existence'.[20] Living through the duration of the film, in this view, puts the spectator in touch with a spiritual sense of time as eternity. This theoretical structure is also echoed throughout the criticism on Tarkovsky. Petric, for example, writes that slow motion has a strong emotional impact, partly because it makes viewers aware of 'the *passage of time* and its *rhythmic pressures*'. In order to experience this, however, we must paradoxically look 'beyond' the image to a point where 'numerous layers of ineffable transcendental signification can be found'.[21]

For Deleuze, however, the long-take is not just experiential, but also makes immanent a conceptualisation of passing time. Deleuze's writings on the time-image, and particularly his association of temporality with various modes of thought, can productively be put into dialogue with *Mirror*. Deleuze believed that calling upon transcendent significance in fact arrests movement, drawing attention away from movement itself to a static structuring. As Deleuze has argued, while post-war cinema tends to abandon metaphor and dislocate the 'internal monologue' of the film, it also becomes 'more demanding, more constraining, in some sense *theorematic*'.[22] While not restoring fixed knowledge or internal certainty to the image, the process of thought becomes immanent to the image. In the post-war cinema of the time-image, the descriptions of space which are usually undertaken by a camera are subordinated to the functions of thought through time. The camera's focusing, moving, and irrational lengths of shots are equated to mental connections that it enters into. According to Deleuze, the camera probes a space to become questioning, provoking, theorematising, and experimenting, a process that can happen within the duration of a long-take.[23] *Mirror* announces this immanence of cinematic association in its first post-credit sequence, with a seemingly innocuous movement. As Maria sits on the fence of her home conversing with a visiting doctor, he examines her hand and notes that she is not wearing a 'ring' (*koltso*). When this word is pronounced, the camera begins to ring around Maria and ends focused on her hairstyle, which is arranged in coils or rings around her head, as though creating an association between dialogue, movement and mise-en-scène.

The long-take may encourage a different pace in which thought develops. In the long-take, according to Totaro, 'the thought process can peak at any moment within the shot, and often gains in intensity precisely as a result of duration'.[24] The long-take in *Mirror*, however, does not just invite thought *in* time, but also *of* time. Tarkovsky has claimed that in his filmmaking, he is 'sculpting in time', removing from the pro-filmic any elements which are not fundamentally necessary to a scene so as to rarefy and draw attention to those that are.[25] It might, however, be just as accurate to say that his films show that it is *time* that sculpts, and that objects and people are subject to the vicissitudes of time, rather than time being something that can be mastered and controlled, as the notion of spatialised or clock time suggests. *Mirror*'s long-takes thematise and enact a sense of time passing indifferently to our presence. As Rodowick has stated, when spaces are no longer rationally linked in post-war cinema, the quality of movement in relation to time changes; 'to the extent that time is no longer the measure of movement as indirect image, movement becomes a perspective on time'.[26] The way in which movement can become a perspective on time is made visible in an early scene in which Maria announces to her two small children that a fire is burning in the barn outside. The characters leave the room to watch the fire, but the camera does not immediately follow them. Instead, it pans slowly out of the room. Just as it is about to reach a point in the corridor when we would no longer see the entrance to the room, a glass bottle lying on the edge of a table in the room falls on to the floor.

There are several things to note about the movement of the camera and the movements within the frame. First, the camera's attention does not stay with a narrative presentation that would ordinarily follow the characters to the emergency that concentrates their energies. Instead, as with *L'Avventura*'s camera movements, which encourage us to become aware of temporal rhythms other than our own, and other than those of the characters, we are asked to share a moment of 'enforced patience', to use Mullarkey's words.[27] Furthermore, our attention is not directed to the bottle's movement through a process of editing. A montage sequence might present this movement as a series of moments in succession. By not doing so, the long-take itself enacts a thematic performance of time passing, indifferent to human endeavour. As Colebrook writes, 'time is *not* a sequence of one thing following another *within* some actual common ground. There is not a world that contains time; there is a flow of time, which produces "worlds" or durations.'[28] In its everyday form, according to Colebrook, perception 'tends to fix itself as a point from which time and becoming are observed'; a point of view thus becomes abstracted from perception and duration. The moving camera, however, encourages our view to also be moved by the force of time, and no point in time is privileged over any other.[29] In this sequence, this conceptualisation of time is literally contrasted to the spatialisation of clock time, signalled by the chiming of a clock.

The film encourages us to think about time as heterogeneous and variable. In parts, for example, the editing together of archival images presents modern temporality as a series of perceptual shocks. Montage sequences of newsreel footage primarily show the effects and processes of the Soviet Union's various conflicts, such as the siege of Leningrad, border skirmishes with Maoists, and the death of Hitler. The footage from the Spanish Civil War is edited into fragments and sped up in places; as Synessios writes, it is 'staccato, sharp, confused, erratically moving'.[30] The Spanish song that is played over these images also has a quickened pace and an urgency, associated, furthermore, with a moment of shock and physical violence – it is the same music that a Spanish girl, a guest of Natalia's, had been dancing to when her father slapped her, abruptly cutting off the song. These documentary sequences are evocative of Benjamin's idea of modernity as itself a series of shocks. As Doane has written, 'the very rapidity of the changing images in film is potentially traumatic for the spectator and allows the cinema to *embody* something of the restructuration of modern perception'.[31] The montage sequences thematise and enact the overwhelming time of modernity, in which time is associated with an 'understanding of temporality as assault, acceleration, speed', with trauma or shock in the increase of the intensity of stimuli.[32] In another sequence, we see Maria running through the rain to the printing press where she works. This sequence presents a different conceptualisation of temporality, but also one associated with a tyrannical regulation of time. The printing presses activate a kind of temporality which is linear, directional, and inexorable. Possible mistakes cannot be rectified. If a mistake in editing has been made by Maria, as she fears, it cannot be reversed. The presses, as a worker tells her, have been running all night. This machinic temporality proceeds under the fierce gazes of Stalin and Felix Dzerzhinsky, head of the Soviet secret police (Cheka) represented in posters on the walls.

Contrasted to this sense of time as an overwhelming flow or a series of shocks is the idea of natural rhythms, thematised through dialogue. The doctor that visits Maria, for example, associates nature with slow temporality in the very first post-credit sequence. Speaking of his pleasure at landing among roots and trees, he says '[plants] don't run about. Like us who are rushing, fussing, uttering banalities. That's because we don't trust the nature that is inside us. Always this suspiciousness, haste, and no time to stop and think.' This dissatisfaction with continually 'rushing' and 'hurrying' in modern society is expressed twice more in the film. When Natalia spills the contents of her handbag, she chides herself gently for being 'always in a hurry'. A worker at the printing house, played by one of Tarkovsky's favourite actors, Nikolai Grinko, says 'everybody's rushing, no one's got any time', and very little else. It is as though the characters were yearning for a kind of uchronia, the temporal equivalent of a utopia. According to Nowotny, a uchronia tends to be imagined in culture at historical moments when the pressure of time is intensifying, to allow for an escape from rationalised time.[33] Uchronia 'feeds on ideas which start from a change in temporal rhythms and strives for a new balance between the linearity of mechanised and homogenised time and the unexpected element, the spontaneity of the "vicissitudes of life"'.[34] If the uchronia 'argues for the creation of new periods of time in which vicissitudes can occur', then this is to provide a slow-moving temporality outside of rationalised, violent, or mechanistic time.[35]

If we return to the printing-press sequence and re-examine some of the archival sequences, we can see that other rhythms of duration are made to operate through them as though to re-claim this temporality, to salvage duration from tyrannical, regulated time. The scenes in which Maria is running through the corridors of her workplace are conveyed in slightly slowed motion, a rhythm which is set against the machinic time presented by the presses. In the documentary sequences, orchestral music is sometimes used to bind the images into a more unified sequence. The music can create a sense of flow rather than disjunction. As Altman writes, if 'the image displaces us incessantly, offering us diverse angles on objects located at radically different distances', sound can be used to restore balance, generating a 'continuous experience'.[36]

The documentary sequences bring to the fore another troubling temporal configuration: that associated with indexicality. As Doane writes, 'the indexical sign is the imprint of a once-present and unique moment, the signature of temporality', and is thus fundamentally linked to the desire to capture and archive passing time.[37] The poem that is heard over the footage of soldiers crossing Lake Sivash, for example, invokes this desire:

> All are immortal. All is immortal
> ... I will call up any century,
> Go into it and build myself a house.

>   . . . one table for great-grandfather and grandson.
>   The future is accomplished here and now.

Significantly, Tarkovsky claims that when he came across this footage, he realised that it 'had to become the centre, the very essence, heart, nerve of this picture that had started off merely as my intimate lyrical memories'.[38] He was drawn, it seems, both to the unique, aesthetic quality of time that ran through the newsreel footage, and the fact that, 'once imprinted on the film', the footage 'ceased to be simply like life', and instead became an expression of both sacrifice and immortality.[39] This paradoxical relation is inherent in the promise of indexicality, which is one of 'the rematerialisation of time', the restoration of a continuum of time which is also thematised through the Narrator's attempt to capture memories of his childhood.[40] From its inception, cinema has been seen in terms of a 'prophylactic against death', ensuring the ability to 'see one's loved ones gesture and smile long after their deaths'.[41] This archival desire is given material form in the photographs that recur throughout *Mirror*.

The attempt to salvage time through indexicality is, however, complicated by the inevitability of passing time and the association of photographic reproduction with death. Indexicality is marked by temporal displacements, as evidenced, for example, in Barthes' statement that the photograph articulates a 'this was now', which is intended to imply that the moment of registration which was, is now present here. As Ann Banfield writes, Barthes' use of deixis 'marks a point at which language may simply not be adequate to describe the photograph's tense'.[42] Barthes associates the photograph's punctum with an overwhelming consciousness of death, a sense that the photographic subject is at once dead and going to die, indicating '*a catastrophe that has already occurred*'.[43] More recently, Mulvey has described cinema as 'death 24x a second', due to its uncanny position between life and death, animate and inanimate, past and present.[44] As Doane writes, once the present has been seized in film, it becomes something 'past'. It also becomes something 'strangely immaterial; existing nowhere but in its screening for a spectator in the present, it becomes the experience of presence'. This presence, however, is disjunctive, it is one 'haunted by historicity'.[45]

Rather than focusing upon a moment of capture, however ambivalent, as promised by the still photograph, Tarkovsky's film attempts to slow down the progress of time, to express a temporality away from the spatialisation and rationalisation of chronology, and allow for the play of memory. It is only within this slow duration, it seems, that the attempt to immortalise childhood and its objects, textures, and figures can be undertaken. The film's final sequence exemplifies this in its presentation of the non-chronological coexistence of characters from different time periods in the same 'logically incompatible' space that cannot be rationally accounted for.[46] While the film has been wavering between capturing a time of, and for, childhood memories, and their continual disruption and transfiguration, the film ends on an image of a seemingly harmonious uchronia. As Synessios has argued, a 'small corner of eternity' appears at the film's conclusion that it seems to have successfully – in this particular scene – carved out.[47]

Unified by the same piece of music, this series of shots begins with a pan across a field that shows the house standing against the forest, and ends focused on Maria and the father lying in the field, talking about having children in the future. Maria looks away as the film cuts to a view of these future children who are being led by the much older mother from the Narrator's 'present'. After the cut back to Maria, with her ambivalent expression, we see the older Maria leading the children through the field, and a continuous take reveals the younger Maria standing in the far background, *within* the same shot as her future self. Deleuze's notion that a reorientation in time and space is necessitated by the moving long-take is powerfully activated in this sequence. The unique 'event' of Tarkovsky's long-take provides an experience of duration and necessitates a re-orientation to match the continual re-framing. Comprehending such sequences 'requires a considerable effort of memory and imagination'.[48] Reorientating ourselves throughout the duration of the moving long-take necessitates the activation of the viewer's memory, such that, as in *L'Avventura*, a 'coalescence' of the perceived with the remembered is reproduced in ambiguous landscapes.[49] The landscape, panned across and moved within by the camera, enacts an interrelation of memory and perception as we are confronted with the placement of characters from different generations within it. Throughout the film, however, as I discuss below, the relationship between time, memory and space is more disjunctive than this apparently fluid finale suggests.

Memory and Narration

The voice-over that begins after the credit sequence seems to imply that the images that we are seeing are derived from a memory of the Narrator's experience. The woman sitting on the fence outside her home in the country is his mother, hoping that she will one day see her husband return home from the war. The Narrator speaks of a time in his childhood when he would watch people approaching their country house. If they took a certain fork in the path, then it could only be the father returning home. What we see during this speech, however, is a stranger (the country doctor) taking this fork in the path and approaching the dacha, suggesting that the Narrator's voice is 'unseeing' rather than omniscient.[50] This is an early indication of a troubled and disjunctive relationship between sound and image. Later in the film, the Narrator recounts that:

> With an amazing regularity I keep seeing one and the same dream. It seems to make me return to a place, poignantly dear to my heart, where my grandfather's house used to be . . . Each time I try to enter it, something prevents me from doing that. I see this dream again and again. And when I see those walls made of logs and the dark entrance, even in my dream I become aware that I'm only dreaming it. And the overwhelming joy is clouded by anticipation of awakening. At times something happens and I stop dreaming of the house and the pine trees of my childhood around it. Then I get depressed. And I can't wait to see this dream in which I'll be a child again and feel happy again, because everything will be still ahead, everything will be possible.

The Narrator's attempts to re-experience the atmosphere, space, and time of his childhood, his memories, and even dreams, is one of the film's primary concerns. In voice-over, he expresses his fear that he will never again be able to live within the dream of his childhood. What we see during his speech, however, is in fact the interior of the dacha in a long-take, which shows the Narrator as a child inside the house. While we see the house and its inhabitants, diegetic sound is muted, replaced by the Narrator's voice. In both sequences, the voice does not seem to be able to 'see' the images, suggesting a fundamental discontinuity that divides voice and image into two separate temporal strands with an unbridgeable interval between them, never to be combined into a homogenous diegetic space or unique duration. This is a characteristic of time-image cinema, in which, as Rodowick writes, 'discontinuous distributions of narrative space' are produced, that 'keep forking, varying, and repeating without resolving in any single explanation'.[51]

The way in which the film's sequences shift almost indiscernibly between apparent memories of the past, dreams, and the Narrator's supposed present has nevertheless led some critics to state that the Narrator is successful in his endeavour to immerse himself in his past or in his memories and dreams. For Truppin, for example, the Narrator's 'entry into memory is total'.[52] This emphasis upon an immersion within a virtual space fails to properly account for the various rhythms of duration that operate in the film which continually destabilise the film's spaces. The force of *time*, as Deleuze has written in relation to post-war cinema, dislodges coherent presentations of *space*. *Mirror* emphasises that there is no actual "space" of memory to which one can return; there are only heterogeneous reflected and refracted images that circulate with one another. In *Mirror*, elements from what have been termed the past and the present are continually intruding upon each other in a manner that suggests the impossibility of accessing a pure memory of the past. As Bird has pointed out, Tarkovsky continually 'underscores the inseparability of images from the imagination that retains and identifies them'.[53] The Narrator complains that, for example, whenever he tries to remember his mother, she always has the face of his wife Natalia (they are both played by Margarita Terekhova). Remembered images and sequences tend to modulate into and out of scenes from artworks. In one scene, for example, wartime constraints force Maria to try to sell a pair of earrings to the doctor's wife. The camera focuses upon the bare, muddy feet and dirty clothes of Maria and her son (Alexei, the Narrator as a young boy). By contrast, the doctor's wife is wearing an improbable purple satin dress and headscarf that gleam in the dim lamplight. Turovskaya attributes her appearance to the fact that, as is suggested by the recurrence of a Leonardo da Vinci book throughout the film, the Narrator's childhood was influenced by art. In his memories, the doctor's wife, home and 'cherubic baby swathed in lace, unexpectedly assume the colours and textures of the High Renaissance'.[54] A filmed landscape of children playing on a snow-covered hill has drawn comparisons to Brueghel.[55]

Throughout the duration of the film, memory does not lend itself to an unproblematic capture. Brief flashes of memory-images recur throughout *Mirror* to disrupt this apparent attempt to absorb oneself within a stable chronology of memory: a hand warmed against a fire, which later reappears as part of a memory-sequence linked to the young Narrator; wind rushing through trees; and a fire burning on a hill. These flashes of recalcitrant images interrupt a continuous sequence and disrupt the Narrator's attempt to salvage a homogenous duration of memory. The concreteness of cinematic space is destabilised throughout the film's duration. The childhood home is constantly seen by means of different angles, lights, and filters; it is sometimes unclear whether we are seeing the same house throughout the film. The home is recreated in each sequence, drawing attention to the fluidity of memory and the impossibility of ever grasping or returning ourselves to the past. Particularly when filmed by a moving camera rather than framed in static shots, the spaces of the film appear impossibly fluid, suggesting endless uncharted mazes of rooms and corridors. *Mirror* also presents a continuous confusion between 'real' and 'reflected' space. The sequence that presents a fire burning in a neighbouring barn is a revealing example of this. In this scene, the slow moving camera pans out of the room that two children (the young Narrator and his sister) have just left, passing across a mirror that shows them watching the fire with their backs to the mirror. We hear a panicked call of 'Dounya!' from some distance as a different boy walks out from a space seemingly behind the mirror and enters a space where he can see the fire burning a short distance away. He is reunited with those who called him, who are suddenly much closer than the sound of the cry would have suggested. To get to the fire, however, he has walked in the opposite direction to where the mirror has suggested it is burning: he seems to have walked to the side of the mirror to see what it reflects, rather than away from it.

The way in which the characters occupy the film's spaces is fundamentally precarious. The adult Narrator, for example, although aurally present, is largely absent from the visual images, allowing the camera to glimpse a part of his body only once. Characters are framed against thresholds throughout the film, beyond which they cannot seem to pass. In the Narrator's apartment, for example, his son Ignat discovers an unknown woman in one of the rooms. She asks him to read an extract from Pushkin as he stands at the doorway. Hearing a knock at the door, Ignat finds an old woman – his grandmother – standing at the entrance to the apartment. Misrecognising him, however, she does not enter the apartment and leaves. When Ignat returns to the room, he finds that the woman he has been reading to has disappeared. The camera focuses upon the indexical heat-stain made by her teacup as this material trace of her presence rapidly fades. In another sequence, noted by Synessios, the Narrator as a young child cannot open the door to the room where his mother is and then, when it opens on its own, cannot enter, but remains standing on the threshold.[56]

The unity of the narrating consciousness itself is ultimately thrown into question. We might assume that the Narrator who introduces the film to us at the beginning, and then is partially seen at the end, presumably on his deathbed, is the psychological source from which the images emanate. The sequence near the film's conclusion appears to go some way towards attempting to anchor and explain the source of the images that we have seen. The Narrator's doctor, his authority in these matters suggested by a white lab coat, asserts that the Narrator has become obsessed with his memories owing to his guilt for some wrong done to his mother, which is not entirely clarified. The discrepancies and disjunctions between sound and image mentioned above, however, continually complicate easy attributions, destabilising a sense of a unified and coherent narrating consciousness. The film, furthermore, sometimes seems to encourage us to attribute the procession of scenes to characters other than the Narrator; that is, particular characters appear to be somehow aligned with specific series of images. A long documentary sequence, for example, is mostly associated with the young orphan, Asafiev. In this scene, Asafiev, a survivor of the siege of Leningrad, throws a grenade onto the shooting range. The instructor launches himself upon it, and the camera, in close-up, focuses on a point on the back of his head, which visibly pulsates, punctuating this duration of mortal fear. The grenade does not explode. The film then shows us a red-haired girl, who reappears throughout the film, laughing and touching a wound on her lip, before the scene changes to the brief documentary footage of the siege of Leningrad. The camera then finds Asafiev again, as he stands on a wooden platform and looks towards it. The Lake Sivash documentary footage is inserted here. When it ends, we see him coming up a snowy hill towards the camera, whistling. He positions himself in close-up, then suddenly stops whistling and turns his head to the side, as though his attention has been attracted by something beyond the frame. Instead of the conventional reverse-shot, which might be used to show us what he was looking at, we are shown documentary footage of bombs exploding and artillery in war-time. Shortly after, there is another cut to Asafiev, standing further away from the camera, but briefly looking straight towards it before he turns away. It is as though he were somehow seeing the images or at least being aware of their being visible to us, and challenging us with his direct look to respond to them.

A similar example of a series of images being aligned with a particular character occurs near the end of the film, when Maria is asked by the father whether she would like a boy or a girl. Her expression changes slowly; at first she smiles, but then bites her lip as though to keep from weeping. The symphonic music steadily builds in tension as she turns to look back towards the house. In the next shot, aligned with the entry of operatic voices, the camera tracks though the forest, and eventually shows the decaying foundations of the house and its well, where the old Maria and young children appear. There is then a cut back to Maria in exactly the same position that she had been in previously, that is, with her head turned away from the camera. She now looks back to the camera, attempting to smile through tears, and turns away again, as though to see more. The images are thus infused with a disorientating sense that they have been seen or imagined by her.

The proliferation of these instances where images seem to be attached to characters *within* the diegesis does not rule out the possibility of a single narrating subject whose imagination encompasses the entire film, of course, but it does destabilise this attribution. On the other hand, neither does aligning characters to various sequences mean that the film, rather than having a single narrator, simply has several. It is useful, at this point, to consider Deleuze's assertion that, in time-image cinema, time no longer flows unproblematically in succession to provide us with a sense of mastery over it, or a subjective 'ownership' of time. As Rodowick clarifies, temporal sequences are thus no longer unifiable from the point of view of a narrator who could 'synthetically authenticate their veracity or sequencing'.[57] No one character can verify the historical truth of a memory, nor can the spectator judge the veracity or probability of one narration over another; rather, 'there is a set of transformations where narrations continually falsify one another in a series that may just as easily contradict as corroborate one another. There is no point – fixed, intemporal, ahistorical – outside these series that enables us to make a subsumptive judgment that transcends and unifies them in a position of truth.'[58] The film shatters the unity of the narrating consciousness, unleashing instead a stream of thematically resonant, aesthetically fluid, moving images.

Reflections on the Camera

The destabilising of the source of narration is related in significant ways to the movements of the camera. The camera does not simply give us the vision of a character and his or her world, a 'mindscreen' as Kawin has termed the field of cinematic subjectivity,[59] but continually imposes other visions 'in which the first is transformed and reflected'.[60] As in *L'Avventura*, *Mirror*'s camera frequently makes obvious its detachment from the characters, moving across their perceptions and attentions as well as appearing to have its own focus and attention. When the father returns to the dacha, for example, and calls to the children in the forest, the camera only briefly tracks them as they run towards the house. Instead, it pans downward to the open Leonardo da Vinci book showing a bearded God- or father-like figure. In the next scene, when the Narrator and Natalia talk in his flat, the camera zooms past her and focuses its attention out of the window. Such examples abound throughout the film, establishing the camera as an independent entity.

Sobchack has suggested that camera movements can indicate that cinematic technology, like human materiality, is always 'lived' in terms of its 'concrete bodily situation and finitude' constantly intending towards the world.[61] 'Whatever its material difference from the human body', she writes, 'the film's body functions like our own, evolving through its perceptive activity an expressed bodily style of being in a world'.[62] Like the movement of the human body, cinematic movement enables 'the accomplishment of perceptive and expressive projects'.[63] Sobchack likens the passage of images through the camera and projector, which are still but perceived as moving, to human respiration or circulation, 'the lungs fill and collapse before they fill again. The valves of the heart open and shut and open again. Both respiration and the circulation of blood are not continuous but segmented and rhythmic activities', which we nevertheless do not perceive as 'intermittent'.[64]

Her vocabulary here is strikingly similar to Tarkovsky's own writing on the 'body' of the film. Throughout *Sculpting*, Tarkovsky often refers to the film, or artworks in general, as animate entities, in terms that recall human properties: 'works of art ... are living organisms with their own circulatory system which must not be disturbed'.[65] Editing, he writes, 'organises the unified, living structure inherent in the film; and the time that pulsates through the blood vessels of the film, making it alive, is of varying rhythmic pressure'.[66] His account of the completion of *Mirror* is couched in terms of a natural, if miraculous, birth: 'the material came to life; the parts started to function reciprocally, as if linked by a bloodstream; and as that last, despairing attempt was projected onto the screen, the film was born before our very eyes'.[67]

Sobchack does stress that the film's technological embodiment and human embodiment is different. This is felt most strongly, according to Sobchack, when the film in fact pretends to have a human body in space (such as taking on the direct point of view of a character within the film). Such a pretence is inevitably felt as false, and accentuates the difference between the camera's and a human's embodiment. Descriptions of the film as a 'body', even taking into account an emphasis on its difference from our own, nevertheless falls short when faced with the complex camera movements of *Mirror*. Rather than camera movements that express an intention and being-in-the-world that is reminiscent of human intentionality, we are presented with movements that continually trouble this theoretical alignment. As Daniel Frampton has pointed out, phenomenology productively allows Sobchack to see film as a unique intending being, 'but then limits her analysis to human-like terms (subject, vision, experience)'.[68] Rather than underscoring its relation to human embodiment, and despite Tarkovsky's statements, *Mirror*'s camera highlights its separation from a unified and coherent human 'body', in ways that are alternately fascinating and disturbing.

We can see this in several scenes featuring the adult Narrator. Because we never see him, and only hear his voice, which is always slightly louder than other characters' voices, hence seeming somehow closer, we may be tempted to equate the camera to his body, or, rather, his body's position in space. However, the camera appears to be aligned to the Narrator only to highlight the impossibility of equating the camera consciousness with a subjective narrator within the film, as well as rendering problematic the idea of possessing a human-like body in space. When the Narrator is talking to his mother on the phone, for example, we see neither character; rather, the camera performs a gliding, machinic tracking shot through his apartment similar to, but much longer than, the enigmatic tracking movement in *L'Avventura*. Yet the Narrator's voice is somehow attached to the camera, locating it in the same space, for while the camera moves, the sound of his voice remains close and stable; the mother's voice, incidentally, locates her definitively within a different space, as it is recorded with the volume and frequency which we might expect from a voice heard through a telephone.

Another striking example involves Maria, after she has washed her hair in the dacha. From a close-up of Maria there is a cut to a large mirror, reflecting or perhaps containing what appears to be a painted landscape. We see a figure approaching this mirror: the older mother, who appears here for the first time in the film. Her reflection, slow gliding movement, and the grey tones of the filtered image render her appearance ghostly and unsettling. As she moves towards the mirror, her reflection looking towards the camera, the camera also zooms slowly in, continuing its movement after she has stopped. Suddenly, a hand comes out from beneath the camera and audibly rubs over the reflection of the older mother's face. This hand belongs to her; it is visibly aged and matched perfectly to the reflected image. However, its appearance disturbs any stable understanding of the camera's movements and its attachment to a body in the diegesis. Owing to the oblique angle of approach to the mirror that the camera had taken, it had not been evident that the camera was aligning itself with the older Maria's point of view, but had rather been a slow mechanical movement that continued to move after Maria had stopped. The appearance of the hand problematises this relation, as it suddenly places the camera at the point of view of the older mother (albeit with the slight disjunction that the camera is somewhat to the side of her). Despite the earlier mechanical movement, we are not, of course, seeing the camera in the mirror in a self-reflexive gesture. Instead, the position of the camera is invisible, and also impossible, replaced by a fragmented human body and an ephemeral reflection.

We can compare this to another scene towards the end of the film, after Maria and Alexei are walking home from the doctor's house. The images are overlaid by a spoken poem, which continues over another shot of the wind emerging from the forest and blowing over objects on an outdoor table. As the poem continues, there is a cut showing the younger Alexei entering a doorway, in sepia and slow motion. The camera initially tracks him as he walks through the darkened house; as the poem ends, however, it pans left to show curtains and sheets of varying textures and transparencies caught by a gust of wind, then pans right again to follow this movement. It then tracks slowly forward, towards a small mirror at the end of the room, and comes up against a translucent lace fabric that is suddenly jerked away, allowing unimpeded passage. Continuing its slow track, another lace fabric is brushed aside, as though by an invisible hand. When the camera nears the mirror, we can see reflected in it a very large, bright light, reminiscent of lights seen on film sets. Without pause, the camera tracks obliquely around the mirror into the dark room, and the next shot returns the young Alexei to view. In this sequence, there appears to be a gesture towards reflecting back the mechanical (the large light), as well as an uncanny sense of using invisible hands to brush fabrics out of the way.

This confusion of the human and the mechanical is echoed in diegetic instances. When Maria is washing her hair, she is shown with the long, wet strands covering her face; her arms hang crookedly out to her side, so that she appears frightening and uncanny. Filmed in a slow motion overlaid with ominous electronic notes, her figure seems not quite human. As Mulvey has pointed out, the blurred threshold between the animate and inanimate is a constant source of human fear and fascination, one that was also in evidence in early cinema: 'a mechanical replica of the human body and the human body from which life has departed both threaten the crucial division between animate and inanimate, organic and inorganic'.[69] This shot of Maria belongs to a tradition in which, to appropriate Mulvey's words, 'replicas of the body acquired the appearance of life, for instance, in the marionette theatre, clockwork toys, or the fantastic stories of automata'.[70] The movements of the camera similarly refuse to rest within the boundaries of what we might think of as 'mechanical' or 'human-like', but move within and through these continually in time.

Texture and the Senses

As well as an emphasis upon duration, critical writing on *Mirror* is unusual for its emphasis upon the film's sensual immediacy. The intense focus on natural landscapes and textures is frequently linked with Tarkovsky's apparent refusal to present symbolic meanings. Tarkovsky himself is the main proponent of this view. In *Sculpting*, he disparages the intellectual montage tradition associated with Eisenstein as propagandist and prescriptive. As Ian Christie has argued, much of Tarkovsky's argument stems from a reaction to doctrinal Soviet cinema that had fallen out of favour by the time he started to make films.[71] His intense hostility to any interpretations of his films that claim to reveal a hidden meaning developed from his experience of working in Soviet cinema, whose symbols and allegories were seen to appeal continually to a purely intellectual experience, each sequence, according to Tarkovsky, having its own 'exact, word-for-word solution'.[72] When interviewers would question the meaning of the natural elements in his films, Tarkovsky was wont to reply something like: 'water is simply water and rain is intended to convey the experience of rain'.[73] Consolidating this view in *Sculpting*, he claimed that 'the poetics of cinema, a mixture of the basest material substances such as we tread every day, is resistant to symbolism'.[74]

Tarkovsky emphasised the immersive possibilities inherent in the natural elements depicted in his films. 'The screen', he writes, 'brings the real world to the audience, the world as it actually is, so that it can be seen in depth and from all sides, evoking its very "smell", allowing audiences to feel on their skin its moisture or its dryness.'[75] At the very beginning of *Sculpting*, Tarkovsky includes some remarkably emotive letters purportedly from viewers of his films, which similarly exhibit this desire for an immersive viewing experience: 'I want to get right inside it, so that I can really be alive'; 'a film I can't even talk about because I am living it'; 'the frames of the screen move out, and the world which used to be partitioned off comes into us'.[76] Tarkovsky's writing has encouraged a similar phenomenological bent in his critics, who link the intense, insistent concentration upon the natural environment to a pure materiality of the image that, like the long-take, is experiential rather than symbolic. In Peter Kral's assessment, for example, 'it is apparently a matter of simply taking on board the strangeness of the world, without coming to terms with it, but making it one's own'.[77] Le Fanu, similarly, notes a consistent failure on the part of the film to make the crossing from image to meaning. Rather than seeing a universe replete with symbols, in which fire signifies the characters' passionate emotions or sexual desires, such images function as a 'discovery of colour'.[78]

The feeling of being immersed within *Mirror*'s filmed worlds is echoed throughout the writing on his film. Synessios writes of being able to feel the weight of water falling upon her own shoulders in scenes featuring rain, and of being 'surrounded' by aural echoes of birdsong, wind and other sounds of the natural elements. The film engages 'our sensory, sensual and emotive faculties, inviting us to enter, ponder, and observe the world unfolding on the screen'.[79] For Synessios, *Mirror* 'was more than a film; it was a reality that I could inhabit'.[80] Le Fanu describes that upon viewing the film he 'felt possessed by the sensation that you occasionally come across in dreams, of an understanding so complete that you yourself become part of the dramaturgy'.[81] An intense sense of topophilia is particularly associated in critical writing on *Mirror* with the childhood home of the Narrator. As Le Fanu writes, for example, the wooden materials of the home evoke a powerful feeling of sensory presence: 'we can almost smell the polish on the old dressers'.[82] Critics such as Dalle Vache have argued that the recurrent use of certain objects, such as the dilapidated plaster and wood in which we can see every scratch and can 'almost' feel our hands running over them, are not to be seen as abstract symbols, but are 'physical entities with a tangible texture and imaginable weight', condensing within them a sense of 'intense physicality'.[83]

The feeling of entering into a filmed world and a direct contact with filmed textures recalls theories of embodied phenomenology and haptic spectatorship. Giuliana Bruno's writing, in particular, is fundamentally concerned with the experience of being 'within' a cinematic space: 'one lives a film as one lives the space that one inhabits: as an everyday passage, tangibly'.[84] Sobchack, similarly, emphasises the immediacy of the sensual contact the viewer has with cinematic spaces and objects. While we cannot touch, smell, or taste in the cinema, she argues, our haptic experience is partly intensified when our sensuous intentions 'rebound' from the screen back to our own bodies.[85] The 'carnal sensuality of the film experience' in itself constitutes 'meaning' without the intervention of intellectual signification.[86]

In *Mirror*, the sense of touch is appealed to through the continual presentation of a variety of textures. The walls and other surfaces are rarely smooth; covered in protrusions, furrows, and wrinkled grooves, they may evoke a powerful tactile response. The sensory possibilities of filmed textures are developed and elongated as the camera passes slowly over the spaces, using the camera to, as Marks puts it, 'graze rather than gaze'.[87] The movement of the camera may even be more effective in evoking a sense of texture than a static focus on an object; our kinaesthetic identification with the camera's movement may evoke a sense of brushing against objects. Through the slow motion and long-takes, and elongated tracking shots, the film literally gives us time in which to discern the texture of objects or to experience the varied rhythms of movement, such as that of the falling rain or plaster. Tarkovsky often employs a slow motion that is barely perceptible, such that we may experience the movement directly before we are aware of the discrepancy.[88] As Christie has written, this expresses Tarkovsky's desire to encourage audiences to see things in their own right, rather than as symbols, 'to attend *first* to the rhythm and framing of the images, to experience the film on an aesthetic-intuitive level, *before* considering it intellectually'.[89]

Mirror's continual movements between the sensory and the thematic, however, encourages an analysis that will formulate a relationship between them. A desire for full sensory plenitude and a haptic immersion in an illusory space, which is posited in critical writing on *Mirror* as a viewing experience, resonates diegetically and thematically throughout the film, as I have suggested in relation to the Narrator's desire to immerse himself in memory and dreams. The same technique used to brush against the textured surfaces, the long, slow panning or tracking shot, is also, as I have suggested, thematically evocative. The time passing through the shot, and the dilapidated surfaces it is passing over, encourage a thematic engagement with temporality. Nostalgia, duration, temporality and transformation are enacted and conceptualised; the disintegrating entropic textures of the film express the liminality of objects passing into other states through time. Rooms whose dimensions are engulfed by textures may invite the sense of touch or a feeling of inscription within the filmed space, but they also partake of a thematic presentation in which we see the walls literally decaying and falling down around the characters, suggesting the paradoxical impossibility of retrieving the past while registering its trace and echo.

An analysis of *Mirror* demonstrates the importance of considering embodiment and hapticity within a temporal context. To illustrate this, I take the example of the repetition of an image of a young girl warming her hand against a fire. Towards the beginning of the film, a close-up image of her hand appears as a flash between two longer sequences. Decontextualised, it may provoke the kind of powerful tactile response, sympathetic to the warmth and glow of the flames, which Sobchack has written of in relation to seeing fingers laced over the camera in *The Piano*: '*my fingers knew what I was looking at* . . . *grasped* it with a nearly imperceptible tingle of attention and anticipation'.[90] At the same time, however, the shot is sensually evocative partly because of its sequential placement: it follows the sequence where the older Maria sees herself reflected in a mirror and reaches out her hand to touch it. The edit is matched on these two hands: the first is ghostly, filmed in monochrome and slow motion; the second appears in bright colour which makes the hand glow in its sensual response to the flame.

However, the fact that this image is narratively disconnected from the images before it, emerging from an unknown space and time in what might be memory, reality or fantasy, also invites a more comprehensive questioning. The image may be sensory, but it is also perplexing. As Bird has written, 'the surface of Tarkovsky's screen uses subtle variations in texture and colour to puzzle our vision and elicit from us a more assertive posture of viewing'.[91] Marks has argued that, faced with an image which we cannot understand, such as images which are defamiliarised through the passing of time, we are 'forced to search our memories for other virtual images that might make sense of it'; if we are unable to do so, we confront the limits of our knowledge.[92] The fleeting nature of the image is unlikely to encourage the attribution of fixed symbolic meaning, yet the provocation to thought may be as powerful as the evocation of tactile response. Towards the end of the film, the image recurs, this time in its context, as part of a sequence showing the red-haired girl as the owner of the hand, a sequence framed by Andrei's looks in the mirror in the doctor's house. The recurrence of the image of the hand may evoke the viewer's memory, influencing the perception of the present image. This sequence provides us with a context into which we may wish to reintegrate the previous image, activating a participatory mode of spectatorship. In providing the potential to reactivate viewers' memories, shots such as this may recreate the object for perception as we thicken it with our own associations.[93]

Aesthetic Transfiguration

Critical writing around the sensory aspects of *Mirror* posit an experiential quality to the images, but also frequently frame them within a discourse on spiritualism and the metaphysical. That is, the images are not just material or haptic, but are seen to move beyond this to provide an experience of transcendence. Alternatively, the images of the natural environment and the Narrator's home are associated with a childhood vision. Below, I outline some of these suggestions, before presenting an analysis of the images of textures and natural elements that is based neither on spirituality nor childhood vision, but on aesthetic transfiguration.

At once unburdened with symbolic meanings and simultaneously endlessly meaningful, Tarkovsky understands his images of natural phenomena and simple objects to evince the presence of the transcendental, effecting a revelatory cinematic experience. 'What you see in the frame', he writes, 'is not limited to its visual depiction, but is a pointer to something stretching out beyond the frame and to infinity.'[94] This transcendent emotion is the 'great function of the artistic image', which becomes 'a kind of detector of infinity . . . towards which our reason and our feelings go soaring with joyful, thrilling haste'.[95] Tarkovsky believes in the power of the artwork to raise humanity to a higher level of spirituality, assuming an idealist notion of the harmonious artwork as elevating the soul in which 'the conception of images is governed by the dynamic of revelation'. He states that 'in the case of someone who is spiritually receptive, it is therefore possible to talk of an analogy between the impact made by a work of art and that of a purely religious experience. Art acts above all on the soul, shaping its spiritual structure.'[96] In Tarkovksy's view, the elements and objects on screen are designed to provoke not a pure experiential presence in the absence of meaning or interpretive value, but rather the possibility of transcending the everyday.

Of course, as Schrader notes, 'although transcendental style, like any other form of transcendental art, strives towards the ineffable and invisible, it is neither ineffable nor invisible itself'.[97] It is, rather, a particular type of filmmaking which uses specific means for its purposes: 'the concept of transcendental style is more useful if seen from within the context of pre-existing aesthetic systems; it can be thought of as form, symbol, or expression'.[98] Tarkovsky, beyond the fact of the ambiguity of the material image, has been fairly reticent about the actual filmic techniques used to express the ineffable. We must not, he writes, be distracted by form, which should remain invisible in the film so as not to 'stick out like the springs of a sofa' – a kind of travesty that he associates with Eisenstein.[99]

Many critics have been content to take for granted this spiritual presence within the film, and echo it in their analyses. According to Petric, for example, 'the cognitive ambiguity of Tarkovsky's shots is meant to shift the viewer's attention from the representational to the transcendental meaning of the recorded event'.[100] Synessios argues that Tarkovsky wished to show not just nature, but 'nature ensouled'. The wind which is repeatedly filmed bending the trees and the grass is, in its invisible power, 'the most overt manifestation of animated nature'; 'it is the nearest possible embodiment of the divinity, of the spirit of place and of things'.[101] Truppin parallels the necessity for the viewer to posit sources for off-screen sounds with a religious acceptance of an unseen 'spiritual' world: 'the use of ambiguous sound plunges the audience into a never fully resolved struggle to believe in the diegesis, much as the films' characters struggle with their own ability to have faith'.[102]

For Dalle Vache, the natural elements in the films are not intended as symbols but as 'primal images, so natural and therefore so inexhaustible in their signifying power that they are capable of reorienting our imagination away from a rational, technocratic world view toward something infinite and unspeakable'.[103] Dalle Vache argues that Tarkovsky's images are akin to religious icons, 'not a sign standing for something else but a site where something other or divine, lost or repressed, manifests itself directly in first person, for our eyes'.[104] According to Dalle Vache, while Tarkovsky seems to inherit a Bazinian interest in cinema as a window upon 'life itself', in the immediacy and movement of the cinema expressing existence 'as such', he is also fundamentally concerned with conveying something transcendental and spiritual, to 'release the mystical core stored in the Bazinian realist approach'.[105] Critical writing on both temporality and the sensory in Tarkovsky's film thus tends to posit the possibility of a freedom from symbolisation or fixed and determinate meaning, but seems unwilling to dwell in this realm, pushing both towards a transcendental or spiritual experience.

Critical writing on *Mirror* also frequently links the 'primal' and 'uninterpretable' images with the innocent gaze and direct impressions of nature that supposedly belong to the child. For Le Fanu, dwelling on the image without fixing meaning onto it is equated with a return to childhood and associated with the fascination of seeing things for the first time. The childhood home is experienced 'with the child's quiet wonder'.[106] Similarly, for Turovskaya, the 'clues to the single images in Tarkovsky's work which bear within them the secret of a thousand interpretations' can be found in the way we experience the film through 'the impressionable soul of a child, the sharpness and freshness of its perceptions', where any image can be interpreted with a wealth of cultural and semantic detail while remaining a solid and physical world, 'a world open to that natural freedom of association seen through the eyes of a child'.[107] Peter Green also notes that 'in *Mirror* the view Tarkovsky seeks is that of the child, with which we glimpse Utopia or paradise'.[108] *Mirror* thus appears to utilise the figure of the child in a similar way in which *L'Avventura* used the figure of Claudia – as a kind of filter, encouragement, and thematisation of a particular way of looking at the world, and at the film. The critical statements about childhood vision are reminiscent of the way in which the figure of the child was sometimes drawn upon by early writers on film to explain the transfigurative power of cinematic framing. Aragon, for example, wrote that

> children sometimes fix their attention on an object to a point where the concentration makes it grow larger, grow so much it completely occupies their visual field, assumes a mysterious aspect and loses all relation to its purpose . . . likewise on the screen objects that were a few moments ago sticks of furniture or books or cloakroom tickets are transformed to the point where they take on menacing and enigmatic meanings.[109]

In *Mirror*, observation, memory, and nature also seem to be coded as part of a realm presided over by a maternal figure. From the very first post-credit sequence, as Synessios writes, 'nature and the elements are intimately connected with the mother in the film'.[110] Kral, similarly, believes that women are 'omnipresent as the privileged guardians of the material world and its day-to-day memory'.[111] This employment of women and children may appear to thematise, as perhaps the film's title may suggest to some viewers, a realm before the 'mirror stage', before the acquisition of rational language. Lacanian scholarship has pointed out a cultural disposition that identifies the Word, Logos, as masculine, as the Word of God or the Law of the Father. In this paradigm, women and children are linked with the visual realm, with beauty, silence, and non-sense.[112]

Significantly, it is always women that we see talking or laughing but cannot hear: the red-haired girl in the grenade sequence, and Maria and the doctor's wife in the earring scene. This latter scene has been commented on by Kral, who writes that 'as they try on earrings, the women, excited by the darkness, exchange whispered confidences to do with their femininity and their lot as wives and mothers'.[113] This eroticised interpretation is misleading: for one thing, only the doctor's wife tries on the earrings, for another, Maria displays more contempt than sisterly affection towards the doctor's wife. It is, however, a potent example of not only the simplification of the role of women in writing on Tarkovsky, but also of the ambivalent presentation of women in the films themselves. The father, on the other hand – in his incarnation as the poet, the Narrator, and Maria's husband, who identifies himself through calling the name of his child – asserts his presence primarily within the aural realm. Chion has pointed out the interdiction against looking that permeates most religions, which transforms God or the spirit into an acousmatic voice, a voice whose source is not visualised on screen.[114] In this interpretation, then, it is significant that the narrative voice-over is abandoned in the first post-credit sequence of the film and barely resurfaces; in fact, it ends on the words 'father will never come home'. Kozloff has noted an interesting trait of silent cinema that largely carried over into sound film: silent film was traditionally seen as the realm of what Freud defined as 'primary process thinking', or the unconscious, which was often equated with the magical thought processes of young children. The theatrical style of monologue or dialogue was, on the other hand, associated with conscious thought processes that recognised rationality and the reality principle.[115] The critical writing on *Mirror* that emphasises this pre-rational realm where things do not 'mean' but simply 'are' can thus be seen in the context of this traditional configuration which equates the pre-linguistic with childhood, women and nature.

The pre-credit sequence of the film, in which a young boy is cured of a stutter by hypnosis and triumphantly announces, 'I can speak!', has thus sometimes been seen as existing in contradistinction to this pre-linguistic emphasis. As Turovskaya writes, for example, the prologue expresses a striving towards liberation from wordlessness, the effort to break into speech which is directly associated with the appearance of the film's title, and thus seems to 'remain on the level of that allegory which the director always claimed to dislike so much'.[116] According to Synessios, the boy's 'I can speak' 'is akin to the biblical "In the beginning was the Word"', and suggests that Tarkovsky has discovered 'a way to express adequately the things that trouble and excite him'.[117] It is interesting to compare this to the use of the biblical line in Tarkovsky's last film, *The Sacrifice* (1986).[118] At its conclusion, the previously mute child, lying under the dead tree that his father told him to water, says: '"In the beginning was the Word." Why is that Papa?' The child's questioning has here an added poignancy, as the father is no longer around to answer, and the viewer is left to puzzle not only over the answer to the boy's question, but also to its relation to the film. We are, in other words, left in a state of indeterminacy and faced with a lack of definitive meaning.

Suggesting that *Mirror* solves this problem of expression in its first scene is, I believe, overly optimistic. The film is, of course, expressive in multiple ways, but this process of expression is more akin to the stuttering that has apparently been healed than to the speech heralded by the boy. The film in fact repeats this stuttering temporal rhythm structurally and cinematographically throughout. The shot of the wind emerging through the trees in black-and-white is seen twice, interrupted abruptly both times before it can properly unfold. There are many examples of these 'stuttering' shots that are cut midway through a potentially complete action, such as a shirt flying across the room and a chicken breaking out of a window in the house. The brief shot of a hand being warmed against a fire, which is later repeated in its wider, longer context, also works towards this stammering impression inherent in the editing. The Spanish documentary footage flashes across the screen briefly twice before it is played out in full. Diegetically, the film ends in silence. The music played over the final sequence is muted, followed by the boy's wordless yell and a silence punctuated only by the sound of a child's pipe that had recurred throughout the film, as the camera returns to the forest from whence it emerged in the opening post-credit sequence.

Viewing the pre-credit sequence in its duration, furthermore, rather than focusing on its final moment, can be seen to suggest a rather different emphasis, namely, on the emergent possibility of a cinematic aesthetic. The film in fact begins when Ignat switches on a television, already putting the possibility of visual mediation to the fore. The ensuing images of the hypnotism might be assumed to be those emanating from this television, as is possibly suggested by their sepia tone, direct style of interview and the staging of the speech therapy. However, it is notable that we hear the beginning of the interview while watching Ignat, and the television flickers with a blue background without depicting any images. We never, that is, see the hypnotism from his television, and the clarity of the sound does not 'match' its flickering. This immediately brings to the fore the heterogeneity of the film's temporal rhythms and their complex process of unfolding in the film. During the hypnotism sequence itself, the camera continually zooms in and out, moving around the hypnotist and her patient, drawing attention to its own process of imaging. Furthermore, the shadow of recording equipment is clearly visible on the wall behind the characters. Rather than effecting the kind of distance and alienation often associated with an awareness of the cinematic apparatus, however, the scene appears to celebrate the possibilities of cinematic rendering with a triumph affectively, rather than symbolically, aligned with the boy's cure.

In *Mirror*, a fascinated gaze at images is invited through, and at, aesthetic devices. While the film encourages a focus on natural textures, the aestheticised rendering of natural phenomena is also effective in rendering unfamiliar what is actually portrayed, and hence not necessarily encouraging a fulfilled tactile response to the image, but rather inciting a contemplation of *how* things are represented, both in what we might think of as the Narrator's memories and fantasies, and in Tarkovsky's film. Filters, disorientating tracking shots, slow motion, sound discrepancies, and other extra-diegetic devices draw attention to the processes of cinematic imaging itself, as well as to what is portrayed 'through' them. As Bird has argued, 'Tarkovsky never lost sight of the fact that he showed the world not as it is, but as it appears when distorted by refractive media.'[119] Like *L'Avventura*, *Mirror* performs a cinematic creativity in its aesthetic processes of imaging. It seeks to 'redefine the viewer's . . . attitude towards images, not as the storehouse of the known, but as a possibility for envisioning the new'.[120] In fact, the intense fascination that the film continues to provoke in many audience members seems to have much to do with this activation of aesthetic affect. For a willing viewer, it exerts a particularly cinematic fascination that is engaging at an aesthetic level. Through the intertwining of recognisable images and their estrangement, the natural elements filmed by Tarkovsky are, as Petric notes, 'experienced on the screen as *cinematic* phenomena rather than perceived as a natural power'.[121]

Significantly, transfiguration and transformation emerge in *Mirror* as a *theme* in the words of the first poem spoken near the beginning of the film. The poet speaks of his lover awakening and immediately transforming 'the language humans think and speak'. In her speech, the word 'you' acquires a new sense, now meaning 'Tsar'. 'Everything on earth was transfigured', the poet continues, 'even simple things: the basin, the jug'. The poem's subject is the transfigurative power of love, something that is also explicitly emphasised when Maria is seen levitating above the bed after unwillingly killing a chicken at the doctor's house. She says to the father: 'at last I soared up . . . don't be surprised. I love you.' Kral has written that, in Tarkovsky's films, 'people and things seem to us to have an exceptional clarity, urgency, and grace, as if we ourselves were in love and suddenly experienced the world with redoubled intensity'.[122] While the expressed or implied emotions of the characters may indeed resonate with those of viewers towards the film (not just 'love', but also nostalgia and longing), the transformation of everyday objects such as 'the basin, the jug', which feature heavily in Tarkovsky's films, are, I believe, more to do with his cinematic aesthetic of transfiguration.

In *Mirror*, the natural elements themselves are used to transfigure the visible world. As Bird has pointed out, the first poem comments upon the image which it accompanies, that of rain falling outside the dacha, which dematerialises objects, making us aware of water itself as a medium.[123] The 'basin, the jug' are transfigured 'when layered and rigid water stood between us', suggesting a mediated screen through which objects are perceived. This technique is refined in Tarkovsky's next film, *Stalker*, which showcases several beautifully slow pans over a close-up view of gleaming objects and fish underwater. The natural elements in *Mirror* often act as frames themselves, within the frame of the screen. The fire in the barn, for example, is itself set within a cool blue and green frame of the forest and the sky. We perceive it through the rain and with other, surrogate, spectators in front of us. This is a 'natural' frame within the cinematic frame, but acquires its own aesthetic value. These frames are continually in motion, subject to the mobility of the camera and the vicissitudes of passing time.

This motility is evident with the various visual 'quotations' of paintings that transfigure the presentation of the natural world. Unlike filmmakers such as Peter Greenaway or Jean-Luc Godard, Tarkovsky rarely allows his quotations of artworks to approach stillness or emerge as *'tableau vivants'*. Instead, the figures within the frame and the frame itself are continually fluid, modulating in and out of, or through, the artworks. As in *L'Avventura*, the inclusion of paintings and drawings partly operates to highlight the affectivity of cinematic temporality and movement. This is the case not only when the film shows a moving embodiment of an artwork or an era of painting, as in the aforementioned earring sequence or the Brueghelian winter landscape, but also when we see an original painting that the camera has filmed. After the father is reunited with his children in a burst of operatic song from the St Matthew Passion, for example, the film cuts to Leonardo's portrait of 'A Young Lady with a Juniper', which according to Tarkovsky served the dual function of 'introduc[ing] a timeless element into the moments that are succeeding each other before our eyes' and comparing the woman with Margarita Terekhova, who apparently had 'the same capacity at once to enchant and to repel'.[124] What is extraordinary about the introduction of this painting, however, is the complex way that it is shown, in an aesthetic process of imaging rather than through a simple straight cut to the portrait. As the Bach music continues, the film suddenly cuts to an extreme close-up of a painted landscape barely recognisable through a blue flare from the camera lens that takes up more than half the screen. As the camera pans left, the face of the portrait comes into view as the reflected flare also moves left, across the face, disappearing only as the camera zooms slowly out from the extreme close-up, announcing a specifically cinematic rendering of this portrait. What is also important is what follows: a cut to Natalia in midshot as the camera zooms towards her face to frame her in close-up. These camera movements away from, and towards, the painted and filmed faces transfigure the painting cinematically.

Contrary to what has sometimes been written, Tarkovsky does not present images akin to 'still life' painting.[125] The conglomeration of objects that he frequently places together, such as glass milk jugs, bread, lamps, mirrors, and cloth, are always seen through the transfigurative force of the camera's movement and focus in time. In the earring scene, for example, the film shows Alexei seated in the centre of one of the rooms, filled with various sheens and textures of half-hidden objects in a brown-hued gloom. There is then a cut that singles out several elements in extreme close-up: two potatoes and a small puddle of milk on a dark wooden shelf. As we watch, a drop falls to join the puddle, then another, and the camera begins to slowly pan down the shelves, past a gleaming copper receptacle, to locate the bottom of this milky waterfall, where another puddle is being enlarged with more drops of milk. This sequence can be seen to perform, cinematically and through time, something that is in fact a concern of still life painting: decay and deliquescence, more aptly expressed by the French term *nature morte*. The passing of time that it suggests, however, is cinematic, in the use of a cut from a long-shot to a close-up, the pan, and the isolated sound of the dripping milk. In the last few seconds of this shot, furthermore, symphonic music is heard, which will overlay Alexei's look into the mirror and his memories of the red-haired girl, continuing the theme of the desire to somehow capture time, or a memory of a moment in time, which slips irretrievably from our grasp. Even if a composition is relatively still, such as the shot of a cup, saucer and plate on the table in front of the woman who asks Ignat to read Pushkin, the indexes of passing time are still registered; in this case, in the steam visibly rising from the cup.

The presentation of textures in the film should also be seen in relation to the way in which they are aesthetically transfigured. Some critical writing on *Mirror*'s textures can give the impression that the images appear in a naturalistic form. For example, the scene in which plaster falls from the ceiling of a room in the childhood home, according to Synessios, evokes a powerful feeling of immersion in which we can feel the film's textures as the characters do.[126] Simultaneously, however, the process of cinematic imaging itself comes to the fore: this scene is among the first changes to black-and-white and slowed motion. The affective power of the scene resides in its incredible cinematic rendering, as well as its tactile effects. The recurrence of the image of the wind bending the tops of trees through its force should also be considered in this way. The importance of such images lies not merely in their powerful material evocations, but also in the quality of movement and temporality that they perform.

Diegetic prompts relating to the sensory appeal of the film are conveyed by the film's dialogue. Although dialogue is frequently denigrated in the study of cinema, many accounts of the experience of viewing the film seems to incorporate, almost unwittingly, the information provided by it.[127] *Mirror*'s dialogue is often opaque, yet the repetition of certain phrases and concepts resonate throughout the film and affect the way we may experience visual images. The mystical conception of nature that critics find in the films, for example, does not simply manifest itself automatically, but is suggested through dialogue. In the first post-credit sequence, the doctor who appears at the dacha explicitly draws attention to the anthropomorphic aura of nature, saying, 'Has it ever occurred to you that plants can feel, know, even comprehend?' The affective relation between natural and cinematic phenomena is powerfully enacted in this sequence. After the mother displays little interest in him, the doctor begins to walk away from the dacha through a field in front of the house. After several steps he pauses and turns to look back at her just as a sudden gust of wind, an inexplicable phenomenon in an otherwise perfectly still landscape, and whose path we can precisely trace across the grass as it comes towards the camera, blows over him and passes. There is a cut to the mother surrounded by still tree branches; their disruption by the wind is slightly delayed. The scene cuts again to the doctor walking away before the exact conjunction of elements is repeated. It is almost impossible to determine whether this actually happens twice, diegetically, or whether we have seen a repetition of the same scene. The fascination exerted by a natural phenomenon is thus overlaid by a captivating cinematic representation of naturalistic images.

From its inception, film criticism has harboured a fascination with two related concepts: the aforementioned tension between an absorption into the cinematic frame and an ejection from it, and the relationship between the materiality and solidity of things on screen, which elicit tactile responses, and their ephemerality. As Stern writes, 'while the indexicality of the cinematic image creates an effect of material presence, the movement of the image simultaneously renders that presence potentially unstable and ephemeral'.[128] Mulvey has also written that movement has always given an elusiveness to the filmed image, 'like running water, fire, or the movement of trees in the wind, this elusiveness has been intrinsic to the cinema's fascination and its beauty'.[129] Running water, fire, and the movement of trees in the wind, all images favoured by Tarkovsky, are central to conveying the simultaneously elusive and material nature of cinema. These 'cinematically destined' images seem to be privileged to show the destabilising tension between presence and absence.[130] Water (or, as is often the case in Tarkovsky's films, milk) flowing, pouring, or dripping in time, is 'mobilised performatively', drawing our awareness to a palpable duration through the camera's intensive focus.[131] The flow of water seems eminently suited to suggest the passing of time in cinema. In fact, so powerfully linked do the two seem to be in Tarkovsky's films, that the films take on the qualities of water in some of the theoretical configurations surrounding them. Dalle Vache, for example, comments that Tarkovsky's camera in *Andrei Rublev* (1966), as it moves through spaces and rooms, 'acquires the fluidity of water running through a maze of interconnecting channels'.[132] *Mirror*, according to Green, 'shares the quality of [Tarkovsky's] beloved element water, flowing in and out of dreams and recollections'.[133]

Films evoke the solidity and tactility of things at the very moment of their passing: 'in the cinema solid things turn into phantasms, touch turns into memory'.[134] This aesthetic concern resonates with the thematic concerns of the film. In *Mirror*, the full sensory plenitude of the Narrator's childhood has passed into memory, one which is perhaps capable of evoking the tactile and proximal senses, but only in vacillation with an ejection from memory, an infection of the past by the present, and an inability to enter spaces and touch things. A tension is enacted between the full sensual pleasure of textures and the temporal destabilisation of a space that we might image entering. The film tends to indicate a sensual fulfilment only through a veil of extra-diegetic awareness.

Rather than equate aestheticisation or 'defamiliarisation' with detachment or alienation, however, much of the affective power of the film seems to come from this oscillation between sensual closeness and aesthetic rendering. As early film critic Dorothy Richardson wrote, 'distance *is* enchantment. It is a perpetual focus.' Distance can provide an escape from an 'obstructive' discontent, a state of 'deadness' to the habitual object.[135] This is not the distance posited by writers on *L'Avventura*, but a re-engagement with the film's aesthetic processes of imaging. According to Susan Sontag, becoming conscious of form may lead to a kind of detachment, in so far as 'our emotions do not respond in the same way as they do in real life'. Aesthetic emotions for Sontag are, however, often strengthened: 'such distancing is a source of great emotional power'. 'The detachment or retarding of the emotions, through the consciousness of form', writes Sontag 'makes them far stronger and more intense in the end.'[136]

Audiophilia

Sound is also used throughout the film to perform a vacillation between materiality and its destabilisation. On the one hand, sound can be used to give a palpable texture to scenes, and a corporeal and 'realistic' presence to spaces and objects; the floor seems tangible and concrete, for example, when we hear a milk bottle rolling across it.[137] At other times, however, sound becomes ambiguous and defeats what Altman has called the 'sound hermeneutic', which matches sound to a source in the image, and hence 'provides a sense of closure that allows perception of the depicted world as coherent'.[138] As Truppin notes, Tarkovsky's sounds 'destabilize, they make the coherent and comfortable seem suddenly strange and disorientating'.[139] Tarkovsky manipulates the spatial signature of sound, that is, the combination of aspects such as reverberation level, volume, and frequency that allow us to place it in a particular physical environment. The film's sounds seem diegetic because they have highly specific spatial signatures, yet these often do not seem to coincide with the space from which the sound is apparently emanating.[140] An example of the destabilising tensions between sound and image occurs during the sequence in which the mother returns to the printing works. All the sounds are muted, except for her clearly audible breathing, and the sound of the printing presses, which increases as she walks towards them. These sounds place us aurally alongside her subjectivity and what Altman has called 'point-of-audition'. He applies this concept to moments where there is an impression of auditory perspective created by changes in volume and reverberation levels, presenting sound as it would be heard from a point within the diegesis and hence relating us to the film as 'internal auditors'.[141] The visual representation of Maria, however, dislodges the stability of this response: the sound of her footsteps does not match up to her movements, which are in slightly slowed motion.

Formal discrepancies are often established between the image and the soundtracks, as when, for example, we see characters talking but cannot hear them, or, as in the case of the Narrator or the voice reading Arseniy Tarkovsky's poems, hear them speaking but never (wholly) see them. The poetry spoken over certain scenes, which are often shot through moving long-takes, creates a tension between being drawn 'into' the image and a sense of being kept back from its threshold. The voice and the image continuously join and separate from each other within the temporal movement of the film, establishing and dissolving resonances between them. When the first poem is recited, for example, the line 'on waking up, I said "God bless you"' coincides with an image of the children sprinkling sugar on the head of a kitten, as though in a refracted blessing of nature and childhood.

Both image and voice in their own way invite a fascinated attention; the former through the kinaesthetic movements of the long-take, and the latter through its declamatory, sensuous incantations in which we can hear the speaker drawing breath. The absence of visual images of the speaking voices has the paradoxical effect of emphasising the materiality of the sound, reminiscent of the way in which Barthes locates pleasure in 'the grain of the voice' and in a vocal physicality, 'language lined with flesh'. The speaking voice of the poet can, to appropriate Barthes's words,

> make us hear in their materiality, their sensuality, the breath, the gutturals, the fleshiness of the lips, a whole presence of the human muzzle . . . to succeed in shifting the signified a great distance and in throwing, so to speak, the anonymous body of the actor into my ear.[142]

In phenomenological theories of spoken poetry, the listener is sometimes said to be more affected bodily by the sound of the words than by their meaning. For Mikel Dufrenne, words can become 'palpable and tasty as fruit'; these are words that we 'savour' rather than 'use'.[143] Rather than clarifying the image, the voice-over often renders both image and voice opaque in their relationship to each other, making it difficult to focus wholly upon one or the other. The very palpability of the voice emerges almost as a barrier to immersion in the visual space. As Deleuze argues, 'so far as [sounds] rival, overlap, cross and cut into each other, they trace a path full of obstacles in visual space'.[144] Robert Bird has also commented on this, arguing that 'the effect of sound in Tarkovsky's films is . . . not to render the image emotionally or intellectually transparent, but to intensify its density and opacity to the point that it begins to exert an almost material resistance'.[145]

Despite the importance of music and sound to Tarkovsky's cinema, it is often overlooked in critical analyses of his films. Tarkovsky argued that music does not only intensify the impression of the visual image, but also 'opens up the possibility of a new, transfigured impression of the same material: something different in kind'.[146] If the music were absent 'the visual image would not just be weaker in its idea and its impact, it would be qualitatively different'.[147] Significantly, much of the music in *Mirror* is heard not during sequences of dialogue between characters, to heighten the emotional intensity of an encounter, narrative development, or characterisation, but rather to underscore the transformative propensities of aesthetic and rhythmic effects. In other words, it is associated primarily with the aesthetic aspects of the film. Tarkovsky somewhat denigrates the emotional effect of music created when scenes are 'propped up with a musical accompaniment which reiterates the main theme in order to heighten its emotional resonance'.[148] Nevertheless, his use of classical music heightens affective responses, albeit not necessarily or only to characters and narrative situations, but to the cinematic processes of imaging.

Considering the affective and important relation between the musical score and Tarkovsky's films, it is perhaps somewhat surprising that, like Antonioni, Tarkovsky has stated his preference for films with no music at all. As he writes in *Sculpting*, this is because both music and film transfigure the world, and thus conflict with one another in their juxtaposition. Instead of advocating the use of music, he writes that 'properly organised in a film, the resonant world is musical in its essence – and that is the true music of cinema'.[149] Sound, he argues, must also be 'sculpted', isolated and manipulated rather than simply 'recorded' in order to form part of an aesthetic experience: 'accurately recorded sound adds nothing to the image system of cinema, for it still has no aesthetic content'.[150] He praises Bergman for isolating and 'hyperbolising' sounds to make them expressive. In his own films, sound itself is transfigured, often isolated from its habitual sources and modes of hearing it, amplified, and thus 'properly', aesthetically, 'organised'. *Mirror* evokes a kind of cinephilia of sound, an audiophilia.

Given that cinephilia is so often associated with the cinematic rendering of natural phenomena, such as the wind in the trees, and water flowing or dripping in various forms, it seems only apt that these provide the two most important sources of sounds in *Mirror*. These sounds, as I have already mentioned, are often divorced from the temporal rhythm of the images that they are usually attached to, which encourages us to attend to the sound with more interest than if it had been registered as merely emanating from a stable source. A recurring phenomenon in *Mirror* is to introduce a sound at the end of a particular scene that belongs to the next scene. At other times, the sounds are preceded by a momentary silence, such as the water dripping from the mother's hair when she washes it. Many sounds are isolated and amplified to drown out other sounds, such as the sound of boots crunching snow or the instructor's heartbeat in the shooting range sequence. The film also uses point-of-audition to draw attention to sound. In the scene of the burning barn, the film noticeably employs the mother's point-of-audition to isolate the crackling roar of the fire, which increases as she approaches it. The burning building is thus made forcefully present to us aurally. A more extraordinary example occurs in the Sivash footage sequence. In the first few shots of this footage, the soldiers pass close to the camera, and we hear their boots squelching through mud in an audible close-up. In a shot that shows the soldiers from some distance, the sound is suddenly muted, and only returned to full volume when the soldiers are shown closer again. Tarkovsky made certain that the sound, recreated and recorded for the film, is matched to the footage, in a disturbing alignment of naturalistic, vibrant sound to the procession of the ghostly, though not-yet dead.

The manipulated naturalistic sounds are also sometimes intertwined with more obvious electronic sounds. In the example above, the sloshing footsteps are soon joined on the soundtrack by portentous drums and electronic strains. When the mother takes a shower at the printing works and the water runs out, the dripping of the shower modulates into an electronically manipulated gurgling and the resonant sound of whining pipes. Similarly, the first time the wind is seen emerging from the trees in an uncompleted action, it is heard over an ominous electronic score. All of these techniques work to foreground sound, dislodging it from a naturalistic recording and locating it within an aesthetically designed sound spectrum.

The use of canonical, classical music is a fundamental aspect of Tarkovsky's emphasis upon cinema as art. In *Mirror*, the music is immediately linked to the film as an aesthetic product when a Bach prelude is heard alongside the credits, which run against a black background. It fades as the mother is seen sitting on the fence, tuning out as the camera approaches her and begins its diegetic narrative presentation. The classical music is here immediately linked to the cinematic art form as announced by the credit sequence. The music links particular scenes and sequences that may not otherwise be obviously associated; music transfigures not just 'the visual image' but also our understanding of how and why the images are combined. After the Spanish footage ends, for example, the film presents documentary footage of a man hovering in the air, suspended from an air balloon (the return of Chkalov). The soundtrack continues to be silent over the next shot, of a massive, almost amorphous balloon, with two men attached to smaller ones beside it. At the third shot change, the symphonic Pergolesi music begins, and continues over several more shots showing the balloons and the men gliding in different configurations. The music has an immediate transfigurative effect, changing an event of historical importance into a beautiful, slow balletic performance that brings out the rhythm of floating through its resonant, continuous string sounds. The cut to the footage of a parade is set exactly at the point at which the singing voices are heard in the piece, rhythmically aligned to the editing, and somehow associating the fluttering of the thousands of pieces of paper to the many voices signing in unison. The music continues as there is another cut to the Leonardo da Vinci book. The pages are turned by anonymous hands, soon revealed to be Ignat's. Alongside the music we can also hear the amplified turning of the pages, the different sounds made by the paper and the crinkling of the protective tissue as the boy crumples it with his hands. The music ends as the dialogue between mother and son begins, as, that is, the narrative takes precedence. The music does not prescribe an emotion related to narrative events, but links, in this case, movements of gliding, floating, fluttering, and the tactile sense of turning pages, and transfigures their affective impact.

Mirrors and Crystals

Given the emphasis upon a particularly cinematic transfiguration through movement, sound and colour, of a vacillation between materiality and ephemerality that cinema can perform so powerfully, it is interesting that most of the criticism and theory that has been written about *Mirror* evinces a tendency to describe the film as something other than cinematic art. Tarkovsky's films have been variously compared to a canvas, a mosaic, a symphony, a poem, and a literary narrative.[151] Synessios, for example, writes that, like Chekhov, who eliminates the 'first page' of his stories in order to eradicate the '*why*', Tarkovsky 'himself removes pages throughout the story, leaving us with fragments, whose meaning and motivation is not easily decipherable'.[152] Le Fanu describes his mosaic metaphor thus: 'as you move round inside it and over it, different facets – different clusters of tessera – catch the light and gleam momentarily'.[153] Kral echoes this description of the film as a near palpable object, writing that the images are organised 'in layers formed one on top of another'.[154] At times, such metaphors become hybrid, Synessios for example, writes that 'literary references, too, colour the canvas'.[155]

Mirror, eliding many of the structural and narrative conventions of classical cinema, appears to somehow overflow and exceed the boundaries of cinema itself in much of the critical writing on the film. This persistent attribution of metaphors, as Sobchack has pointed out, indicates that there is a gap in language and expression with which to speak about the film experience, hence encouraging writers to borrow from the language of other art forms and media.[156] Tarkovsky's pronouncements on this issue are, as is often the case, contradictory. He himself uses various metaphors to describe artistic experiences, although these are more frequently of a religious or spiritual nature. At the same time, however, he argues that the idea of a 'composite cinema', which states that cinema is an amalgamation of other art forms, denies the validity of cinema as an art form in itself, and 'implies that cinema is founded on the attributes of kindred art forms and has none specifically its own; and that is to deny that cinema is an art'.[157] While Tarkovsky has, as Bird argues, contributed to the interpretation of his films as 'woolly mystical fables' through the self-important tone of his writing, it remains essential to remember this assertion of the artistic element of the cinematic experience: 'the meaning or significance of Tarkovsky's films are accessible only through their direct apprehension as art works'.[158]

The title of Tarkovsky's film names possibly the most infamous cinematic metaphor: the mirror. Synessios writes that Tarkovsky was fascinated with the semantic roots (for example the word 'zret') of the Russian word for mirror ('zerkalo') which imply not merely looking, but looking intently and perspicaciously. The verb 'zret' also means to ripen and mature, 'therefore the word itself reveals a way of looking, and, by aural association, a process of maturing, ripening'.[159] Furthermore, the same roots underlie the word for 'audience' ('zriteli'). The mirror, however, has been the metaphor for disembodied viewing par excellence, most commonly, but by no means only, in psychoanalytic criticism. Theorists of embodiment have unsurprisingly criticised the way in which this metaphor reinforces the alienation of vision from the body, rendering the viewer a passive receptacle for the film's deceptive and illusory images.[160] As Sobchack has pointed out, the metaphor of the mirror confines the film to the screen rectangle and discusses it as a static viewed object.[161] In Deleuze's writings, however, the mirror has resurfaced as part of his conception of the crystal-image, although he does not, as Emma Wilson has noted, engage in depth with psychoanalysis in his work on cinema.[162]

MIRROR: TRACES AND TRANSFIGURATION 127

According to Deleuze, the crystal-image defines a characteristic of post-war cinema in which the actual and virtual become indistinguishable from each other. The actual image is put beside 'a kind of immediate, symmetrical, consecutive, or even simultaneous double'. The actual image has a virtual image which corresponds to it as a double or reflection, and there is a coalescence between the two: 'it is as if an image in a mirror, a photo or postcard came to life, assumed independence and passed into the actual'.[163] As Deleuze writes, perception and recollection, the real and imaginary, the physical and mental, 'or rather their images', continually follow each other and refer back to each other 'around a point of indiscernibility . . . the actual optical image crystallizes with its own virtual image'.[164] Objects which are by nature doubling, such as mirrors, perform these exchanges within the film:

> the mirror-image is virtual in relation to the actual character that the mirror catches, but it is actual in the mirror which now leaves the character with only a virtuality and pushes him back out-of-field . . . the character is no more than one virtuality among others.[165]

Deleuze sees *Mirror* as 'a turning crystal, with two sides if we relate it to the invisible adult character (his mother, his wife), with four sides if we relate it to two visible couples (his mother and the child he was, his wife and the child he has)'.[166]

Owing to the brevity with which Deleuze outlines his ideas on particular films, they will require expanding. It is certainly the case that the characters in *Mirror* are caught up in a proliferation of reflections within the pro-filmic space. We are presented with characters that seem to walk out of mirrored reflections, such as the boy at the fire, and with tracking shots that seem impossibly to show us the same character next to him- or herself, such as Maria in the sequence in which she washes her hair. In most instances, however, the reflections are not self-identical: other elements continually intrude upon an ideal mirroring. The mirrors reflect an image of the looking subject as being fundamentally transformed by the force of time. They fuse the present with a past and future, in the way that, for example, the same actors play characters from different time periods, and are also present in the same scenes and eras. During the hair-washing sequence, Maria is seen next to her reflection, then next to herself; there is then a cut to the older Maria looking at herself in the mirror, closely associating these virtual images. The older Maria is also shown in photographs next to the young Maria, which Natalia finds in the Narrator's apartment. The older mother, at the end of the film, seems to step out of her reflection and replace the younger mother: one of the two young children calls her 'mother' and draws attention to this replacement. When Alexei, similarly, looks into the mirror, he sees reflected in it not just himself but his memories of the red-haired girl. When Natalia looks in the mirror this provides a trigger of association for the Narrator, who sees not just her reflection, but also his mother. The mirrors encode memory within themselves, showing not a pure reflection on a surface, but an image of a non-chronological temporality. The mirrors can be seen as recollection objects that literally inscribe memory within themselves. According to Marks, the recollection object is an 'irreducibly material object that encodes collective memory', allowing 'unresolved pasts to surface in the present of the image'.[167]

These examples suggest another way of interpreting Deleuze's statements that what the crystal-image shows is 'a little bit of time in the pure state', and 'it is time, that we *see in the crystal*'.[168] What we see in the mirror is actually the subject *in time*, as continually transformed by time. The reflections and repetitions of the characters in many ways embody Deleuze's understanding of the subject as split and fragmented. For Deleuze, the subject is divided into a passive Ego (*moi*) that is in time and constantly changing, and an I (*je*) that actively carries out a 'synthesis' of time by comprehending this division of past, present and future. In this schema, according to Deleuze, 'I am separated from myself by the form of time.'[169] Time continually modulates between various differences within subjectivity itself. The splitting of time which doubles perception with memory also constitutes a fundamental division of the subject. While it is unrolled in time, our actual existence duplicates itself along with a virtual existence, a mirror image. The mirrors thus reflect back not an image of a unified and coherent 'self', but encourage a recognition of the plurality of 'selves'. If we think of identity as continually changing, it is as though the mirrors capture a moment from that continuum, to reflect the looking subject as it was or will be. In this regard, we can see the reflections as images of spatialised time, moments isolated briefly from duration, even as heterogeneous temporality is suggested thematically.

Deleuze's analysis is, like *Mirror* in his description, closed in on itself, a turning object. What Deleuze does not elaborate on in his idea of a crystalline object is how the 'virtual' images and mirrorings unfold through time in ways that are likely to disorientate viewers. Shots in which characters seemingly walk out of their reflections or that show us the same character next to themselves are likely to necessitate a reorientation of filmic time. The reflections seem to emerge as powerful moments, yet it is also important to consider them in the context of the duration of the film, as they encourage us to engage our memories. The first appearance of Natalia, for example (who is, incidentally, reflected in a mirror), follows a scene which had featured Maria, encouraging us to mis-recognise Natalia as Maria. This confusion is not allowed to prolong itself, as the Narrator quickly addresses Natalia as his wife and comments on her resemblance to his mother, necessitating a re-engagement of our perception. Our habitual sense perception, which allows us to recognise the woman in the mirror is, in the context of the film, misleading rather than affirming. When the Narrator claims that, when he imagines his mother, she always has Natalia's face, the images of Natalia in the Narrator's flat are suddenly replaced by those of Maria at the childhood home, as though mirroring the recollection process. Rather than showing Maria's face, however, as might be appropriate or logical for the comparison, we see her walking away from the camera, from behind. When Natalia later looks at photos of the Narrator's mother, we can see that they are, indeed, identical. At this stage, however, the Narrator inexplicably denies their resemblance. The reflections, which are often explicitly commented upon in a diegetic prompt, thus necessitate a continual movement through, and re-creation of, our memories of the film and our perception of the image unfolding before us, disturbing frames of reference and thickening perception with memory.

The film continually echoes and reflects its own past images in a series of rhythmic repetitions and patterns. Several scenes appear to be linked by visual and aural repetitions and thematic associations. The echoing rhythms of footsteps, for example, link several moments of the film. At the shooting range, Asafiev's boots crunch loudly on the wooden planks covered in snow, with the only other sound heard on the soundtrack being the muted one of crows calling. In the documentary footage that soon follows, from the siege of Leningrad, several naked men, the sound of their bare feet in the mud and lake audible, accidentally overturn a cart. The scene changes back to the shooting range, as Asafiev climbs the stairs, his boots audible in the snow to the exclusion of all other sounds. The Sivash footage, documenting another tragedy of the Second World War, begins immediately after; for almost two minutes before the voice begins reciting poetry, we hear the sound of the many soldiers' boots squelching though the mud and water.

Other scenes, or camera movements within scenes, appear to cluster around the images and sounds of falling water. During the first poem recited, for example, Maria stands watching the rain at the window of the dacha, the tear falling down her cheek echoing the trickling rain outside. In the next sequence, the characters watch the fire in the barn, its force muted by the falling rain. The conjunction of fire and water recurs immediately after, as water and plaster within the house fall down around the flickering flame of a lamp. While these elements are not seen in the next sequence (the Narrator's telephone call to his mother), water returns in the printing works scene, soaking the mother with rain as she runs there. The poem spoken over her journey through the factory's corridors resonates evocatively with the deluges of water seen. The poet speaks of his frustration at missing a meeting with his lover on a sunny day, as she comes instead on an 'utterly gloomy and cloudy day. It rains, and it's getting unusually late, and rain drops down the cold terrain, unsoothable by word, unwipable by hand . . .'. The poem recalls Maria waiting at the dacha, watching the rain, her tears unsoothable, for a lover who never appears. When she subsequently tries to take a shower at the printing works, the water literally stops flowing, and it does not appear again until the Sivash footage, approximately halfway through the film.

An important recurring image is that of hands. The hypnotist in the film's first sequence cures the stuttering boy through an intense focus on his hands. When hands attached to an unseen character (Ignat) are turning the pages of the Leonardo da Vinci book, they stop at a sheet showing the artist's sketches of hands, themselves already repeated on the page in various poses. The film here mirrors the many drawn hands with a living, moving embodiment. I have already commented on the other important reappearances of hands – that of the older Maria touching her reflection, the momentary flash of the hand warmed against a fire, and a repetition of this (although not in a close-up, but in a mid-shot) as part of a wider narrative context. These repetitions do not necessarily have a particular meaning, but their constant reoccurrence may prompt a flow of associations, perhaps provoking viewers to an engagement that increases in affective force throughout the duration of the film.

A possibly more obviously meaningful pattern or mirroring occurs throughout the film in the positioning of Natalia, the younger Maria and the older Maria in the frame. Natalia's crouching position on the ground as she gathers her belongings, for example, is repeated when we next see the mother, crouching on the ground sawing firewood. When we last see her in this sequence, it is in a close-up, as she watches with ambivalence the reunion of her husband with his children. In the following scene with Natalia, the camera zooms towards her face as she says, 'you could have come more often. You know that he's missing you', a statement that has equal relevance to Maria's situation, as though Natalia is continuing, or perhaps initiating, a dialogue between Maria and her husband. In one of the film's final sequences, the camera approaches the older Maria from behind, her hair coiled in a bun, smoking. The configuration of this scene recalls the camera's movement at the film's beginning, when it focused upon the younger Maria's coiled hairstyle. Such moments of near-mirroring echo the film's desire to have all the generations at 'one table', as Arseniy Tarkovsky's poem expressed it.

The presence of mirrors as actual objects within the film is also insistent; they seem to be more than just reflective surfaces. The mirrors are both ephemeral and tactile objects that draw attention to themselves through their ornate decoration and the stains and dirt which often cover them, literally overlaying them with traces of 'time'. The focus upon them allows time for our eyes to move between seeing the mirror as an object and seeing it as a reflective surface. Tarkovsky's last film, *The Sacrifice*, provides an example of how this movement might be envisioned by a camera. The camera tracks across a littered street from above, eventually passing over a pane of glass placed somewhere above the street. As it emerges into the foreground, it reflects what is above the street (the tops of buildings) in a double exposure, until the camera begins to focus upon the glass itself and the unidentified dark liquid, possibly blood, which is splattered across it. The possibilities of this sort of perceptual movement between foreground and background, enacting a temporality in our process of looking, must also be taken into account when thinking about the reflections in *Mirror*.

Perhaps the most disturbing image in which a mirror occurs is that of a fleeing woman in the Spanish footage who carries a mirror: it is broken, and it reflects nothing. Considering the film's stuttering editing and the similarly scattered, refracted past moments that are impossible to regain in their pure pastness, the broken mirror might be seen to resonate with the cinematographic and diegetic concerns of the film. While the film continually destabilises and disorientates, however, it also evokes an aesthetic fascination and a sense of joyful creativity. Its cinematic rendering of natural beauty and gestures towards the creative fluidity of remembering can provide a deeply affecting experience. The remarkable ability of cinema to generate an aesthetic fascination amidst a diegetic landscape of loss, sorrow and mourning is also powerfully enacted in Krzysztof Kieślowski's *Decalogue*, to which I now turn.

Notes

1. The complex process of production is beyond the scope of this chapter, but is thoroughly documented by Synessios.
2. Natasha Synessios, *Mirror* (London: I. B. Tauris, 2001), pp. 11–12.
3. Andrei Tarkovsky, *Sculpting in Time* (Austin: University of Texas Press, 2010), p. 120.
4. Ibid., p. 117.

5. Ibid., p. 116.
6. Synessios, *Mirror*, pp. 7, 38.
7. Tarkovsky, *Sculpting in Time*, p. 183.
8. Ibid., 183.
9. Deleuze, *Cinema 2*, p. 39.
10. Ibid., p. 39.
11. Ibid., p. 28.
12. Donato Totaro, 'Muriel: Thinking With Cinema About Cinema', *Offscreen* (July 2002), www.horschamp.qc.ca/new_offscreen/muriel.html.
13. Jon Beasley-Murray, 'Whatever Happened to Neorealism? – Bazin, Deleuze, and Tarkovsky's Long Take', *iris*, 23 (1997), p. 37.
14. Ibid., p. 39.
15. Ibid., p. 49.
16. Ibid., p. 39.
17. Synessios, *Mirror*, pp. 50–1.
18. Vlada Petric, 'Tarkovsky's Dream Imagery', *Film Quarterly*, 43.2 (1989), pp. 28–34 (p. 28).
19. Tarkovsky, *Sculpting in Time*, p. 117.
20. Ibid., 83.
21. Petric, 'Tarkovsky's Dream Imagery', p. 30.
22. Deleuze, *Cinema 2*, p. 168.
23. Ibid., p. 22.
24. Totaro, 'Muriel'.
25. Tarkovsky, *Sculpting in Time*, pp. 63–4.
26. Rodowick, *Gilles Deleuze's Time Machine*, p. 81.
27. John Mullarkey, *Philosophy and the Moving Image: Refractions of Reality* (Basingstoke: Palgrave Macmillan, 2010), p. 166.
28. Colebrook, *Gilles Deleuze*, p. 42.
29. Ibid., pp. 42–3.
30. Synessios, *Mirror*, p. 63.
31. Doane, *Cinematic Time*, p. 15.
32. Ibid., p. 33.
33. Helga Nowotny, *Time: The Modern and Postmodern Experience* (Cambridge: Polity Press, 1994), p. 132.
34. Ibid., p. 137.
35. Ibid., p. 138.
36. Rick Altman, 'Sound Space', in Rick Altman (ed.), *Sound Theory, Sound Practice* (New York: Routledge, 1992), p. 62.
37. Doane, *Cinematic Time*, p. 16.
38. Tarkovsky, *Sculpting in Time*, p. 130.
39. Ibid., p. 130.
40. Doane., *Cinematic Time*, p. 10.
41. Ibid., p. 22.
42. Banfield cited by Mulvey, *Death*, p. 57.

43. Barthes, *Camera Lucida*, p. 96. Original italics.
44. Mulvey, *Death*, p. 15.
45. Doane, *Cinematic Time*, p. 23.
46. Vida T. Johnson and Graham Petrie, *The Films of Andrei Tarkovsky: A Visual Fugue* (Bloomington: Indiana University Press, 1994), p. 194.
47. Synessios, *Mirror*, p. 79.
48. Noel Burch cited by Deleuze, *Cinema 2*, p. 235.
49. Deleuze, *Cinema 2*, p. 235.
50. To use the terms suggested by Michel Chion, *The Voice in Cinema* (New York: Columbia University Press, 1999), p. 24.
51. Rodowick, *Gilles Deleuze's Time Machine*, p. 104.
52. Andrea Truppin, 'And Then There Was Sound: The Films of Andrei Tarkovsky', in Rick Altman (ed.), *Sound Theory, Sound Practice* (New York: Routledge, 1992), p. 243.
53. Robert Bird, *Andrei Tarkovsky: Elements of Cinema* (London: Reaktion, 2008), p. 127.
54. Maya Turovskaya, *Tarkovsky: Cinema as Poetry* (London: Faber & Faber, 1989), p. 67.
55. Synessios, *Mirror*, p. 60.
56. Ibid., p. 75.
57. Rodowick, *Gilles Deleuze's Time Machine*, p. 100.
58. Ibid., p. 101.
59. Bruce F. Kawin, *Mindscreen: Bergman, Godard, and First-Person Film* (Princeton: Princeton University Press, 1978).
60. Deleuze, *Cinema 1*, p. 76.
61. Sobchack, *Address*, p. 209.
62. Ibid., p. 212.
63. Ibid., p. 207.
64. Ibid., pp. 207–8.
65. Tarkovsky, *Sculpting in Time*, p. 124.
66. Ibid., p. 114.
67. Ibid., p. 116.
68. Daniel Frampton, *Filmosophy* (London and New York: Wallflower Press, 2006), p. 46.
69. Mulvey, *Death*, p. 38.
70. Ibid., p. 47.
71. Ian Christie, 'Introduction: Tarkovsky in his Time', in Maya Turovskaya, *Tarkovsky: Cinema as Poetry* (London: Faber & Faber, 1989), p. xvii.
72. Tarkovsky, *Sculpting in Time*, p. 118.
73. Tarkovsky cited by Angela Dalle Vache, *Cinema and Painting* (London: Athlone, 1996), p. 137.
74. Tarkovsky, *Sculpting in Time*, p. 116.
75. Ibid., p. 213.
76. Cited by Tarkovsky, pp. 10–13.

77. Peter Kral, 'Tarkovsky, or the Burning House', *Screening the Past* (2001), http://www.latrobe.edu.au/screeningthepast/classics/cl0301/pkcl12.htm.
78. Mark Le Fanu, *Cinema of Andrei Tarkovsky* (London: BFI, 1987), p. 79.
79. Synessios, *Mirror*, p. 70.
80. Ibid., p. 3.
81. Le Fanu, *Cinema of Andrei Tarkovsky*, p. 69.
82. Ibid., p. 80.
83. Dalle Vache, *Cinema and Painting*, p. 153.
84. Giuliana Bruno, *Atlas of Emotion: Journeys in Art, Architecture and Film* (New York: Verso, 2002), p. 65.
85. Sobchack, *Carnal Thoughts*, p. 77.
86. Ibid., p. 77.
87. Marks, *The Skin*, p. 162.
88. Synessios, *Mirror*, p. 51.
89. Christie, 'Introduction: Tarkovsky in his Time', p. xviii.
90. Sobchack, *Carnal Thoughts*, p. 63.
91. Bird, *Andrei Tarkovsky*, p. 18.
92. Marks, *The Skin*, p. 47.
93. Ibid., p. 147.
94. Tarkovsky, *Sculpting in Time*, p. 117.
95. Ibid., p. 109.
96. Ibid., p. 41.
97. Paul Schrader, *Transcendental Style in Film: Ozu, Bresson, Dreyer* (Berkeley: University of California Press, 1972), p. 5.
98. Ibid., p. 84.
99. Tarkovsky, *Sculpting in Time*, p. 51.
100. Petric, 'Tarkovsky's Dream Imagery', p. 33.
101. Synessios, *Mirror*, p. 69.
102. Truppin, p. 235.
103. Dalle Vache, *Cinema and Painting*, p. 137.
104. Ibid., p. 138.
105. Ibid., p. 137.
106. Le Fanu, *Cinema of Andrei Tarkovsky*, p. 80.
107. Turovskaya, *Tarkovsky*, p. 82.
108. Peter Green, *Andrei Tarkovsky: The Winding Quest* (Basingstoke: Macmillan, 1992), p. 85.
109. Louis Aragon cited by Christian Keathley, *Cinephilia and History* (Bloomington: Indiana University Press, 2006), p. 69.
110. Synessios, *Mirror*, p. 66.
111. Kral, 'Tarkovsky, or the Burning House'.
112. Sarah Kozloff, *Overhearing Film Dialogue* (Berkeley: University of California Press, 2000), p. 11.
113. Kral, 'Tarkovsky, or the Burning House'.

114. Chion, *Voice*, p. 19.
115. Kozloff, *Overhearing Film Dialogue*, p. 11.
116. Turovskaya, *Tarkovsky*, p. 64.
117. Synessios, *Mirror*, p. 71.
118. *The Sacrifice*, film, directed by Andrei Tarkovsky. Sweden/France: Svenskafilminstitutet, 1986.
119. Bird, *Andrei Tarkovsky*, p. 13.
120. Ibid., p. 145.
121. Petric, 'Tarkovsky's Dream Imagery', p. 34.
122. Kral, 'Tarkovsky, or the Burning House'.
123. Bird, *Andrei Tarkovsky*, p. 165.
124. Tarkovsky, *Sculpting in Time*, p. 108.
125. A claim made by Le Fanu, *Cinema of Andrei Tarkovsky*, p. 88, and Johnson and Petrie, *The Films of Andrei Tarkovsky*, p. 128.
126. Synessios, *Mirror*, p. 50.
127. Kozloff, *Overhearing Film Dialogue*, p. 6.
128. Stern, 'Paths', p. 320.
129. Mulvey, *Death*, p. 66.
130. Stern, 'Paths', p. 320.
131. Ibid., p. 337.
132. Dalle Vache, *Cinema and Painting*, p. 154.
133. Green, *Andrei Tarkovsky*, p. 92.
134. Stern, 'Paths', p. 354.
135. Dorothy Richardson, 'Narcissus', in James Donald, Anne Friedberg and Laura Marcus (eds), *Close Up 1927–1933: Cinema and Modernism* (Princeton: Princeton University Press, 1999), p. 201.
136. Sontag, *Against Interpretation*, p. 181.
137. Truppin, 'And Then There Was Sound', p. 247.
138. Altman cited by Truppin, p. 236.
139. Truppin, 'And Then There Was Sound', p. 237.
140. Ibid., 241.
141. Altman, 'Sound Space', p. 60.
142. Barthes cited in Charles Affron, *Cinema and Sentiment* (Chicago: University of Chicago Press, 1982), p. 114.
143. Mikel Dufrenne, *In the Presence of the Sensuous: Essays in Aesthetics* (New Jersey: Humanities Press International, 1987), p. 123.
144. Deleuze, *Cinema 2*, p. 224.
145. Bird, *Andrei Tarkovsky*, p. 152.
146. Tarkovsky, *Sculpting in Time*, p. 158.
147. Ibid., p. 159.
148. Ibid., p. 158.
149. Ibid., p. 159.
150. Ibid., p. 162.
151. Symphony: Synessios, *Mirror*, p. 48. Mosaic: Le Fanu, *Cinema of Andrei*

Tarkovsky, p. 87; Johnson and Petrie, p. 116; Green, *Andrei Tarkovsky*, p. 92. Poem: Turovskaya (throughout).
152. Synessios, *Mirror*, p. 52.
153. Le Fanu, *Cinema of Andrei Tarkovsky*, p. 87.
154. Kral, 'Tarkovsky, or the Burning House'.
155. Synessios, p. 60.
156. Sobchack, *Carnal Thoughts*, p. 81.
157. Tarkovsky, *Sculpting in Time*, p. 113.
158. Bird, *Andrei Tarkovsky*, p. 21.
159. Synessios, *Mirror*, p. 84.
160. Sobchack, *Address*, p. 17.
161. Ibid., 15.
162. Emma Wilson, *Memory and Survival: The French Cinema of Krzysztof Kieślowski* (London: Legenda, 2000), p. 9.
163. Deleuze, *Cinema 2*, pp. 66–7.
164. Ibid., p. 67.
165. Ibid., p. 68.
166. Ibid., p. 73.
167. Marks, *The Skin*, pp. 77, 84.
168. Deleuze, *Cinema 2*, p. 79.
169. Deleuze cited in Rodowick, *Gilles Deleuze's Time Machine*, p. 129.

CHAPTER 4

Signs and Meaning in the *Decalogue*

By the time Krzysztof Kieślowski made the *Decalogue*, he was a well-known film director in Poland, having begun his career making documentaries that focused upon the injustices and absurdities of life under Socialism. He made his first feature film, *The Scar*, in 1976, and had made five feature films before he began the *Decalogue* project.[1] The series marked a shift away from the political concerns that had been visible in his earlier films. Kieślowski has stated that during the imposition of martial law in Poland (1981–3) he realised that politics cannot answer 'any of our essential, fundamental, human and humanistic questions'.[2] The *Decalogue* was planned by Kieślowski and his co-scriptwriter, lawyer Krzysztof Piesiewicz, who is often credited with the idea of creating a film series based on the Ten Commandments. Originally, Kieślowski intended to supervise the project while allowing each episode to be directed by a different director. However, he found himself becoming too attached to the project to give it away.[3]

The series was filmed over eleven months in 1987 and 1988 in a single apartment building complex in Warsaw, a grey residential high-rise block typical of Socialist architecture in Eastern Europe.[4] Each was filmed by a different cinematographer, except *Decalogue 3* and *9*, which were both filmed by Edward Sobociński. Although it was intended as a television series, the *Decalogue* premiered in a Warsaw cinema between 20 and 24 October 1989, and appeared at international film festivals (Berlin, San Sebastian, Venice) before that. The Warsaw cinema screening became an important cultural event, as is documented in the press.[5] Kieślowski has admitted that when shooting the television and film versions of *Decalogue 5* and *6*, the two got mixed up in editing, such that scenes from the TV version went into the film version and vice versa, a process that Kieślowski labelled 'a pleasant game in the cutting room. The nicest moment.'[6] We are already confronted, here, with in-betweenness, between cinema and television.

If my analysis aims to be sensitive to the various rhythms of cinematic time, the nearly ten hours of footage that constitutes the *Decalogue* presents an interesting challenge. Each of the ten episodes that make up the series can be seen to constitute their own unique duration, yet each also contains echoes, traces and foreshadowings of other episodes within the series. Furthermore, two of the episodes, *Decalogue* 5 and 6, were expanded into the films *A Short Film About Killing* and a *Short Film About Love*, respectively, while several of the characters in the films, such as the singer with the heart condition in *Decalogue 9*, look forward to characters in Kieślowski's later films (in this case, Weronika/Veronique in *The Double Life of Veronique*, which Kieślowski made after the *Decalogue* series in 1991).[7]

This chapter attempts to capture something of the fluidity and gradual development of meaning and significance in the duration of the films. Meaning in the *Decalogue* series, I suggest, is not fixed and static; images, instead, continually resonate with an *uncertain* significance, and indicate the limits of meaning, both for the characters who question what is meaningful and significant in their lives, and potentially for viewers who are encouraged to question what is meaningful and significant in the films. I draw upon the argument of Trotter concerning the hermeneutic threshold in cinema, that may prevent a crossing over into definite meaning or symbolisation.[8] As Trotter has outlined, there may be moments in film where meaning is resisted, even as interpretation seems to be encouraged. One of the key characteristics of the *Decalogue* films is not the transcendent symbolism, but the continual unfolding of uncertainty – uncertainty of interpretation, knowledge, meaning, and chronology. The temporal unfolding of the films renders symbolic association fluid, and in many cases ultimately unattributable. In this respect one of the most significant assertions about Kieślowski's films, albeit in this case about *The Double Life of Veronique*, is Wilson's, who refers to the 'risk of the spectator's attempt to find logic and veracity where the filmmaker has left lacunae and doubt; this risk must necessarily increase in proportion to the very indecipherability of a particular film'. Wilson suggests that 'this has specifically been the fate of *Le Double Vie de Veronique* where viewers attempt to understand a film which simply does not make sense'.[9] I argue that an analysis of the *Decalogue* series should remain sensitive to the possibility that meaning and significance may, in the duration of the film, continually dissolve. As I suggested in the Introduction, Massumi's writing on affect is suggestive for films such as the *Decalogue*, which frequently elide explanatory narrative development, while resonating with unlocalisable intensities.

Like *L'Avventura*, the *Decalogue* series has evoked powerful responses on opposite sides of the affective spectrum. As Woodward writes, there is a particular class of critic who 'begrudgingly admits Kieślowski's importance while finding the films almost unwatchable'. David Thomson apparently finds the films 'so cold as to forbid touching . . . to see a Kieślowski film for me requires a steeling, as if I were going into torture or church'.[10] On the other hand, Kieślowski's films have inspired adoration; continual retrospectives of, and tributes to, his work are visible across the world. Ultimately, however, the affective and emotional force of the *Decalogue* films is rarely analysed, remaining a repressed underside of writing on the *Decalogue*. This chapter attempts to locate a complex knot of potential affect and emotion in several of the films, with a particular focus on how these may be elongated through the slow passage of cinematic time.

Because of the sheer length of the series, it may be helpful to make a brief sketch of each of the films' narratives to encourage readers' familiarity with them.

> *Decalogue 1*: A young boy, Paweł, receives a pair of ice skates as an early Christmas present. His father, Krzysztof, calculates on a computer that the lake is frozen enough for Paweł to skate on; nevertheless, the ice breaks and Paweł dies.
>
> *Decalogue 2*: Dorota is pregnant by a man other than her husband, Andrzej, who is possibly dying in hospital. Dorota demands that his doctor tells her with certainty whether Andrzej will live; if so, she feels she must abort the child. The doctor eventually announces that Andrzej is sure to die. Dorota does not abort the child, but Andrzej eventually recovers.
>
> *Decalogue 3*: On Christmas Eve, Ewa requests that Janusz leave his family to help her find her missing husband, Edward. Ewa and Janusz have not seen each other since their affair ended three years ago. After searching all night, Ewa reveals that Edward in fact left her the same night that her affair with Janusz ended.
>
> *Decalogue 4*: Anka, whose mother died just after her birth, enjoys a close relationship with her father, Michał. When he returns home from a trip, she reveals that an old letter from her mother claimed Michał is not her real father, leaving them free to become lovers. Michał refuses, and Anka subsequently reveals that she made up the contents of the letter.
>
> *Decalogue 5*: Jacek, initially seen wandering through Warsaw and asking to get a young girl's Communion photo enlarged, murders a taxi driver, Waldek. He is defended in court by a lawyer, Piotr,

who learns that the young girl in Jacek's photograph was Jacek's sister, who was killed years ago by a tractor driver. Jacek is then executed.

Decalogue 6: A young man, Tomek, is in love with his neighbour, Magda, and spies on her with a telescope. After revealing this to her, she agrees to go out with him. They have a sexual encounter that embarrasses Tomek, and he slits his wrists. A remorseful Magda awaits his return from hospital, but he reveals he no longer spies on her.

Decalogue 7: A little girl, Ania, has grown up thinking that her grandmother, Ewa, is really her mother, and her real mother, Majka, is her sister. Majka kidnaps Ania with the intention of taking her abroad. She is betrayed by Ania's father and Ania is returned to Ewa.

Decalogue 8: A Polish-Jewish visitor from America, Elżbieta, returns to Poland and attempts to determine why a woman, Zofia, now an ethics professor, agreed to hide her when she was a child during the Holocaust, and then refused at the last moment.

Decalogue 9: Romek, a heart surgeon, has learnt that he is impotent. He spies on his wife, who is having an affair. He attempts to commit suicide, but survives.

Decalogue 10: Two brothers, Artur and Jurek, are shocked to inherit an incredibly valuable stamp collection. Although going to great lengths to protect the collection and to extend it, it is stolen, and each brother suspects the involvement of the other.

Significance: Omens, Objects and Patterns

Associative Networks Across the Series

The *Decalogue* series inevitably raises questions about the extent to which the episodes can be seen as interpretations of each commandment. Perhaps the most innovative analysis has been conducted by Slavoj Žižek, who posits that 'one should emphasize the *strict* correlation between the episodes and the Commandments'. In his view, each film refers to only one commandment – not the one correlating to the number of the film, but rather to the number of the commandment after that. *Decalogue 1*, in this schema, refers to the second Commandment, *Decalogue 2* to the third, and so on until *Decalogue 10*, which refers to the first Commandment, 'Thou shalt have none other Gods but me.'[11] Other writers, correctly in my view, posit a more fluid relationship between the Commandments and the films. Annette Insdorf, for example, writes that 'rather than asking us to be literal-minded, *The Decalogue* provokes contemplation of how the spirit of the Commandments might still be applicable to our daily lives'.[12] Tadeusz Lubelski has written that the Commandments mark out the 'direction of ethical reflection of the viewer'. The films, he continues, are not religious *as such*, but 'bring the viewer close to a religious reflection'.[13] The fact that the series is numbered rather than named explicitly encourages viewers to make their own links and interpretations when considering the relationship to the Commandments. According to Kieślowski, the lack of titles for the *Decalogue* films came about from not wanting to 'name' things, forcing viewers to look for the Commandment themselves, to an effort of thought.[14]

At times, several of the films may suggest particular engagements with religion, ethics and morality through dialogue. Having kidnapped Ania in *Decalogue 7*, for example (the seventh Commandment being 'thou shalt not steal'), Majka poses the question: 'Is it possible to steal something that is yours?' At other times, engagements with ethics may emerge in a more general way, as in *Decalogue 8*, when two characters discuss whether good and evil exist, and what situations may bring these out in particular people. At yet other moments, religious imagery and settings, such as those in *Decalogue 1*, encourage a consideration of religion and its importance to the characters and to the film (I return to this particular case later). One of the pleasurable aspects of the *Decalogue* is that it encourages a continual interpretive process of conjoining film and Commandment into a meaningful form, while recognising those moments in which a strict application of Commandment to film is resisted.

The *Decalogue* series may encourage a kind of exegesis, but the question of the relationship of the Commandments to each film in no way exhausts the questions surrounding the films' meanings. Indeed, it is the nature and possibility of meaning itself that forms a recurrent thread in critical and theoretical writing about the *Decalogue* in particular, and Kieślowski's films in general. The questions around meaning that recur in critical debates can be formulated as follows: is the universe ordered and controlled, predestined by whatever higher being or force we can imagine, or are events random, not guided by anything but occurring by chance? Each theorist has a different way of phrasing this question, but their concerns are very similar. According to Žižek, in Kieślowski's films we find an 'oscillation (and coincidence) between the reign of chance and the underlying secret interconnection between events . . . is there a deeper meaning beneath contingency, or is the meaning itself the outcome of a contingent turn of events?'[15] According to Kickasola, there is a 'metaphysical quest' that runs throughout Kieślowski's films:

there is a strong sense of telos in the human person that makes us feel such things are not random, *could not* be random, and that meaning is not something we merely project onto the surface of things, but rather . . . a message being delivered to us.[16]

For Sobchack, 'the ambiguity and paradoxical nature of happenstance as it both provides open possibilities and countless "chances" for subjective being to "become" and yet closes in on and fixes us with every objective move we make to determine our "fate" preoccupies Kieślowski'.[17]

These questions of meaning are valid as much for the characters of the *Decalogue* films, who continually experience transformative encounters that, in their universe, may or may not be random, as for the viewer and critic, who may wish to determine whether particular moments or events have an overarching significance or are in place simply by chance. As such, the question that I posed above could be reformulated as follows: are the events and images in the films always and completely controlled within a particular system of signification and meaning, or are the images and events sometimes, perhaps often, random, occurring by chance and not indicating any particular meaning?

There are moments in the films in which the questions of meaning and signification seem to crystallise. One such is the reappearance of an unknown man, played by Artur Barciś, in each episode except the seventh, where, apparently, the quality of the footage in which he appeared was unusable, and the tenth, where the atmosphere of dark humour rendered his appearance inappropriate.[18] Kieślowski has described him in the following way: 'There's this guy who wanders around in all the films. I don't know who he is; just a guy who comes and watches. He watches us, our lives. He's not very pleased with us.'[19] Kieślowski has also referred to this character as the 'motor of thought' that forces the characters to rethink their actions or plans.[20] In each film in which he appears, he is in a different guise; in *Decalogue 2*, for example, he seems to work at the hospital where Andrzej is lying, in *Decalogue 5*, he appears in the prison before Jacek's execution carrying a stepladder and is presumably a tradesman. He never speaks, but looks at the characters, and sometimes towards the viewer, at particular moments that seem to be significant for the characters and for the narrative.

Several writers have been compelled to attribute a spiritual or mystical force to this figure. Haltof describes him as an 'enigmatic angel-like character' who 'glues the series together and adds an almost metaphysical dimension'.[21] Kickasola terms him 'Theophanes', writing that he 'appear[s] to be a reference point for the biblical themes embodied in the films . . . one might say he is the *Dei oculi*, the "seeing" dimension of God's connection with the world'.²² Without wishing to underplay the religious or theological aspects of the *Decalogue*, this dimension has been eloquently discussed elsewhere (for example by Kickasola and Garbowski).²³ For my purposes, the man played by Barciś is referred to simply as 'the unknown man', another reminder of the limits of knowledge and understanding. While his appearances force the characters to pause and reflect, they also seem to demand analysis, encouraging us to interpret the reason for his appearance at a particular moment as something other than random coincidence. However, it is not always clear what particular significance the film is directing us to. Furthermore, there tends to remain a question as to whether he reappears at moments that are already more significant than others, or whether it is his reappearance that renders the moments more significant.

Characters from individual episodes of the *Decalogue* also often appear briefly in other episodes, thus bringing various episodes, narratives and themes into dialogue with each other. According to Biro, these reappearances may afford the viewer the 'pleasures of surprise and recognition', as well as offering 'a more complex sense of continuity'.²⁴ Kieślowski reportedly paid careful attention to which character appeared where; he hung a chart to this effect on his wall.²⁵ Perhaps the most obvious case of infiltrating an episode with the resonance of another is not a reappearance as such but the recounting of a story. In *Decalogue 8*, Zofia asks her class for examples of 'ethical hell'. One student recounts the story of *Decalogue 2*: a woman is pregnant by a man other than her husband, who lies dying in hospital, and is considering aborting the child. Zofia in response states that she knows how this story ends: the child lived. She is right: at the end of *Decalogue 2*, the couple are to have a child, and we see the more heavily pregnant Dorota briefly in *Decalogue 5*. In relation to introducing the story of *Decalogue 2* into *Decalogue 8*, Kieślowski stated that he wanted the audience to think, 'I already know this story, it happened to a friend of mine . . .', as though the films are to insinuate themselves into the memories of the audience, in ways that do not allow us to immediately realise whether we have seen it on film or heard about it in 'real life'.²⁶ The introduction of Dorota's story into Elżbieta and Zofia's places even greater emphasis upon Zofia's failure to rescue Elżbieta as a child.

The resonances that a particular character from one *Decalogue* film may bring to another can completely change our experience of viewing the moment of their appearance. In *Decalogue 9*, for example, Romek and Hanka decide to adopt a child. Soon after, Romek watches a young girl playing in the courtyard. Paul Coates writes that the girl 'represents the child that will make all the difference to the marriage, the child Romek and

Hanka never wanted but are now preparing to adopt'.[27] Things are not so straightforward, however, if we consider that the girl in question is Ania from *Decalogue 7*, or at least someone who resembles her closely, recalling the fraught nature of parenthood and displaced childhood that this film presents. As he watches, Romek pours milk from a glass bottle into a pan, recalling, perhaps, the first time a milk bottle appears in the series, when, in *Decalogue 1*, frozen liquid in a glass bottle suggests to Paweł and Krzysztof that it may be frosty enough to go skating, and the subsequent pain of the father at his child's death.

Omens

Critical writing on the *Decalogue* tends to emphasise the moments where the images seem to have a symbolic or allegorical meaning, something that emerges most clearly in relation to *Decalogue 1* and *2*. Early on in *Decalogue 1*, for example, Paweł asks his father what death is, to which Krzysztof replies matter of factly: 'the heart stops pumping blood'. Soon after, Krzysztof pours milk, which has clearly soured, into his coffee, about which Kickasola writes: 'on a symbolic level, the milk is sour, just as the father's explanations are impoverished in the light of the eternal questions'.[28] When Paweł finds a dead, frozen dog near the apartments shortly before his own death, Žižek suggests that it is a 'premonition of *his own* frozen state after his drowning'.[29] While Paweł is skating on the ice, Krzysztof is working in his apartment and cleaning up an ink stain that has spread over his papers. Insdorf has stated that 'since, in retrospect, this occurs at the very moment Paweł is on the ice, it functions as a foreboding: liquid is out of control'.[30] After Paweł's body is removed from the lake, Krzysztof flees to a nearby church under construction. There, he overturns an altar covered in candles and holding a painting of the Virgin Mary; the wax drips down the face in the painting as though she is weeping. Krzysztof then puts his hands in the stone basin for holy water, which is frozen in a disc that he picks up and places against his forehead. For Coates, this disc's shape is 'a metaphor for the candle he would light upon Paweł's grave'.[31]

While each of the symbolic associations that writers find in Kieślowski's images are valid interpretations, their intent is not necessarily to approximate the development of meaning through duration, but rather to present it as relatively determined. The fixation of symbolic meanings to moving images loses something of the process and duration of how films may unfold and resist meaning through time. As Craig Owens has written, allegory conducts a spatialisation of time, a division of duration into discrete instants of meaning:

allegory concerns itself, then, with the projection – either spatial or temporal or both – of structure as sequence; the result, however, is not dynamic, but static, ritualistic, repetitive . . . it arrests narrative in place.[32]

Despite seeing some of *Decalogue 1*'s images as signs of something other, Žižek also offers another approach to the possibilities of signification in the film, examining the functioning of symbolism itself. In Kieślowski's films, according to Žižek, 'a pre-symbolic motif . . . insists and returns as the Real in different symbolic contexts'. He finds an 'intermediate domain of transversal links, associations, echoes, which are not yet properly signifying in the precise sense of a differential symbolic network that generates meaning'.[33] Žižek's interpretation, particularly his concern with the Real, should be read in the context of his other philosophical writings. As Mullarkey explains, for Žižek, the Real cannot be known in itself, 'the Real simply persists, undifferentiated, while language and imagination try to capture and categorize it'.[34] According to Žižek, the *Decalogue* films are 'full of the ominous intrusions of the extra-narrative, raw Real that can be (or not) read as a sign'.[35] The relation that Žižek posits between the images in the films (specifically, *Decalogue 1*) is more metonymic than metaphorical. The melting wax that drips 'tears' down the painted face of the Virgin Mary, he writes,

> is the last link in the chain of metonymic displacements of the motif of melting down: firstly, the frozen milk melts; then, the ice that covers the nearby lake melts, causing the catastrophe, finally, the wax melts.[36]

Referring back to the question of meaning posited near the beginning of this chapter, he then asks 'is *this* the final answer of the Real, the proof that we are not alone . . . or just another stupid coincidence?'[37] A kind of metonymic relation is suggested by other writers, such as Coates, who describes the 'transformations of liquid the film effects'.[38] Žižek, however, expounds upon this most fully.

Seeing a metonymic rather than metaphorical relation between the liquid elements in the film – at times frozen, melting, swirling, spreading – is reminiscent of Barthes's analysis of George Bataille's *Story of the Eye*, and particularly of the way in which it was taken up by Rosalind Krauss and Yves-Alain Bois in their expanded exhibition catalogue, *Formless: A User's Guide*. In *Story of the Eye*, 'a story of an object' rather than of characters, Barthes traces the trajectory of a migration of the object from image to image.[39] According to Barthes, the metaphorical composition of the story involves a term, the eye, which is 'varied through a number of substitute objects . . . The Eye's substitutes are *declined* in every sense of the term: recited like flexional forms of the one word.'[40] The text's metaphors and images do not refer to a transcendental symbolic system; rather, 'each of its terms is always the significant of another term (no term being a simple thing signified)'.[41] Krauss and Bois developed Bataille's writing to describe an operation of formlessness in modern art that continually displaces meaning. The *informe* is described as 'whatever does not lend itself to any metaphorical displacement, whatever does not allow itself to be in-formed'.[42] What the repetition of such an image can provoke is a rhythmical pulsation that, instead of directing us toward an abstract meaning, 'puts into action an infinite permutation that . . . annuls metaphor through metaphoric excess'.[43] This slippage between different elements reveals a fundamental elasticity of meaning in contrast to a transcendental allegorical schema 'from which nothing escapes being impressed into the service of meaning . . . the formless is inimical to this drive towards the transcendental'.[44]

The modulation of *Decalogue 1*'s liquids – milk, coffee, water, ink, wax – into and out of different forms, then, may gesture towards some kind of symbolic meaning, but not necessarily towards clearly determined signifieds to which these signifiers may refer (for example, that the souring milk symbolises a spiritual lack). In so far, then, as there may be nothing definite implied in the chain of fluids, apart from the existence of the chain itself, *Decalogue 1* may be seen to lend itself to the kind of functional destabilising of meaning that is present in the *informe*. The repetitions of fluid materials may destabilise rather than concretise the field of meaning. Putting the operation of the *informe* into dialogue with the films might enable us to understand them as 'declining' series of objects rather than establishing allegorical equivalents for them. It is then particularly apt that the film repeatedly features fluid materials that can continually transform into different shapes. As Luce Irigaray has written, as a physical reality, fluids 'resist adequate symbolisation and serve as a constant reminder of the powerlessness of the logic of solids to represent all of nature's characteristics'.[45] Fluid structures, as Olkowski emphasises, 'are part of an ontology of change'.[46] An analysis of the film may thus highlight the repetitions of objects and images – in the transmutation of *Decalogue 1*'s fluids, for example – without necessarily relating them to a transcendental schema. However, there is a limit to the extent to which we can 'apply' Krauss and Bois's ideas concerning the *informe* itself, which is arguably just as totalising a system as allegory. A formless image corrodes the meaning of all others; there can be no theme or narrative outside the chain of declined motifs.

Another theoretical approach, one that is closer to my own, is suggested by Sobchack, whose writing on the *Decalogue* is more focused upon meaning and time than her writing on the sensory appeal of cinema in general. Rather than assigning a particular meaning to each image, Sobchack relates the process of making meaning in *Decalogue 1* to the more general questions surrounding chance and fate, accident or purpose, that she sees as an overarching concern in Kieślowski's films. Citing the moment of (and moments after) Krzysztof's awareness of the ink stain, she writes, 'with the emergence of the ink stain every empirical object and sound becomes sensed (both by Krzysztof and us) as an ominous sign of something more than it empirically is, a portent of something awful, something "other" that ruptures the fixed rationality and order of things'.[47] While the events following the spreading of the ink may seem random, such as a little girl ringing the doorbell and asking for Paweł, or an ambulance passing by, these occurrences become 'cumulatively informed by dread and cumulatively weighted as "fateful"'.[48] Indeed, I argue that the cumulative sense of ominousness and uncertain significance is a process that begins from the film's very opening scenes.

What is lacking in the metaphoric and the metonymic approach is the theoretical and critical consideration of the possibility of between-moments in a film's unfolding, those moments in between those that seem to be significant for the narrative, symbolically meaningful, or part of a system of repetitions and variations; that is, those moments which do not seem particularly concerned with meaning at all. Both Žižek's and Sobchack's writings contain tantalising suggestions that there may be room for these between-moments in film analysis. Žižek's suggestion of a 'pre-symbolic realm', describing objects that do not quite yet signify, and which may eventually signify 'or not' implies this, as does Sobchack's description of moments that become 'cumulatively' suggestive; there is a temporality to her analysis that is not quite fully sketched out, but important nevertheless. In Kieślowski's films, she writes,

> things are pregnant with possibility; they swell in existential stature. Indeed, neither are they merely the practico-inert, nor are they safely secured as poetic symbols; rather, they exist and take on weight and value in a continuous motion of postponement.[49]

At this point, I would like to briefly remind readers of what I suggested about critical writing on *Mirror*, which tends to focus upon the materiality of filmed objects and textures. I argued in Chapter 3 that while *Mirror*'s images appeal to the senses, there is also a thematic process at work. A desire for sensory plenitude and its denial is thematised through the Narrator's voice-over and enacted through the continual presentation of textures of decay and deliquescence. Critical writing on the *Decalogue* is in some way on the opposite end of the spectrum to that on *Mirror*: objects tend to be seen as symbols, and their materiality is frequently overlooked. To address this imbalance, I turn again to Trotter, and in particular his discussion of tangibility in cinema. Trotter has argued that filmed objects can fail to be 'fully intelligible'; they can instead resonate with material plenitude, with what he calls 'sense', rather than meaning.[50] In cinema, 'the palpable is the hidden "other side" of our relentless determination to attribute meaning and value to events of the lived world'.[51] In relation to the *Decalogue*, what is at stake is less the appeal to touch per se, and more that material objects seem to refuse to be co-opted into a higher symbolic structure, protruding from the diegesis, asserting themselves in the frame as stubbornly material, obtuse objects. Such objects may not necessarily be a 'symbol nor an element of "simple realistic diegesis"' but rather a plenitude filling the screen, asking 'to be understood in [their] unruliness, and in [their] near tangibility ([their] bristling or thrusting out at the viewer)'.[52]

If we closely examine the development of *Decalogue 1* through duration, we may have a better understanding of the continual process that defers meaning, destabilises symbolisation, and highlights a stubborn tangibility. The film opens on to a close-up view of a body of water. Most of it is frozen over, but a segment still ripples at the left-hand side of the screen, a portion that escapes fixation. A spiky cluster of broken reeds protrudes from the water's surface. As we hear an extended flute note, the camera pans slowly across this semi-frozen expanse, the rippling segment of water always visible at the left-hand side. Panning up, the camera locates a man sitting on the snowy banks of the lake in long-shot, before cutting to the reverse shot, taken with his back in view. The film then cuts to a close-up of his face, framed by the brown and black matted furs that he is wearing, as his eyes come to rest directly towards the camera, a look that commands our attention and seems to inscribe significance on to this moment, though it is not clear what this significance is. The scene changes to night time, as a lateral tracking shot taken from behind glass shows us a woman walking on a street. She walks towards the camera until the frame holds her in close-up. She is looking slightly above the camera's position, and the film then cuts to what she is looking at – a mounted television, viewed from a diagonal angle, which shows a group of children running towards the television camera. The film's camera zooms in on this image, singling out one child in particular, before cutting to the woman who now has tears in her eyes. A cut back to the television screen shows the footage being slowed down as one child runs towards the camera, until the footage is stilled and the child's blurred face is visible in close-up. There is another cut to the unknown man as he gazes into the camera, as though the previous scene has somehow been seen by him; indeed he too appears to have tears in his eyes, which he wipes away.

The film will soon reveal that the child on the television set is Paweł, who will die when the ice melts on the pond, and the woman is his aunt Irena. However, the chronology of this sequence and the varying temporal rhythms are likely to resist a fixation of stable meanings on to the sequence, instead putting our thoughts and interpretations into flux. The scene with Irena takes place after Paweł's death, while it is impossible to say whether the scene with the unknown man takes place before or after Paweł's death, whether he weeps (if he weeps, for indeed the tears may be caused by the fire's smoke) from knowledge or foreseeing. The temporal chronology raises more questions than it determines meanings. If the unknown man weeps, and he does so before Paweł's death, does this suggest that Paweł's fate is predetermined?

There is also uncertainty hovering over the television images taken of Paweł, which we are later shown being filmed in his school, thus giving us retrospectively a context in which to put these images. The images on the television are slowed down, but it seems impossible to determine whether this is a glitch in the television images or whether the footage was intentionally slowed, whether this is how Irena, and/or the unknown man is seeing or imagining this footage, a subjective slowing, or whether this is only slowed for our benefit. Furthermore, what is it that actually slows in these moments – the television footage or the filmed footage itself? While eliding definite interpetations, what emerges powerfully is affect, a sense of great sadness that is not yet tied into narrative process and thus not localisable as emotion. The affect emerges through the tears of Irena and the unknown man, the slow-motion movement of the boy on the television screen which presents an as-yet unidentifiable sense of loss, the frozen landscape associated with a kind of stillness and death, but most importantly the flute music, which resonates with melancholy and somehow also an undertone of fear.

Many other moments in the film have an uncertain significance. Not long after the opening sequence, for example, we see Paweł walking to the shop, greeting a friend, then crossing a snowy expanse in front of a church in long shot. When he is nearly out of frame the flute music begins again and continues over the next cut, a shot of the unknown man. This shot interrupts Paweł's narrative diegesis for the viewer, and once again seems to encourage us to acknowledge the significance of this moment – but what exactly *is* the significance? Perhaps the next shot can suggest an answer: a close-up of a frozen, dead dog. The shot after this is a close-up of Paweł, looking at the dog. This is a reverse of the conventional shot/reverse-shot, whereby we would first see Paweł looking, and then what he is looking at. This, as well as the unknown man's look, seems to be aiming for a heightened awareness in viewers. The moment has an uncertain resonance, slowing narrative progression, at the same time as it slows Paweł's own daily activities. Significantly, Paweł reaches out to touch the dog, which is both a gesture of mourning and a reminder of the dead animal's tangibility.

Returning home, Paweł begins the aforementioned conversation about death with his father, and the camera lingers on the coffee glass, in close-up, steam pouring from its top, as the milk swirls around within it. This moment both interrupts their conversation ('the milk is soured') as well as the narrative flow for the viewer, pausing and lingering on the metamorphosing object. Following the incident with the dead dog, the soured milk has an ominousness about it that perhaps would not have been present otherwise. Soon after his conversation with his father, Paweł asks Irena about God. Irena hugs him and explains that God is in the love that he feels for her at that moment. From this image, the film cuts again to the unknown man, seen from behind tending a fire, and the cold frozen landscape around him adds an element of counterpoint to the warmth of the previous scene. It constitutes an indeterminate intrusion between two scenes of familial bonding – that between Irena and Paweł, and that between Paweł and his father at a chess tournament, which follows.

Paweł and Krzysztof are fascinated by their computers, which they use at home to solve mathematical problems. Arriving home after the chess tournament, Paweł and Krzysztof speak to Irena on the phone. They are both in frame in the darkened room, lit from the glow of what we soon see is the computer. As Krzysztof talks to Irena, Paweł begins to look towards this light source (seemingly located behind the camera). The frame at this point seems to carry two separate rhythms and points of attention: Krzysztof in a sense continues the earlier conversations about religion with Irena (giving his permission for Paweł to attend religion classes), while Paweł simply stares, his attention clearly elsewhere. Once Krzysztof also looks to where Paweł is looking, the film cuts to the computer, glowing with a green light. Paweł denies switching on the computer that he is not allowed to touch. Krzysztof looks at it and asks, 'Hey, friend. What do you want?', as the film cuts back to the computer. Words in black type appear on its surface: 'I am ready.' Krzysztof switches it off, as Paweł asks, 'What if it really wanted something?' Once again an object forces a slowing down of time in a moment that resonates with uncertainty, which in this case the characters voice for us: did it turn itself on? What does it want? As Insdorf writes, 'screens, like other surfaces, are full of mysteries in [*Decalogue*] 1'.[53]

The following day in a lecture, Krzysztof speculates on how in the future computers may have their own personalities and aesthetic preferences. As the class packs up, the film cuts to the unknown man as the flute music is heard again. The music continues over the next shot: a glass milk bottle, cracked and full of frozen liquid. As with the dead dog, we see the bottle before the characters do, as though it must be significant for us also. For the characters, it is a sign of the temperature ('Look! After only an hour outside!' exclaims Paweł), but before this suggestion of its signification, it remains a mute object of somewhat ethereal beauty, glowing dimly in the dark and then brightly illuminated as the window is opened. After calculating on the computer whether the ice will be able to hold Paweł's weight, Krzysztof goes out onto the ice to check for himself. The flute strains begin again as he slides and jumps on the frozen pond. He sees the unknown man and his fire; the editing suggests that they exchange looks. This is the first indication that the man may be sharing the same space and time as the characters.

In the final twenty or so minutes of the film, Krzysztof is seen working on his papers before becoming concerned for his son and searching for him. The sequence begins with an aural intrusion of off-screen sound – an aeroplane passing. As the clock strikes, Krzysztof looks down at the stain that appears through his papers, spreading quickly. He picks up the bottle and the ink spills in a trail across his work. He is shown washing his hands in close-up, blue ink streaking across the white basin. A siren wails and the hands become motionless; Krzysztof looks up into a mirror, before we see him watching the ambulance from the window, his expression perhaps slightly puzzled. A neighbour rings asking whether Paweł is home as her son is missing; she ends the call with 'something's happened . . .'. As Krzysztof is going out of the door, a woman screams out a name, 'Jacek!', and tumbles down the stairs. As Sobchack has written, each moment deepens a sense of dread;[54] even though the events seem random and possibly irrelevant, they are woven into a temporality of expectation and momentousness that increases through time.

While these moments build a powerful tension, both Krzysztof and the camera delay being drawn toward their centre – the pond. One of the difficulties I have watching this sequence unfold is witnessing Krzysztof's reluctance to similarly rush off to *see*, drawing out the moments before he knows about, and before we are confronted with, the death of Paweł. As ambulances and parents rush to the scene, he attempts to remain calm, and the camera excruciatingly follows his attempts to track down Paweł, first at his teacher's flat, then with a radio, which only responds with the terrifying emptiness of static. When Krzysztof finds himself wanting to rush up the stairs, he pauses and makes himself count to ten to calm himself, a futile effort to impose a rational order on to the ceaseless, uncontrollable flux of time. Krzysztof enters the lift with an elderly gentlemen, who only wants to go to the first floor, and takes an age to shuffle out of the lift, starting back at the stoic Krzysztof. Even when Krzysztof appears at the lake, watching the emergency services working on the catastrophe, a hint from Paweł's friend takes him away again to the block, following a child who may know something about Paweł but whose hysterical mother refuses to allow to speak. This time he does not attempt to calm himself but hurtles up the stairs as they are taking the lift. As we watch Krzysztof speaking to various neighbours and searching for Paweł, it is impossible to pinpoint the moment at which he comes to realise that Paweł has suffered some catastrophe. As Wilson writes, 'we do not see the accident on the lake; instead it *bleeds* into the consciousness of Pavel's father'.[55] It is also difficult to pinpoint one single moment in which the death of Paweł is revealed; instead, this seeps through the images slowly and painfully like the gradually spreading ink stain.

    The devastating scene at the pond where Paweł's body is recovered has an aura of something mystical, as the gathered crowd kneel slowly in the dark. Krzysztof returns home to find the computer has turned itself on again. 'I am ready' it proclaims. The green screen of the computer is framed at one point so that it fills our screen also, such that our frame (of the film screen, television screen, or computer screen) constitutes its frame. In the context of Paweł's death, this moment of the computer's seemingly animate sensibility gains an inexplicable dimension that is both banal and terrifying. The scene changes to the church in the process of construction, bathed in blue light, as Krzysztof approaches the altar. The camera pans up to the painting of the Virgin Mary, before cutting to Krzysztof as he overturns the altar, sending the candles on top of it flying. In close-up, a candle tips over and begins dripping; the next shot, of the Virgin Mary's painted face with the wax dripping down on her cheek as though weeping, is an impossible shot in terms of diegetic spatial coherence. The candles were at the bottom rather than the top of the painting. Krzysztof takes the frozen holy water out of the stone basin and places it on his forehead. It is as though the film refuses to end, not with the kneeling or Krzystof's realisation, not with the computer, still not with the wax melting, not even with the disc, drawing out seemingly endlessly the pain and despair. The film finally ends as we are returned to the beginning, the television screen with Paweł's face in close-up as he skips through a distorted, slowed-down temporality, off screen.

Various interpretations have been suggested concerning the relationship between science and religion put forward by the film. Has Krzysztof, an atheist, been punished for his faith in technology rather than in God, to echo the question that Insdorf posits?[56] Is this the meaning that the Commandment, 'Thou shalt not have no other Gods but me?' colours the film with? Žižek argues that the 'lesson' of *Decalogue 1* is

> *not* that, when our reliance on the false idol of science fails us (embodied in the father's personal computer), we are confronted with a 'deeper' religious dimension; on the contrary, when science fails us, our religious foundation is also shattered – *this* is what happens to the desperate father at the end of *Decalogue 1*.[57]

However, I am more in agreement with Coates, who wrote in relation to the possibility that the computer somehow caused the accident on the lake, that 'the questions cannot be answered, or the film totalized'.[58] Extracting a 'lesson' from the film fails to encompass its uncertain temporal process, where images and events seem to continually seep out from the meaningful containers we may attempt to make for them. Ultimately, the painting of the Virgin Mary stares back at us just as opaquely as the 'ready' computer, and can neither comfort Krzysztof, nor provide viewers with a satisfactory conclusion. The film is full of images that, on the one hand, seem to taunt us with their richness of potential meaning – the dead dog, the milk bottle, the green computer screen, and finally the painted eyes of the Virgin Mary – while on the other hand are opaque, unknowing and unknown. Like Krzysztof, who was misled by signs that told him the lake was frozen enough, the viewer must also face the possibilities of uncertain signification.

Decalogue 2 has also been interpreted as a work full of symbolic meaning. The film begins as the building caretaker finds a dead rabbit on the ground, which has presumably fallen from one of the flats above. Commenting partly on this, Michael Timm writes 'when the heavens give some kind of sign, it is in the form of a rag, a rabbit (!) or suchlike, that falls to the ground. These objects are signs in a moral alphabet.'[59] Near to the beginning of the film we see Dorota plucking leaves off a plant and twisting the stalk downwards. It slowly begins to unwind upwards again. According to Insdorf the plant 'moves back up of its own accord, suggesting the life force that will reanimate her husband'.[60] At one stage Dorota puts out her cigarette in a box of matches, igniting them. The fire, Insdorf writes, 'flares symbolically'.[61] Soon after, she deliberately edges a glass full of tea off a table, which shatters onto the floor. Kickasola argues that this action marks a rupture to a communal ideal represented by the taking of tea with another person: 'these images carry a heavy metaphorical quality, typically expressing something vital lost (or draining) from a character'.[62] For Coates, a scene near the end of the film where a bee is shown slowly climbing its way out of a jar of compote where it had been drowning has 'the lengthy, contrived air of allegory'; 'allegorically it re-enacts the human escape from "certain" death'.[63] Insdorf agrees: 'like the plant stem, the bee's life force is of course symbolic of the husband's, whose recovery is nothing short of miraculous'.[64]

Decalogue 2 intertwines several stories of loss which resonate with each other. In Dorota's view of her situation, someone will have to die – if not her husband, then her unborn child. The film's gradual unfolding of her problem is interwoven with the doctor's own story of loss, told to his housekeeper in two 'instalments'; 'next instalment next week', he tells her, as though he were narrating his own *Decalogue*-type story. The first half of the story is told just after we see his housekeeper dusting around three aged photographs in one frame of a very young child, a baby and a woman. After they sit at a table, the housekeeper asks, 'What was it?', and the doctor replies that the child was teething. There is no other introduction into the story, neither is it placed for us in a temporal context. Simply, he continues that while the baby was teething, his father had lost a tooth, which his wife took as a bad omen: 'too many teeth in this household'. The story, for now, ends there. The doctor later turns the photograph to the wall when Dorota comes to question him, yet however much he may attempt to separate his own past from Dorota's present, the film will suggest that they are linked. In the next instalment of the story the doctor narrates how he went to work at the hospital, and when he came home, there was only a hole where the building had been: his family had been killed during the Second World War. As the doctor tells it, the surplus of teeth, the sign of impending disaster for his wife, was indeed a true omen.

The indeterminacy of potential signs of death or life is to a certain extent thematised in *Decalogue 2*. The doctor initially refuses to give a verdict on whether Andrzej will live or die, saying that he has often seen patients who should have died but nevertheless lived, 'and others die without reason'. Andrzej's prognosis is uncertain, but at a later stage, slides under a microscope indicate to the doctor that there is a 'progression', presumably of the illness. After the doctor narrates the ending of his story to his housekeeper, Dorota tells the doctor that she is having an abortion in an hour. He is now able to tell her that Andrzej has 'no chance' of living. Despite the fact that the film shows us the medical evidence, there are many rich resonances here that emerge from the story of the death of the doctor's own baby. As usual, Kieślowski does not push the connection or direct it in any one particular fashion, but it lingers over this moment. The doctor rescues an unborn baby but declares the certain death of the father, a reversal of the situation in which he was the sole survivor of the family. At the film's end, Andrzej, having survived despite the signs, comes into the doctor's office to express his gratitude, and says in a tone of wonder, 'We're going to have a baby . . . do you know what it means to have a child?' The camera focuses on the doctor's face as he says briefly, 'Yes, I do.' The film fades out. This resonant, lingering sadness comes in the midst of the affirmation of life – Andrzej's, and the child's. The moment is powerfully inscribed with the story of the loss of the doctor's family; this loss returns to haunt this scene with sadness.

Throughout the film, things seem to hover on some kind of threshold between existence and extermination, and if we are to see them as signs or omens of some kind, many do not point to one or the other, death or life, but rather modulate throughout the course of the film. The 'signs' of life or destruction have their own temporal narratives that interweave with one another. They have trajectories and paths that can change direction, just as Andrzej's movement towards certain death is seemingly reversed. If the doctor's cactus is appropriate to his prickly nature, as Insdorf states, it is also an object on a trajectory towards death.[65] It is 'sick', he tells his housekeeper, but she manages to salvage it. The leaves of Dorota's plant, deprived of life, are left at the bedside of her husband, who nevertheless regains his life. As Kickasola has pointed out, to simply interpret this image symbolically is to 'limit its power. Clearly there is a life–death image here . . . there is nothing quite like seeing it unfold, however'.[66]

Other objects move on inexorable paths towards destruction, for example, Dorota's flaming matchbox. The camera captures this in close-up in a slightly slowed motion as the flames leap from the box. There is a delay in the sound of the matches igniting which encourages us to attend to the aesthetic, cinematic presentation of this moment. Soon after, she rests her head on the table and pushes a full glass of tea towards its edge. The film cuts to the floor, where in slow motion we see first the saucer break, and then the glass, scattering fragments in all directions and splashing the liquid towards the camera.

One of the most frequently cited 'symbolic' moments in the film occurs when a bee struggles out of a compote jar, a movement from near death to life that has been said to parallel Andrzej's. Certainly, there is a resonance, although it can only be concretised retrospectively, once the film presents to us the recovered Andrzej. This symbolic association is only one way of considering this moment, however, and one that is rather reductive of its temporal progression. The moment of the bee's struggle is in fact embedded in a longer sequence, a duration marked out by one piece of music, but containing several different temporal rhythms. The sequence begins as Dorota stands in front of her Venetian blinds at night time; the camera is on the outside looking in at her. We hear extended violin notes, as there is a slow, long pan down the building. The camera takes in the dark greyness of the walls, drawing out those moments in between the times when it focuses on a face, or on an object, or something of importance to the narrative. We then see the doctor, his face distorted by a strange red light, seemingly looking directly into the camera. The violins continue as the camera pans sideways, blurring the surfaces from grey and black to white, again drawing out moments of illegibility. The camera then finds itself looking at Andrzej's face – it has condensed space through this continuous temporality marked by the music. As Andrzej turns his head tentatively, a piano sound enters the musical piece, the same as that heard on the soundtrack when Dorota destroyed her plant.

The camera pans across the room, blurring the space, eventually showing the watery, red compote with a spoon in it from which a bee is struggling against being submerged in the liquid. There is a cut back to Andrzej, before we see the bee slowly clamber up the spoon and onto the top of the glass. As the music continues, there is a cut to an orchestra; panning across the musicians in mid-shot, Dorota is soon shown amongst them, playing the violin. This shot reveals a schism between diegetic and non-diegetic music, a betweenness, whereby, although the music did not emanate from the previous images, it is endowed retrospectively with a diegetic purpose. The musical piece, drawn out in a continuous duration, has masked the condensation of narrative time. Dorota looks up from her violin and seems to smile towards someone in the audience, the next shot, however, brings us back to the hospital, as Andrzej shuffles into a doorway, knocks on a door, and the piece ends. The music has traversed from Andrzej's near-death, the bee's struggle, to his recovery.

Indeterminate Objects

My analysis of *Decalogue 1* may already have suggested the importance that the film, and critical writing on the film, places upon objects which resonate with an uncertain significance – the dead dog, the milk bottle, the ink bottle. These objects are framed in close-up, held in the shot just slightly longer than we are likely to need to simply recognise them. *Decalogue 2* also contains several moments in which the camera movements, slow duration and close-ups develop uncertain affects and significances around particular objects. Objects, or rather parts of objects, in Andrzej's hospital room in particular are endowed with an inexplicable intensity. After Dorota's first visit to the hospital, the film cuts to a close-up of a section of white-painted metal, a pipe or part of a bed frame, as water slowly drips onto it. The sound of the dripping seems amplified, as it traces the trajectory of the movement of the water with what Chion has called sound's 'temporal dynamic'.[67] The dripping water, as an irregular and unpredictable sound, 'puts the ear and the attention on constant alert . . . unsettling our attention through its unequal rhythm'.[68] The film cuts back to Andrzej, who, with effort, moves his head as if to look at the source of the sound, and the metal is then shown again, as though this is a shot/reverse-shot and eye-line match. However, this metal is only ever shown in close-up, and there is nothing to anchor it in a specific place around Andrzej, which unsettles spatial coherence. Andrzej's face in close-up is then shown again, as he turns his eyes upwards. The film then cuts to another detail of the room, an extreme close-up of some peeling plaster seeping water. Andrzej moves his head to the right, and the camera then pans slowly down the water dripping from the wall, until it comes to rest for several seconds on the leaves that Dorota had torn off the plant.

Throughout this sequence, we can hear Andrzej's laboured breathing and the constant dripping of the water. Everything seems to be melting, drop by drop, as we are presented with an intensified focus on tiny details of the space (presumably) around Andrzej. The next time Dorota comes to visit Andrzej, a similar sequence to the one described above is performed. She has already been there for some moments before, inexplicably, we hear a loud dripping sound. This time we see his face before we see the source of the sound, and he seems almost fearful. We can hear the breath catching in his throat. The film then shows us a section of pipe again, then his face, then another fixture in the wall dripping. The camera then pans down for several seconds showing us a white, textured wall, his pained breathing still audible, until we see what the water is dripping into – a reddish liquid that looks like watered-down blood. Several drops fall into this mixture as we watch. The dripping, as Insdorf has noted, is 'a graphic embodiment of slow-moving time'.[69]

Sobchack makes reference to Jacques Lacan's account of his 'epiphanic visual encounter' with a sardine can floating off the Brittany coast, which seemed to 'look back' and displace him, to argue that Kieślowski's objects also seem to 'look back' at viewers:

> a great many of Kieślowski's cinematic objects assert a signifying power and mysterious autonomy that emerge through the hyperbolic excess of ontic presence created

by both the camera's close-up framing of them and its hyperempirical detailing of their material presentness.[70]

The 'look back' of objects 'momentarily startles, intimidates and fixes us with its "irrational" autonomy', refusing 'human comprehension and reduction'.[71] Although Sobchack refers primarily to *Decalogue 1*, the 'mysterious autonomy' of objects is highlighted throughout the series. *Decalogue 4*'s privileged object is the mother's letter, which ultimately refuses to become intelligible. When the letter appears, it is accompanied by a brief musical piece that underscores its moment of appearance. There is a fundamental uncertainty regarding the status of the letter that has not been neatly resolved at the film's conclusion. When her father leaves for his trip, Anka finds the letter in the bottom draw of a cabinet. On the night of revelations, she gives him the letter, with both envelopes; we see this lying on the arm of the couch, and we see him looking at it. She then puts it back in this same bottom draw on top of a pile of objects already in there, not bothering to reinsert it into the larger envelope. When they decide to burn it, she goes to this same draw and pulls it out from the pile of objects. Now, however, we see the envelope and letter in the same state as we saw it by the river – the outer envelope has a slit, from which she pulls the mother's envelope out – as though it has transfigured itself.

In *Decalogue 8*, objects pulsate with memory. As Zofia tells Elżbieta, whenever she saw someone playing with a necklace, it would propel her into her memory of the Jewish child that she failed to hide during the war, who also played with a cross on a necklace. Elżbieta frequently touches two charms on her necklace, Jewish and Christian symbols. Memories around objects are rendered indeterminate, however. An important element that emerges in the story that Elżbieta tells to the class about her wartime experience (albeit in third person) is that she was offered a cup of tea, which she was not given time to drink. She recalls taking a sip of the tea, but then looking at her guardian and putting down the cup. When asked by Zofia whether she remembers any precise details of the apartment, the first thing she recalls are the teacups of fine porcelain, each one different. In Zofia's apartment, when they are about to have supper, the film frames a close-up of a gold teacup, which Elżbieta slowly draws towards her and then picks up. She pauses before drinking and the camera moves up to her face as she contemplates the cup. The clock chimes as she drinks, a reminder of time passing and time past.

Throughout *Decalogue 8*, Zofia is surrounded by objects that do not quite behave as they should: her lights flicker on and off, her car struggles to start. A crooked picture hangs on her wall. She adjusts it, but when she leaves the room it reverts to its crooked state. Elżbieta also adjusts the painting and it slides back off kilter as she leaves the frame. Haltof suggests that the painting indicates that 'the spotless picture of Zofia's life reveals one major stain that cannot be easily fixed'.[72] Although the camera does not focus on the painting unduly, its peculiar movement, as though possessed of an animation of its own, looks forward to *Decalogue 9*'s glovebox, and back to the objects endowed with a resonant intensity – the milk and ink bottles in *Decalogue 1*, as well as the computer that seems to turn itself on, the plant leaves and dripping pipes in *Decalogue 2*, and the letter in *Decalogue 4*. In *Decalogue 9*, as in *Decalogue 1*, objects seem to 'look back' at the characters and the viewer. The glovebox in Romek and Hanka's car behaves erratically, seeming to open and remain closed at will, as though communicating some kind of significance. After Romek has almost crashed his car near the beginning of the film, the glovebox opens in close-up, and refuses to shut again. The next time it opens, it yields up a physics textbook that we soon learn belongs to Hanka's lover, Mariusz. Romek puts it in the bin, but changes his mind and puts it back in the glovebox, which immediately opens again and refuses to close. The next time Romek tries to open it, he must hit it before it falls open, and the glovebox is empty, as though it has ingested the book.

Decalogue 10 is, in many ways, a film about objects that become more important than people, as well as about the peculiar fascination such objects hold. Throughout the film, stamps function as signs with fluctuating meaning and value. Short musical extracts are used to heighten the significance of these strangely beautiful signs. For example, when Artur and Jurek first open the cabinets that contain their deceased father's priceless albums, a high note on the violin extends over three separate close-ups and pans of the albums, medals and books. The music seems to inscribe significance into these shots, but we are not immediately made aware of the true value of the objects. The brothers speculate on their meaning and value; for Jurek, they signify 'all our misery, our mother's wasted life . . .'. Jurek chooses a series of three stamps with a German Zeppelin on them to give to his young son, ignorant of their price; the significance of the stamps is, for now, hidden from him.

A drumming beat is also used at certain points throughout the film. The ominous drum roll first occurs when Artur is entering the hall where the stamp collectors are buying and selling. However, it is difficult to distinguish from the ambient noise, and appears more like a rumble, an underlying threat that is not yet clear or fully audible. Three very brief rumbles, now clearly audible, recur when the brothers learn the value of the collection; one stamp could be (ultimately) exchanged for a car, another three for a flat. The collection itself is worth 'tens of millions'. As Kickasola writes, however, 'the focus, for the head of the Philatelic Association, is clearly not the monetary value of the collection, but the symbolism of the collection – the amount of work and dedication for which it stands'.[73] In the meantime, Jurek's son has done an exchange of his own; three valuable Zeppelin stamps for a large pile of worthless stamps, an exchange that provides physically more but significantly less.

The brothers attempt to conduct their own hermeneutic enquiry over the figures and symbols that fill their father's notebooks, coded text examining the whereabouts of various stamps, including the rose Austrian Mercury, needed to complete a series of three. As Kickasola writes, the signs in the father's journal 'prove a hermeneutic challenge similar to the task of interpreting the Scriptures'.[74] The buyer who had obtained the Zeppelin stamps offers to procure the Austrian Mercury stamp for them, but first requests that they undergo a medical examination. As they meet in the park to discuss the results, the camera watches them from behind a tree. As Insdorf writes, this shot suggests a point of view of someone spying on them, although we never see who, if, indeed, a human perspective is implicated at all.[75] Their meeting in the park reveals the necessity of a convoluted system of exchange – the person with the rose Austrian Mercury wants two stamps, owned by someone else in Szczecin, who wants another stamp, which is owned by the dealer in the park, who in turn wants a kidney for his sick daughter. The signs continue to circulate, each referring to the other, with a meaning that is not fixed, but fluctuates according to circumstance.

As Jurek is in the hospital having his kidney removed, the brothers are being robbed. The film presents a montage sequence of body parts and objects in close-up: hands being washed, a mask being fixed on to a face, a key being turned in a lock, a nurse's hat being discarded, hands being gloved, and then an image that does not seem to belong to this pattern – a blowtorch being fired up and burning through metal. The camera lingers on two halves of a bar topped by a bright orange glow. Cutting briefly to the doctor's face, presumably operating on Jurek, the film then shows us the massive black dog that the brothers had purchased for security being stroked by a gloved hand, continuing the patterning of hands. After this image, bloodied rags are thrown into a bowl, before three stamps are seen in close-up as a magnifying glass passes over each of them. The status of these mysteriously covetable objects is elevated by the music. The close-ups of their details through the glass and the black background detach them from their context while focusing on them intensely.

In the *Decalogue*, objects seem to be endowed with their own spatial and temporal trajectories, as though, to paraphrase Barthes, the films were stories of objects as well as of characters. If there is, as Žižek states, a motif in the *Decalogue* concerned with the 'invisible network connecting people' it is possible to also find such a thread in the *Decalogue*'s objects.[76] However, while the objects may become a sign of something other, we must also contend with their fundamental indeterminacy. Žižek states this in psychoanalytic terms: in analysis, he writes, it is assumed that everything that a patient says has a meaning; however, 'when we pursue the work of interpretation far enough, we encounter *sinthoms* . . . formations with no meaning . . . tics and repetitive features . . .'.[77] Žižek continues, 'underlying the "official" narrative development, these *sinthoms* form a dense texture (of visual motifs, gestures, sounds, colours) that provide substantial "tensile strength" to the narrative line'.[78] The objects that we encounter in the films have a certain flexibility; they may be co-opted into specific interpretations, but they may also resist meaning, remaining tangible, material and opaque.

Viewing Patterns

The *Decalogue* films continually unfold repetitions, doublings, symmetry, and patterns, returning us to questions of meaning and contingency: is there a meaningful relationship between moments, images or objects that are patterned or repeated, or is such symmetry coincidental? If we return to the idea that *Decalogue 1* seems at times to be 'declining' fluids – milk, water, coffee, wax – into different states – solid, liquid, frozen – then we may see a parallel of sorts with the older male figures that continually reappear in *Decalogue 4*. There is, of course, Anka's father, the teacher with whom she acts out a scene from *Romeo and Juliet*, her father's friend, who interrupts their conversation about their relationship, the two men in the photograph, one of whom could be her father, the extra reflection in the telephone, and the men who appear in the massive poster above her bed. Even the unknown man, his canoe echoing those in the poster, becomes part of this network. Is it just a coincidence that these men, real and virtual, circulate around Anka, or is it a 'sign' of her obsession with her father? The film refuses to let us know who her father is, let alone suggest answers to this more general, and perhaps more vexing, question.

Where *Decalogue 4* is peopled with older men, children, and young girls in particular, recur in *Decalogue 5*. For example, we see a picture of a young girl being drawn, before the camera cuts back to the girl herself, a movement from representation, image, to flesh, that cannot be carried out for the photograph Jacek carries in his pocket, which he can only enlarge.

He then attracts the attention of two young girls outside the café window by flinging coffee grinds against it. The taxi driver halts to let a group of children pass, some of whom wave towards the car. Images of young girls are multiplied in the photography store. This scene begins with a close-up of Jacek's face through glass, and then cuts to a photograph of a young girl in traditional Holy Communion outfit: white lace dress, white flowers in her hair, her gloved hands held together in prayer. The camera pans left to reveal more photographs of young girls, all dressed and posed similarly, variations of replicated images.

Patterns and repetitions in the mise-en-scène and editing seem to emerge as meaningful, yet tend to refuse a full explication of their significance, remaining recognisable but not necessarily wholly interpretable. At other moments, however, the way in which images are patterned can be seen to echo the concerns of a particular film. In *Decalogue 9* point of view shots are foregrounded and repeated; not all of them, however, indicate a person who looks. Two early sequences in the film, which structurally mimic each other with an important variation, can be offered as an example. After Romek has attempted to crash his car, the scene changes to night time. From behind rain-streaked glass somewhere inside the apartment, we can see Romek's car outside. There is a cut to the interior of the car (but also seen through the glass of the car window, from outside) of Romek looking back up at the flat window, which we can only see as a blur of lit-up glass through the windows and rain. Once he gets out of the car, Romek looks up again, and we are shown what he is looking at, the window seen more clearly. The next shot is from the lobby, where we can see Romek pacing outside, and soon Hanka enters into this shot as a reflection. Her reflection looks towards the camera, although we know that she is watching Romek. It is unclear how long she has been there; significantly, she says that she 'heard the car' rather than saw him approach. When the characters leave the frame, the camera pans slowly over the darkened building, before cutting to a shot in the lift, of Hanka's face illuminated by light, the rest of the frame in darkness. In the lift, the film performs a beautiful alternation of light and shadow; as the lift rises, Romek and Hanka's faces are illuminated in turn. The lighting is slightly out of sync with their conversation; it has its own temporal rhythm, its own duration.

A sequence the next morning provides an interesting point of comparison. The film frames the car through the apartment window again, as Romek walks towards it. This window then opens from off-screen space, behind and to the side of the camera, providing us with an uninterrupted view of the car, and explicitly revealing that we had been sharing Hanka's point of view. In a movement similar to the previous night's, Romek looks back around the car seat and waves. The reverse shot shows Hanka at the open window, waving back and then closing it. The structure of the shots is very similar to the first, except, this time, Hanka's presence implies that we share her point of view, imbuing the first sequence retrospectively with an even greater sense of uncertainty about who was seeing what. There are moments in the film that suggest a point of view from a specific character, as when Romek hides in the wardrobe and we see his partial view on to Hanka and her lover. Other moments, such as the first sequence described above, seem to suggest someone's vision or vantage point but no character is shown to occupy it. When Romek and Hanka have supper after his return, the camera peeps around a doorway. Several other shots of Romek are taken from behind window glass with seemingly no one looking out at him, for example, when he arrives and leaves the hospital, and when he disposes of Mariusz's textbook. This latter shot is partly occluded by the dark space of the window frame. The film's spaces seem to be surrounded by viewpoints, while deferring answers as to who, if anyone 'within' the film, is looking.

Like *Decalogue 9*, *Decalogue 6* thematises vision. In the film, Tomek spies on Magda from a distance, before collapsing this distance in a way that echoes Metz's fears of what might happen were the distance between viewer and object of vision elided: 'to fill in this distance would threaten to overwhelm the subject . . . to bring him to orgasm and the pleasure of his own body . . . hence putting an end to the scopic arrangement'.[79] Commentators on *Decalogue 6* have frequently drawn attention to Tomek's 'scopophilia'.[80] According to Insdorf, 'Kieślowski extends voyeurism to all the major characters, suggesting how easily one can take the place of the other'.[81] *Decalogue 6*, she writes, invites us 'to vicariously experience a gaze filled with longing'.[82] Haltof writes that 'the events in two-thirds of the film are represented through Tomek's eyes', including 'the voyeuristic shots of Magda in her apartment'.[83] The camera, he continues, 'carefully replicates the perspective of a person watching'.[84] In several moments when he looks through his telescope, the lighting keeps his face in shadow while encircling his eyes, as though reducing him momentarily to a pair of eyes.

We might expect that in this film, where a character is shown obsessively looking, the camera may most powerfully present a point of view associated with the character. The film, however, troubles a secure link between character and point of view. In the opening scenes of *Decalogue 6*, Tomek is seen breaking into a school to steal a telescope, a more powerful replacement, we later learn, for a set of binoculars. Later on, a pattern of shots will be repeated whereby Tomek is shown seated at his desk looking through the telescope, and then shots are seen through the telescope that approximates what he is looking at – Magda in her apartment. However, the scene where he steals a telescope is *already* cross-cut with surveillance images of Magda, similar to those that we later associate with Tomek's look through the telescope. Once again, we are faced with indeterminate images – are we seeing Tomek's future look, or is the camera asserting its own viewing presence? Furthermore, the images that Tomek apparently sees through the telescope, and which the film presumably shows to us, are actually edited, and thus move away from approximating Tomek's gaze. That is, there are cuts within the surveillance scenes themselves, not just cuts from Tomek to Magda's apartment. For example, when Magda is entertaining a man in her apartment, Tomek phones to report a gas leak so that she will be interrupted. We watch Tomek watching the arrival of the workers. The camera approximates his look through the telescope as it pans up the building, locating them in the stairwell. Then, however, there is a cut to Magda and her lover on the floor in the next room, a cut back to the men, a cut back to the couple, and further cuts between Magda's lover and Magda talking to the workers. This is presented, then, as a cinematic construction, not just an approximation of a human perspective. A disjunction appears that dislocates a comfortable alignment between image and diegetic source.

In *Decalogue 6*, a major narrative event is brought about seemingly by random coincidence. Tomek persuades Magda to go on a date with him. Afterwards, they see their bus pulling in to the bus stop. Magda has a proposition: if they make the bus, Tomek can go home with her. They run for the bus but it pulls away, and they seem to miss it. A second later, however, it stops, and Tomek does indeed go to Magda's house. Here he experiences sexual embarrassment and later slits his wrists, an experience which seems to make him stop spying on Magda. The bus incident which led to this seems a random occurrence, and yet a certain patterning of the mise-en-scène elevates particular details of the film as though they were indicators of some kind of meaningful system. Colouring the mise-en- scène with red and blue seems to link the two characters, as though suggesting their meetings are not random but somehow part of a pattern. Circular imagery is prevalent in the film, reflecting one of its major thematic and material foci – the seeing eye. The post office has circles cut out of its glass, through which we see Magda, who has a circular reflector in her window; the round shape of the telescope reflects that of Magda's binoculars, and small red dots even adorn the building doors.

The characters, too, act out circular rhythms: Magda uses a toy on a string to circle around her and Tomek's palm. Tomek runs around in a circle after Magda agrees to go out with him, a movement that the camera mimics. It is as though the characters were unwittingly echoing the shapes of their environment. The narrative itself has something of a circular structure to it. Tomek spies on Magda, then she attempts to look across at his flat with binoculars after he leaves her flat. The unknown man appears twice, first in the moment of Tomek's greatest joy, when he spins wildly in a circle, and second in the moment of his greatest despair, when he flees Magda's flat. Each ventures into the space of the other, first Tomek into Magda's apartment, then the reverse. Spatially we are in the same place at the end as at the beginning – the post office. Temporally, however, the circle does not close. The pattern breaks when Tomek reveals that he no longer spies on Magda. The ending reverberates with the sadness of their missed encounter.

Decalogue 10 is permeated by patterning, doubling and symmetry, by visual and narrative echoes of the doubling of brothers. The stamps come in series which must be completed, each a variation on the other. Scenes proceed according to a repetition-variation. Both brothers go to see the stamp buyer in his shop, both then in succession tell the police officer that they suspect the other. The giant black dog that Artur purchases has its double in the dealer's shop. When Jurek exits the post office towards the end of the film, he sees another stamp collector, who Czesław owed money to, walking an identical dog. Drumbeats and cymbals rumble on the soundtrack as this man meets another, the stamp dealer from the shop, also walking a massive black dog. This is a moment of revelation, it seems, for both brothers, indicated by their expressions, which are seen in close-up, first Jurek then Artur, adding a further symmetry to the scene. At the end of the film, the brothers confess to each other that both had suspected the other. In close-up, the camera shows us three stamps laid out on the table that Artur bought. Jurek then matches them with identical stamps, creating a new series. The film ends on a symmetrical shot of the two brothers, laughing, foreheads pressed together over the stamps. Even the credit music, the rock song which inverts the Ten Commandments in its instructions to kill and steal, returns here to bookend the film, and completes a series of its own – the *Decalogue* series itself.

Music and Sound

The intensity of the films is frequently extended through music and sound. Kieślowski and Preisner had a close working relationship; the composer worked with the filmmaker from the very beginning rather than illustrating the films after they were finished. Each film has a different sound, and the musical motifs used for each tend to have several variants that are played throughout. Claudia Gorbman has argued that music is most commonly used in films 'to ward off the displeasure of uncertain signification'. That is, film music can be so strongly codified that 'it can bear a similar relation to the images as a caption to a news photograph. It interprets the image, pinpoints and channels the "correct" meaning of the narrative events depicted.'[85] Preisner's music and the soundtracks for the films, however, rarely create such an obvious indication of the narrative and thematic 'meanings' of the films, although at times music and sound suggest a direction of thought and of emotion that is traced out in a musical trajectory, as well as extending an affective intensity through sound.

In *Decalogue 5*, for example, the music heard when Jacek is wandering the streets of Warsaw is what Chion has called 'empathetic'. It creates an emotional resonance that persists despite the film's presentation of a visually ugly world 'covered in urine' (an effect achieved by way of a green lens over the camera.) The piano and violin piece has a melancholy tone, echoing visual suggestions of his loneliness and isolation (for example, the film contrasts his solitary figure with a group of laughing youths). The music shares in Jacek's feelings, 'express[ing] its participation in the feeling of the scene', to appropriate Chion's words.[86] Significantly, the music stops abruptly when Jacek moves from doing something seemingly innocent to what might be more closely connected to his future crime. In the first case, the music stops when the film reveals that he is watching taxis, in the second case, it ends more abruptly when he puts the metal bar that he will use for killing on the table at the photography store. If the music is in some way empathetic, then these cessations seem to suggest that empathy will only be taken so far.

In the opening of *Decalogue 3*, the configuration of image and sound echoes the film's concerns with isolation and exclusion. The film opens with an image of blurred coloured lights; on the soundtrack, a drunken man slurs his way through a Christmas carol, before asking plaintively, 'Where is my house?' While the image is obscured, the soundtrack is perfectly clear, and we can hear the man stumbling as he walks. A disjunction thus appears between the audible, concrete aural realm and the blurred visual space. The image eventually resolves into figuration; we do not see the source of the sound, however, but rather city lights. The drunken man is, for now, excluded from our vision, though he will appear later, retrospectively giving this voice a body. Subsequently, viewers are excluded from understanding characters' motivations and actions. The film's narrative may conclude with Ewa and Janusz parting on good terms, but the music played over the credit sequence extends the film's uncertainty through to its very conclusion. It consists of the same Christmas hymn sung by the drunk at the film's beginning. It was also sung at the midnight mass attended by Janusz, his family, and Ewa. This was, indeed, the first sighting they had of each other, before she interrupted his familial idyll. Then it was sung by many voices together in communion, here, a single instrument, a glockenspiel, traces a movement through the hymn hesitantly, as though unsure of the next note. The instrument is then joined by an orchestral or electronic undertone, but rather than complementing the instrument, it adds an unsettling sense of ominousness.

Decalogue 9's music first enters the soundtrack after Romek nearly crashes his car, and it also times the length of his standing in the rain, unable to return home. The piano refrain is extended through time as Romek paces outside. The film specifically draws attention to the affective force of its music. Romek's patient, the opera singer, introduces Romek to composer van den Budenmayer (a fictional musician whose 'works' are composed by Preisner). In Romek's flat, a close-up shows a record player as we hear the same piano piece again. This time, however, the music is allowed to develop, only retrospectively indicating that the refrain we were hearing at the beginning is part of an opera, opening a moment of between-ness when non-diegetic music modulates into the diegetic. The music in the film, to use Sowińska's words, explicitly 'presents itself as a work of art'.[87] In the fictional world of *Decalogue 9*, van den Budenmayer's music is so beautiful that one would risk death to be able to sing it. The singer hums part of a van den Budenmayer opera for Romek. A close-up of his face registers an affective disturbance, after which the camera focuses on the singer, moving across her body as she uses her fingers to count out the rhythm. The camera fixates on her hand in close-up as it comes down to knead her knee, as though the image is to endow the music with a physical, bodily tangibility, as well as reminding us of the fragility of her own body.

An aspect of *Decalogue 9*'s soundtrack that is less frequently commented upon is its use of silence, which draws attention to the passage of time. In the scenes ending with Romek's suicide attempt, the musical sequence is composed of competing rhythms and instruments; initially, it is a low-toned mournful melody, then the high, sharp tones of the violins enter in counterpoint. The film cuts between Romek pedalling furiously on his bicycle, Hanka on the bus (returning from her ski trip in the fear that something has happened to Romek), and the unknown man. The road Romek is on is unfinished and he and his bicycle are propelled over the edge onto the sand below. After he lands, there is silence, a silence shared between all three characters as the camera shows us each one in turn: Hanka in close-up looking straight into the camera, Romek's head on the sand, and the unknown man in the distance. The silence stretches in time, broken eventually by the ticking of the bicycle wheel as it turns over, but then this also comes to a halt, and the silence stretches on as the camera rises above Romek's splayed body, back up onto the road, and begins to reverse along the white painted line. Another interruption cuts into the rhythm of this movement; namely, a cut to a bus along the road, where the camera is still positioned on the roadway. The sound is a startling auditory intrusion into the silence. But then it too is allowed to fade away as it retreats from view, leaving another moment of silence, stretching out the moments before we are returned to narrative concerns.

Temporality, Narrative, and Affect

Developing Uncertainty

The films of the *Decalogue* series develop gradually, allowing insights into the identities of the characters and their relationships to emerge slowly. Slow temporal progression, in which narrative meanings are withheld or rendered uncertain, can serve to move viewers away from 'actualised objects', to use Colebrook's words, towards an attention to 'the very flow of images', and to the experience of passing time.[88] The films unfold narratives and significances, but through the very gradualness of their development, highlight this very operation of unfolding, of hesitation, in which, as in duration, 'not everything is presented all at once'.[89] As Kickasola has written, Kieślowski often sacrifices clarity of plot and characterisation 'for the sake of pace and resonance', while also 'preserv[ing] other long moments of experience' that contribute little to narrative progression as traditionally conceived.[90]

In *Decalogue 2*, meaning and significance develop slowly and are allowed only gradually to build upon each other, while the time of both ordinary and unusual actions is extended and often intensified through close-ups. In the early scenes, the doctor is shown performing everyday actions – examining his cactus, turning on the radio, boiling water, filling the bath. At this point he weakens, and the camera captures his hand in close-up as he steels himself against the bathtub. Kickasola interprets this image symbolically. The doctor's hand, he writes, is 'grasping for more than physical support. The dissociated, abstract feeling the shot yields empowers it with metaphorical force . . . the doctor represents old, hardened Poland, weary with fatigue, afraid to hope'.[91] Rather than see it as a symbolic moment, however, we can consider the way in which this weakening – what Trotter has termed a 'residue of undefined feeling' – carries over the subsequent scenes of the film, a film that will crawl thickly through lethargic states, such as Dorota's waiting, her depression and Andrzej's sickness.[92] Through the first ten minutes of the film, the actions proceed slowly. As the doctor leaves his house, a woman is shown smoking in the corridor. The doctor is seen going out and then returning, noting that the woman is still there. She asks to speak to him about her husband but he turns her away. In her flat, she reads a letter, then scrunches it up. To the sound of a bird trilling, the doctor's housekeeper cleans his flat. He begins to tell her the story about his past. Encountering Dorota again, he tells her she can come to see him. We know that she wants information about her sick husband, lying on the doctor's ward, but it is only twenty-seven minutes into the film that we are made aware of the crux of the ethical problem at stake – her pregnancy, and hence her need for the doctor's definitive verdict on Andrzej's chances of life.

Decalogue 3, in which Ewa attempts to endure a measured chunk of clock time amongst the traces of a partially fabricated past, has a similarly gradual temporal development and only slowly reveals elements of narrative significance. The film initially shows Janusz and his family at home, then at midnight mass, where Janusz sees Ewa, and then at home again. The camera focuses on the softly-lit interior of Janusz's apartment from outside the window, until a shadow creeps across this view, between the window and the camera, a shadow soon revealed to be Ewa's silhouette as she watches Janusz from outside and then moves towards the doorbell. Ewa initially appears to Janusz as a reflection in the glass door to the building, an image from his past that materialises in front of him. The film will gradually reveal the details of their past affair to us; we learn, for example, that Ewa suspected Janusz of orchestrating Edward's knowledge of the affair to get rid of her. Tension builds between them as they search for Edward through the night, before arriving at the flat that Ewa and Edward are supposedly sharing. There is a beautiful play of reflections as Ewa is preparing the apartment to look as though Edward still lives there. We see Janusz's reflection in the window as he watches her do this, although she does not see it. Christmas lights, ubiquitous in the film, can again be seen through and reflected in her window. The lighting adds to a sense of insubstantiality, emphasising the fantasy space that she has created for display. Ewa clearly fakes signs of Edward's presence, removing a razor from a cupboard and placing it near the sink. This is perhaps the first definite indication that Ewa may be lying, and viewers are presumably expected to review what they have seen previously in light of this; the past of our viewing must shift in relation to newly revealed significances.

Eventually, Ewa and Janusz end up at a railway station at 7 a.m. and Ewa reveals the truth: Edward left her the night he caught her with Janusz, and now has a new family. Suicidal at the prospect of facing anther Christmas Eve alone, she promised herself that if she could keep Janusz by her side until 7 a.m., by whatever means, she would not kill herself. The revelation of the intentions behind Ewa's actions again encourage a retrospective reassessment of what we have seen previously. Several writers, however, have expressed dissatisfaction with what they believe is, in Coates's words, 'an oversimplified process of "detection"'. According to Coates, the film 'feels laboriously contrived, its ending merely prompting a weary statement: "so that's why she . . .". The film is less an illumination of Ewa's condition than a lengthy postponement of its revelation.'[93] According to Žižek, the film reduces the viewer to 'the position of the observing detective who, on the basis of sparse clues, has to guess what is really going on with Ewa'.[94] Kickasola, on the other hand, has noted the importance of the duration of 'postponement' as theme, arguing that Ewa's salvation is 'a remarkably existential salvation – a duration of time, a getting through'.[95]

Coates and Žižek are in danger of oversimplifying the film, as though solving the 'mystery' of Ewa's actions somehow finalises the film. In fact, the film proceeds at a level of indeterminacy that encourages viewers to be continually and actively questioning the nature and possibilities of significance, not just in the relationships between Ewa, Janusz and Edward, but also in narrative events. For example, before Ewa arrives at Janusz's flat, she parks her car near a snowy lawn with a Christmas tree, and watches as a child in striped pyjamas runs out of a building, across the lawn and towards the large, lit-up tree. The child is caught by someone in uniform and is hauled back again. Towards the end of the film, when Ewa has indicated how isolated she has felt on Christmas Eve, she begins to tell Janusz about the child that she saw earlier, 'when I was driving to the church, I saw a boy'. At this point the film cuts from her face in close-up, to a small figure on the platform below, looking down the tunnel, and who seems to be wearing striped pyjamas. Two security guards approach him, and the film cuts back to Ewa, who continues: 'he escaped from hospital in his pyjamas . . . they caught him'. The small figure on the platform echoes the child in the story and the child we saw earlier. This incident is highly ambiguous, and, just at the moment when Ewa seems to have revealed herself most fully to Janusz, adds an element of inexplicability to the film that seems to mock our ability to wrap things up.

If *Decalogue 3* is in some ways about enduring time, *Decalogue 4* raises questions as to its reversibility, as well as continually reversing narrative information in a way that puts meaning into flux. Before the credit music of *Decalogue 4* has entirely faded away, we hear the opening note of a musical refrain, a low ominous sound. It continues as we see a darkened room and a girl's profile lightening into view as she looks out of a window with Venetian blinds. Over the music, we hear a lighter being struck, before the scene cuts to a man holding a lighter to his cigarette, also facing a window. We see her, that is, and we hear him. From the very beginning, then, a certain permeability of boundaries is suggested – between non-diegetic credit music and film, image and sound, that proleptically articulates one of the film's themes – the crumpling of boundaries between the categories of 'father' and 'daughter'.

At the beginning of the film, a young woman tenderly kisses a sleeping man. The relationship between them is unclear at first. We see the man throw a pot of water on her in an Easter Monday ritual. As she stands cowering in the bath, the man casts an extended look at her figure, her white nightdress becoming translucent from the water and clinging to her frame. It is just after this sequence that she calls him 'dad', which seems to solidify the nature of their relationship. After the father, Michał, goes away for a short trip, Anka becomes obsessed with a sealed envelope she has found amongst his possessions. 'To be opened after my death' is written on the front. After some hesitation, she opens this at the riverbank, and finds inside another envelope with different handwriting, 'to my daughter Anna'. She is about to open this when she sees the unknown man, who has been canoeing on the river. The word 'gondola' can just be glimpsed on the boat, which seems perverse in the bleak riverside setting, but like the *Romeo and Juliet* play that is rehearsed by Anka later in the film (in which she cannot understand as an actress why she loves the younger man but snaps into focus very quickly when the older instructor takes charge of the scene) are allusions to a romantic tradition that becomes relevant for Michał and Anka's relationship. Seeing the unknown man, his face framed against the white diamond shape of his boat, she pauses and we do not see her cut open the letter. Back at home, she sifts through her mother's things in the basement, finding a photograph of her mother with two men and another woman, none of whom are named.

Anka then copies the handwriting on the envelope addressed to her onto an identical envelope that she finds amongst her mother's possessions. The reappearance of the ink bottle from *Decalogue 1* is somewhat threatening, recalling the tragic destruction of family that this film performed. We never see Anka actually opening and reading the letter, but the next scene encourages us to assume that in the ellipsis between one scene and the next, Anka has read and memorised it, as she recites the letter's contents to her father when he returns from his trip. According to Anka's recitation, the letter reveals that Michał is not her true father. The significance of the scenes between father and daughter that we witnessed at the beginning may now shift in our understanding, as we reverse through what we have seen. Simultaneously, Michał and Anka reverse through their relationship as father and daughter, and in some sense reverse out of it, as they reveal a complex mutual attraction that both have struggled with. About the photograph, Michał says that 'one of these two men could be your father'. The question of reversibility is introduced into the dialogue. Michał says to Anka that, 'I was away from home, I left you here alone, because I wanted something irreversible to happen', something that might put an end to the complexity of their relationship. Anka reveals that she aborted a child because, 'I never wanted anything irreversible.'

The next morning Anka panics when she wakes and finds her father gone. She crosses to the window and flings it open, the reverse, as Coates notes, of a scene at the beginning of the film, where, also in her nightdress, she closed the window. In recalling the opening, the ending tantalisingly suggests the possibility of 'the past's undoing' that has been thematised in the film.[96] Spotting her father from the window, she runs after him and tells him that she made up the contents of the letter, and in fact never opened her mother's envelope. The unknown man reappears here, once again carrying his white canoe on his back. The moments of his appearance seem to link two moments in which Anka's conscience gets the better of her. However, it also performs the possibility of reversal again – the first time we saw him, he was walking towards Anka, and towards the camera; this time, he is shown mostly walking away from her and from the camera. Anka and Michał decide to burn the letter, but a tiny fragment of it remains, which Anka reads out loud, an uncertainty in the words themselves as well as in their meaning: '"My darling daughter, I want to . . . show you? ... tell you. I would like to tell you something very important. Michał isn't . . ." the rest is burnt'.

As she reads the letter, the camera moves away from the characters and pans slowly across the space of her bedroom, focusing first on the heavily bearded face of the man in the poster, grinning or grimacing in an athletic gesture. The camera moves down to pick up a smaller image of a man canoeing in the poster, moves across her bed and across the photograph of her mother and her male companions on a chest of drawers, revealing each face in turn. One of these faces seems to double itself, reflected in the red plastic telephone next to the photograph. O'Sullivan has speculated on the photograph and the uncertain significance that comes from this strange reflected face, writing, 'not only are we in doubt, but we are in doubt as to what we are doubting: is it the nature of the thing itself or is it the motivations of the director?'[97] The camera ultimately refuses to show us what the burnt letter will also refuse, the identity of Anka's father. Whether Michał is, or is not, her father, remains indeterminate.

Present Pasts

Several of the films question the integrity of present moments, suggesting instead the possibility that the present always retains 'a reservoir of connections with the past as well as a close anticipation of the imminent future', to cite Grosz.[98] Where *Decalogue 4* questions the reversibility of the present moment even as it retraces the past between a father and daughter, in *Decalogue 5*, the weight of the past presses on to the present, a past that is continuously hinted at but not explicated until the film's final scenes. This is not to say that the past becomes accessible, but rather that its traces continually impinge upon the present. *Decalogue 5* begins with several temporal and spatial inconsistencies. Uniquely in the series, the guitar music that is played in the credit sequence of each film is absent in *Decalogue 5*. Instead, we hear a disembodied male voice speculating on human nature and the law.

When the film begins, we see a man, the lawyer Piotr, reflected in a mirror, although he is not speaking. The temporal status of this voice is ambiguous – is it an interior monologue, or is it a future speech, perhaps from the interview that follows? For several seconds, his voice continues over images of a young man wandering around Warsaw's Old Town, as though designating him as, in part, the subject of his words about the death penalty, which he will indeed later become as he is hung for murder. The 'present' of this sequence thus has, to use Bergson's words, 'one foot in the future'.[99] *Decalogue 5* initially shows us Jacek, Waldek and Piotr in three different spaces. The cross-cutting between them seems to suggest that these various 'presents' are simultaneous. However, this impression may be misleading. Later on in the film, Piotr reveals that he had been in the same café as Jacek on the day of the murder, which places the images of Piotr and Jacek as occurring on the same day, but not, at least at this point, simultaneously.

Before the film brings these characters together (when Jacek enters the driver's taxi, kills him, and is defended by Piotr), there is a slow accumulation of violent and cruel episodes. Waldek abandons the pregnant Dorota and recovered Andrzej who are waiting for his taxi, leers at a young girl working at a grocery stand, and deliberately frightens a man walking his dogs so that one of them escapes. Jacek throws a rock from a bridge, which causes a traffic accident, and pushes a man into a urinal. An expectation of greater violence is gradually created, aided by close-up shots of Jacek winding the rope that he will use to kill the driver around his hand, and cutting it to size in the café. In the series in general, we often watch characters performing actions that will become more significant, though rarely entirely transparent, retrospectively, such that we must bring our own viewing pasts to bear on the present images. During his wanderings through Warsaw, Jacek goes to a photography store where he asks to get a picture enlarged, of a young girl at her Holy Communion. We are not told who the girl is or her relationship to Jacek. However, when he enters the shop and approaches the woman at the desk, he says, 'I have this . . .'. Instead of placing the picture on the table, he puts down the metal bar, then the rope, linking the instruments of his murder with the girl and the photograph.

After his incarceration and just before his death, Jacek reveals to his lawyer that the photograph was of his sister, Marysia, who died when Jacek and his friend became intoxicated, and the friend later ran her over accidentally with a tractor. The fact that he himself has killed a driver is a significant, though unclarified, aspect of the film. According to Esther Rashkin, 'Jacek acts out, in a murderous repetition compulsion, the paradoxically restorative annihilation of the friend who killed Marysia in an internally logical, though completely psychotic, belief that if he kills his friend, Marysia will not have died.'[100] The viewer is thus required to 'perform a retrospective reviewing of the film from end to beginning', which is echoed in the backward looks that recur through the film, such as Jacek looking behind him through the crook of his arm at the taxi rank.[101] Rashkin suggests that 'there are seemingly inexplicable things in the narrative . . . that become explicable or meaningful if read with a backward or retrospective gaze . . . an anasemic move back toward prior unseen dramas and significations'.[102] I am not convinced that things become entirely explicable or meaningful, but they certainly encourage a reflection on the association of past to present, both in Jacek's life and in the timespan of our viewing of the film.

Before leaving the photography store, Jacek asks, 'Is it true that you can tell from a photograph whether the person's dead or alive?', to which the shopkeeper answers, 'Someone's been telling you nonsense.' As Garbowski has noted, the discussion about the photograph is 'a strange twist on Barthes' view of the photograph as a memento mori'.[103] Barthes locates a doubled temporality in the photographic image. Examining a photograph of an assassin about to be executed, Barthes wrote, 'I read at the same time: *This will be* and *this has been*; I observe with horror an anterior future of which death is the stake . . .'.[104] Like *Mirror*'s archival footage of the soldiers at Lake Sivash, the photograph of Jacek's sister intertwines multiple temporalities. Her death has been, but is yet to come in the photograph. It is an image of the past, but, as Mulvey writes, 'once time is "embalmed" in the photograph, it persists, carrying the past across to innumerable futures as they become the present'.[105] It is an image that will return to haunt the film, as, just before his death, Jacek asks to have the enlarged photograph delivered to his mother, after his death.

Decalogue 8 begins with another spatio-temporal dislocation, a sequence that is unanchored to narrative, meaning or theme for the first section of the film. While melancholy, folkish violin music and the sound of footsteps are heard on the soundtrack, we see what briefly seems to be a point-of-view shot – of grey walls shot with a handheld camera – before an adult's and child's hands join in front of the camera as they walk through a courtyard. We get a brief glimpse of a little girl's face as she turns back towards the viewer. There is not much to indicate that this scene is a flashback, it is just something that does not yet fit into the narrative. The following shot is highly contrasting: bright green leaves fill the screen as birds sing.

In her class about 'ethical hell', Zofia asks for contributions from students, and one tells the story from *Decalogue 2*. During this story, the film cuts between Zofia and Elżbieta looking at each other, in moments that are permeated with an, as yet, uncertain significance. At the conclusion of the student's story, Zofia suggests that the life of the child 'is the most important factor'. This seems to prompt Elżbieta to contribute the next story, which she announces to be a true one. A six-year-old Jewish girl being hidden in 1943 by Poles must be moved to another hideout; she is taken by an adult to the home of a young Catholic couple, who then refuse to hide her, giving the excuse that they cannot bear false witness (a direct reference to the eighth Commandment). As she speaks, the camera pans from Elżbieta's left to the end of the lecture theatre, picking up the listening faces. There are some empty spaces at the end of this row. When the camera pans left again not long after, one of these spaces is filled by the unknown man, listening, and then looking into the camera. As the story continues, close-ups on Zofia's face become tighter as her expression becomes more evidently disturbed. In the next shot of the lecture theatre, after Elżbieta has finished her story, the unknown man has gone. The story that is being narrated within the film is given import through the man's presence, his appearance and disappearance remaining a moment difficult to explain in diegetic terms.

Elżbieta's story of the child being led from place to place by an adult may now propel the viewer back into the past of our viewing as well as the past more generally; we may begin to build a context for the opening image. This is assisted by the fact that, as the students file out of the classroom and the camera continues to hold its focus on Elżbieta, the music from the opening sequence returns. All other sounds of the lecture theatre are silenced, making that of the violin stand out. In the next shot, the camera pans across a room to locate Zofia. The violin music continues across these two shots, binding the characters together in a shared history. The jolted hand-held camera movement from the opening shot returns as Zofia walks towards Elżbieta in the corridor. A point-of-view shot from Zofia's perspective moves towards Elżbieta unnaturally quickly, emphasising the sense that things are coming to some kind of important juncture.

Elżbieta and Zofia do not only talk about the past, but literally go over the same ground, as Zofia takes Elżbieta to the building in which she lived during the war, and in which she seemingly abandoned Elżbieta. As Elżbieta walks into the courtyard, short, staccato violin sounds can be heard, imbuing the scene with a tension that not only conveys the dramatic nature of this process of remembering in the physical space of the past, but also a hint of the fear that was present in the original moment. Elżbieta then hides so that Zofia must now find her, as though attempting to somehow reverse the action in which she was abandoned. The truth about why Zofia did not hide Elżbieta follows this seemingly cathartic episode, but, as Zofia states, there are 'banal' reasons for this refusal: they had information that the people who were ultimately to hide her were working for the Gestapo, and would have destroyed the underground network that Elżbieta and her husband were working for, putting many lives at risk. Despite this explanation, the film ends on an uncertain note. Elżbieta has attempted to speak to another former member of the underground, now a tailor, who helped her during the war. He, however, refuses to speak about the war. The two women talk and smile outside his shop, but for the film's final images, the camera remains with the tailor as he watches them. The camera remains, that is, in a space of uncertainty and silence, amidst a refusal to speak and give definite meaning to an experience.

Painful Duration

Negative responses to the *Decalogue* films are not surprising considering that the narratives of the series tend to revolve around death, mourning, loss and sadness. Insdorf has called the *Decalogue* 'ten short films about mortality', and indeed, almost every episode features either a direct exposition of death and/or loss, or the possibilities of death and annihilation, in many cases involving children, which heightens the atmosphere of threat and vulnerability.[106] It is not just the fact of the films revolving around difficult themes that is significant, it is also the way in which such themes or moments are extended, sometimes agonisingly, through time. The extended duration of such moments or sequences can be seen in both affective and emotional terms.

As I stated in Chapter 1, Massumi has defined emotion as a kind of subjective fixing of an experience, an intensity that is recognised as proceeding from a particular cause, an intensity that is thus localised and understandable. Consider, for example, an early moment from *Decalogue 3*, in which Krzysztof from *Decalogue 1* meets Janusz, dressed as Santa Claus, on the threshold to their apartment building. This moment encourages us to recall Krzysztof's recent traumatic loss of his son, as he prepares to spend Christmas Eve without him. The haggard-looking Krzysztof brings an air of mourning with him. After Janusz enters the building, the camera lingers on Krzysztof as he moves around to Janusz's window. We see and hear Janusz's children squeal with delight, but as the camera pans to frame the window from Krzysztof's point of view, the idealised scene is permeated by sadness. It is a kind of sadness which may be located in the contrast between Krzysztof's loss and Janusz's family's happiness. It is, in other words, an emotional moment.

Affect, on the other hand, is a felt intensity that one cannot necessarily pin down to a specific cause, something that cannot be understood as emanating from one particular moment or image, something that grows in force and escapes from emotional categories. One example occurs at the beginning of *Decalogue 10*. The film opens with a burst of sound, a rock band playing to an appreciative audience (apart from a man who is attempting to push through the crowd, which we later understand to be Jurek, the brother of Artur, who is singing). The music fades over a cut to the interior of a small room with a roughly made single bed. As the camera pans relatively slowly over an empty chair and the empty bed, a low musical note is drawn out, before very high synthesised sounds, like electronically manipulated screams, enter the soundtrack. The camera continues to move towards a fish tank, illuminated against a window emitting a blue light of dawn or dusk. The camera moves close to the tank, until it is peering right down into it, as the musical screams gather force until ceasing for a second of silence as we look upon the floating dead bodies of fish. These can be read narratively (no one has been able to feed the fish so they have died) and symbolically (they stand in for the dead man whose empty bed also suggests absence), but neither of these interpretations captures the disquieting force of the camera's slow movement to the strains of the music. There is no emotional resonance per se, as the image is as yet unlocalised, unfixed. Instead, it resonates with pure, indefinable, affect.

In the duration of the film experience, I have argued, affect and emotion cannot be so neatly separated. They continually bleed into one another, and transformations are effected from one to the other. There are many moments in the *Decalogue* films that exhibit this modulation between affect and emotion. In *Decalogue 3*, for example, affect and emotion emerge around a camera movement similar to that in *Decalogue 10*, when Ewa visits her aunt in a care home. This is an emotional scene for Ewa; her aunt is losing her memory and does not recognise her as an adult. She falls asleep while Ewa places a Christmas gift in her lap, a pair of gloves that, as Kickasola writes, resemble 'limp, helpless, empty hands'.[107] Ewa smoothes her aunt's head one last time and exits the frame. The camera remains, focusing over the aunt's head on to the window, towards which it begins to track slowly. We hear Ewa opening the door; a burst of song from the other room (Christmas carols being sung by the other care home residents) is heard on the soundtrack, and fades when the door is closed, continuing in muted form over this sequence.

The sound of communal voices in another space heightens a sense of isolation in the aunt's room as the camera continues to track towards the window. Ewa is picked up in frame again as she gets into her car and drives away. This movement is not, as Insdorf suggests, 'the point-of-view of the aunt who will remain alone'.[108] The camera movement is liberated from a particular observer; the movement itself embodies the progression of time in a space of loneliness. However, there is something in the camera's slow movement, the drawing out of the scene's temporality, that is not adequately classed as emotion, linked to sympathy for the characters. Something in this sequence escapes linguistic fixity, instead resonating with an uncertain affect.

Alongside *Decalogue 1*, the final moments of which extend painfully, *Decalogue 5* and *7* are perhaps the most difficult to endure. The latter has received the least praise and the most criticism out of all of the *Decalogue* films. For Coates, *7* is the 'least satisfactory episode' partly because of its 'excessive verbal exposition of preceding events'.[109] When Majka arrives at Wojtek's house after kidnapping her own daughter, they have a conversation in which they reveal the details of their affair, something that Coates has termed a 'creaky mechanism of retrospective summary . . . perilously reminiscent of prime time soaps'.[110] For Haltof, Majka's question, 'Can you steal something that is yours?' provides a 'literal, perhaps too literal, indication of the film's main concern'.[111] It is interesting to turn at this point to Massumi's discussion of an experiment in *Parables For the*

Virtual. He recounts how a group of children were asked to watch a short film, which is described in the following way: 'A man builds a snowman on his roof garden. It starts to melt in the afternoon sun. He watches. After a time, he takes the snowman to the cool of the mountains where it stops melting. He bids it goodbye and leaves.'[112]

The researchers showed the children three versions of this film; one with an added 'factual' voice-over, one with words expressing the emotional resonances of the scenes, and the original wordless version. The children were asked to nominate the most 'pleasant' version, which was the wordless one, whereas the least pleasant was the factual. When an explanatory voice-over was added to the images, it interfered with their intensity, as measured by the bodily responses of the wired subjects. The experiment suggests to Massumi that 'language . . . is not simply in opposition to intensity. It would seem to function differentially in relation to it . . . matter-of-factness dampens intensity.'[113] Intensity, therefore, 'would seem to be associated with non-linear process', that is, not necessarily with the narrative progression of causal chains of events.[114] Although there is of course no voice-over in *Decalogue 7*, it seems that the film's verbosity and literalness has affected its intensity for the writers mentioned above.

However, the film does not make everything explicit. There is an undercurrent of uncertainty and indeterminacy within the narrative, circling around the figure of the child, Ania, and the limits of her knowledge and understanding. In *Decalogue 7*, a disjunction operates between the reality of the adults' situation, the issue of maternity, past affairs and painful histories, and the limited view of the child. There are continual references to the childhood world of fantasy in which she is immersed, while, as she dreams, something seems to erupt from this and causes her to scream uncontrollably. To an extent, then, unlocalisable affects are thematised, as well as, in my view, evoked in the disjunction between states of knowledge.

Decalogue 7 has possibly the most disturbing beginning of any in the series. After the credit music, there is a silence as the film presents a vertiginous low-angle view of the *Decalogue* building, and begins panning down it. A child's repeated yells punctuates the soundtrack. A light switches on in one of the windows, but the camera lingers on it only briefly. The next cut, rather than showing us the source of the screaming, is to another dizzying pan around the estate. The scene then changes entirely to an office, where Majka is returning her student papers. The sound of screaming is again present in the next shot, a domestic interior, but not the source. The sounds remain displaced, an unlocalised, unanchored moment of emergent affect. The next cut returns us to Majka in another kind of office, this time receiving a passport. The screaming recurs for the third time as we see Ania's hand clutching the material of a bed frame. Majka attempts to calm her, with no effect. The child continues to scream until an older woman (Ewa) pushes her way through to the child. This opening has an uncertain temporal chronology. It is unclear whether the screaming is from one, two, or three separate occasions. Because we hear the sound as we see the building, we may think (rightly) that it emerges from this space. Majka is then seen entering this space, which retrospectively implies that the shots of her in the offices may not have been simultaneous with the yells, as the editing might lead us to assume. This temporal disjunction in the editing echoes the disjunctions in their family life.

In the frequent close-ups of Ania's face throughout the film, it is difficult not to search the subtle changes of her expression for outward reflections of what she understands about her situation. One of the film's early images, as Ewa comforts her from the nightmare of the film's opening, is her tear-stained and bewildered face in close-up; she blinks, as though struggling with the aftermath of the dream or attempting to return from it. 'Were you dreaming about wolves? . . . Mother's told you that there aren't any wolves . . .' Ewa says. If wolves suggest a fairytale world, Ania's red dress and coat are reminiscent of Little Red Riding Hood. There is a fairytale element to Ania and Majka's escape into the woods, amplified as they find a deserted carousel in a clearing. The camera captures her sitting on a carousel horse, laughing as she asks Majka, 'Have you kidnapped me?'

The disjunction between her vision and the events circling around her emerges painfully here. Ania may be entranced by this carousel, but we can see that it is a run-down remnant of an abandoned park, overgrown with weeds, which imbues the images with melancholy. As Majka tells Ania that she is her real mother, Ania's expression is inscrutable. Asleep in her father's house, Ania grabs his finger in her sleep and won't let go. Close-ups again indicate a disjunction between states of affect and knowledge: Ania smiles in her sleep, while her father attempts to wrench his hand free. In the film's final images, the camera maintains an extended and close focus on Ania's face as she looks after the train that is taking away her sister/mother. Frowning, open-mouthed, bewildered and confused, she has been abandoned without understanding why.

Decalogue 5 is perhaps the most discomfiting film of the series, potentially evoking the most negative of affects, such as revulsion or disgust, as well as a measure of pity and sadness, all extended through a slow duration in which we are brought too close to the killer and the killed. It has often been noted that the characters in the film are frequently seen through glass and in reflections. Piotr is first seen as a reflection in a mirror, Waldek is initially seen through glass, which also reflects the image of the building, and Jacek is first seen in duplicate, in front of a glass that reflects his image. Sarah Cooper sees these reflections as problematising distinctions between interior and exterior, reality and image. This 'mirroring', she argues, occurs at various levels throughout the film, such as in the cross-cutting between Jacek, the taxi driver, and the lawyer, which suggests a parity between the two killings.[115] Insdorf also points out the recurrence of reflections in glass and mirrors and how frequently we see characters behind glass, writing, 'these reflections connect to the film's structural mirroring of murders – that of the driver by Jacek, and of Jacek by the state'.[116]

However, what has not been particularly noted is the trajectory that increasingly takes us from reflection to body. *Decalogue 5* begins with a series of disembodiments and reflections before becoming almost excruciatingly corporeal. As the film continues, it increasingly emphasises bodily discharges and sounds: Jacek spitting in his coffee cup with a plop, the taxi driver's gurgles as he is strangled, his blood rushing down his head, the sickening sound of his head being smashed in, and the bucket prepared for Jacek's discharges under the noose. As well as facial close-ups, which privilege expression, the film also presents frequent close-ups of feet: Waldek's feet are shown twice rubbing against each other as his shoes come off, there is a close-up of his dirty foot, toes pointing towards the viewer and filling the screen, and Jacek's swinging feet are shown when he is hanged. These are moments of repulsive tangibility rather than legibility, inversions of the facial close-up.

The preparations that lead up to the killings, and the killings themselves, are agonisingly extended in *Decalogue 5*. After Jacek has given directions to Waldek in the car, it is shown slowing down at an obstruction in the road: the unknown man is measuring something with surveying equipment. The editing suggests that Jacek and the man look at each other, the latter seeming to shake his head slowly. Jacek sits up straighter as though startled by this communication. Ominous music that had been sounding previously is muted, instead, a strange electronic series of high-sounding beeps become progressively louder, a pulsating rhythm that counts out the moments and punctuates the duration of this meeting of the eyes. When it is broken, the inexorable progression towards the murder continues. When they stop near a field, Jacek throws the rope he has been winding around his hand over the neck of the driver and pulls it back, twisting it tight around his neck and around the car seat. The horrific gurgling sound made by the driver as he chokes is almost intolerable. Intercut with the driver and Jacek are three moments of a very different temporal rhythm. There is a long-shot of a man on the ridge of the hill, who is slowly cycling past, an embodiment of a slow, regular forward progression that contrasts sharply with Waldek's dying gurgles and flailing feet.

A similar moment occurs when Waldek manages to find the car horn and leans on it continuously. The film cuts to a grey horse in a muddy field that turns its head slowly towards the camera. Ponderous, dirty, and beautiful, the horse embodies a gentle, calm temporal rhythm entirely at odds with the event taking place in the car. This moment is cut short as Jacek moves to the front of the car and begins beating Waldek's arm with his metal bar; the beeping stops, but the sound is continued by a train horn, which makes the startled Jacek turn around. The camera shows the train, like the cyclist, passing slowly out of frame; as in *Mirror*, these are indications of time passing indifferently to human suffering. As with *Decalogue 1*, the film refuses to end the discomfiting experience of viewing. As Insdorf writes, 'The murder is presented in horrifying detail and length (approximately seven minutes), stretching audience tolerance: it is not meant to be easily digested.'[117] The driver does not die until Jacek smashes his face with a rock. The scene ends as Jacek tears off the taxi radio, which had begun playing a children's song that he presumably could not bear, and throws it into the mud. The camera lingers on this now-mute object in its filthy new habitat, a brown fetid mess.

The preparations for the next killing are also painfully extended. A man arrives at the prison and walks the length of the corridor inside it. Like Antonioni, Kieślowski does not cut any of this action, allowing the awareness of what is to come to intensify through time. Time stretches out as Jacek is taken to the cells, down the same length of corridor that we saw the executioner traverse, and then into the execution chamber. Piotr's fist in close-up taps against the wooden chair, beating out the time. Perhaps even more disturbing than the slowing down of events is the way in which everything suddenly seems to speed up just before Jacek is hanged. There is a burst of action as the executioners shout hoarse directions to one another, then 'wait' as the noose is adjusted. Then there is a brief silence, before a cut shows the trapdoor in the floor opening and Jacek's feet dangling in the gap.

As in *Decalogue 6*, the film's major narrative turn, the murder of Waldemar, seemingly hinges on chance: it is by chance that the driver, rejecting two previous fares, picks up Jacek, and by chance that Jacek chooses Waldek as his particular victim. This randomness and happenstance at the heart of the film introduces a threat to order and meaning. Trotter writes, 'randomness is the means by which daily or familiar life exceeds the categories we impose upon it', and, I would add, by which we attempt to understand at it.[118] Interestingly, Trotter links randomness with mess: 'Contingency's signature, written all over the street, is mess.'[119] Chance encounters leave their various messes, and cinema, Trotter argues via Kracauer, is frequently attracted to the rubbish and waste that we would prefer to ignore in our ordinary existence.[120] As *Decalogue 5* proceeds, the viewer is increasingly confronted with the random mess of existence, and of death: dirt, spit, blood, mud, and bodily fluid, which form a threatening counter-current to the reflections, mirrorings, and indexical images that encourage us to interpret them and to make meaning from them.

The extended anguish present in some of the films begs the question of what makes people return to view the films again, and to write about them. Can we be said to *enjoy* them? We can again return to Massumi's conclusions from the experiment. Massumi describes how the children were asked to rate individual scenes from the short film about the melting snowman on both a scale of 'happy-sad' and of 'pleasant-unpleasant'. The sad scenes were rated the most pleasant, 'the sadder the better'.[121] Massumi argues that there may often be a gap between 'content and effect: it would appear that the strength or duration of an image's effect is not logically connected to the content in any straightforward way'. By content he means the 'indexing to conventional meanings', while 'the strength or duration of the image's effect could be called its intensity'. The relations between content and intensity may be more complex than we imagine, characterised, perhaps, by what he calls a 'crossing of semantic wires . . . sadness is pleasant'.[122] It is beyond my abilities to explain the phenomenon, but in relation to the *Decalogue*, I believe that part of the pleasure, even as we wallow in the affective, emotive, or something-in-between state of sadness, repulsion, or disgust, is the recognition of how forcefully the films can affect us. It demonstrates the power of cinema's intensities. As Colebrook writes, 'intensities skew or scramble the faculties; the eye may desire while memory or judgment recoils in horror'; in viewing films, we may be 'drawn and repelled concurrently'.[123] There is an aesthetic appreciation inherent in this pleasure, a pleasure related to a deeply felt experience that is nevertheless artfully constructed.

Notes

1. *The Scar*, film, directed by Krzysztof Kieślowski. Poland, Zespół Filmowy 'Tor', 1976.
2. Danusia Stok, *Kieślowski on Kieślowski* (London and Boston: Faber & Faber, 1993), p. 144.

3. Ibid., p. 144.
4. Marek Haltof, *The Cinema of Krzysztof Kieślowski: Variations of Destiny and Chance* (London and New York: Wallflower Press, 2004), p. 77.
5. Maria Małatyńska, 'Dekalog, Kieślowski', *Życie Literackie* (19 November 1989).
6. Stok, *Kieślowski on Kieślowski*, p. 153.
7. *A Short Film About Killing*, film, directed by Krzysztof Kieślowski. Poland: Zespół Filmowy 'Tor', 1988. *A Short Film About Love*, film, directed by Krzysztof Kieślowski. Poland: Zespół Filmowy 'Tor', 1988. *The Double Life of Veronique*, film, directed by Krzysztof Kieślowski. France/Poland/Norway: Sideral Productions, Zespół Filmowy Tor, Norsk Film, 1991.
8. Trotter, *Cinema and Modernism*, p. 55.
9. Emma Wilson, *Memory and Survival: The French Cinema of Krzysztof Kieślowski* (London: Legenda, 2000), p. 10.
10. Cited in Steven Woodward, 'Introduction', in Steven Woodward (ed.), *After Kieślowski: the Legacy of Krzysztof Kieślowski* (Detroit: Wayne State University Press, 2009), p. 2.
11. Slavoj Žižek, *The Fright of Real Tears: Krzysztof Kieślowski Between Theory and Post-Theory* (London: BFI, 2001), p. 111.
12. Annette Insdorf, *Double Lives, Second Chances: The Cinema of Krzysztof Kieślowski* (New York: Hyperion, 1999), p. 71.
13. Tadeusz Lubelski, 'Dekalog', in Marek Lis and Adam Garbicz (eds), *Światowa Encyklopedia Filmu Religijnego* (Kraków: Biały Kruk, 2007), p. 103.
14. Michel Ciment and Hubert Niogret, 'Pańskie Filmy są Rentgenogramami duszy...', *Film na Świecie*, 3.4 (1992), p. 31.
15. Žižek, *Fright of Real Tears*, p. 101.
16. Joseph G. Kickasola, *The Films of Krzysztof Kieślowski: the Liminal Image* (New York and London: Continuum, 2006), pp. ix–x.
17. Vivian Sobchack, *Carnal Thoughts* (Berkeley: University of California Press, 2004), p. 85.
18. Kickasola, *The Films of Krzysztof Kieślowski*, p. 163.
19. Stok, *Kieślowski on Kieślowski*, p. 158.
20. Ciment and Niogret, 'Pańskie Filmy', p. 30.
21. Haltof, *The Cinema of Krzysztof Kieślowski*, p. 81.
22. Kickasola, *The Films of Krzysztof Kieślowski*, p. 165.
23. Ibid.; Christopher Garbowski, *Krzysztof Kieślowski's Decalogue Series: The Problem of the Protagonists and their Self-Transcendence* (Boulder: East European Monographs, 1996).
24. Yvette Biro, *Turbulence and Flow in Film: The Rhythmic Design* (Bloomington: Indiana University Press, 2008), p. 146.
25. Ciment and Niogret, 'Pańskie Filmy', p. 30.
26. Ibid., p. 30.
27. Paul Coates, 'The Curse of the Law: *The Decalogue*', in Paul Coates (ed.),

Lucid Dreams: The Films of Krzysztof Kieślowski (Wiltshire: Flicks Books, 1999), p. 110.
28. Kickasola, The Films of Krzysztof Kieślowski, p. 170.
29. Žižek, Fright of Real Tears, p. 98.
30. Insdorf, Double Lives, Second Chances, p. 76.
31. Coates, Lucid Dreams, p. 97.
32. Craig Owens, Beyond Recognition: Representation, Power, and Culture (Berkeley: University of California Press, 1992), p. 57.
33. Žižek, Fright of Real Tears, p. 96.
34. John Mullarkey, Moving Image, p. 65.
35. Žižek, Fright of Real Tears, p. 98.
36. Ibid., p. 123.
37. Ibid., p. 123.
38. Coates, Lucid Dreams, p. 97.
39. Roland Barthes, 'The Metaphor of the Eye', in Story of the Eye, Georges Bataille (London: Penguin, 1982), p. 119.
40. Ibid., p. 121.
41. Ibid., p. 122.
42. Rosalind Krauss and Yve-Alain Bois, Formless: A User's Guide (New York: Zone, 1997), p. 31.
43. Ibid., p. 32.
44. Ibid., p. 146.
45. Irigaray cited by Dorothea Olkowski, Gilles Deleuze and the Ruin of Representation (Berkeley: University of California Press, 1999), p. 63.
46. Olkowski, Gilles Deleuze, p. 68.
47. Sobchack, Carnal Thoughts, p. 88.
48. Ibid., p. 88.
49. Ibid., p. 103.
50. Trotter, Cinema and Modernism, pp. 60 and 70.
51. Ibid., p. 49.
52. Ibid., p. 70.
53. Insdorf, Double Lives, Second Chances, p. 72.
54. Sobchack, Carnal Thoughts, p. 88.
55. Emma Wilson, Cinema's Missing Children (London and New York: Wallflower Press, 2003), p. 19. My italics.
56. Insdorf, Double Lives, Second Chances, p. 74.
57. Žižek, Fright of Real Tears, p. 121.
58. Coates, Lucid Dreams, p. 97.
59. Mikael Timm, 'Przykazania Jako Gra', Film na Świecie, 3.4 (1992), p. 69.
60. Insdorf, Double Lives, Second Chances, p. 78.
61. Ibid., p. 79.
62. Kickasola, The Films of Krzysztof Kieślowski, p. 35.
63. Coates, Lucid Dreams, p. 98.
64. Insdorf, Double Lives, Second Chances, p. 80.

65. Ibid., p. 78.
66. Kickasola, *The Films of Krzysztof Kieślowski*, p. 177.
67. Michel Chion, *Audio-Vision: Sound on Screen* (New York: Columbia University Press, 1994), p. 10.
68. Ibid., p. 15.
69. Insdorf, *Double Lives, Second Chances*, p. 79.
70. Sobchack, *Carnal Thoughts*, pp. 91–2.
71. Ibid., p. 93.
72. Haltof, *The Cinema of Krzysztof Kieślowski*, p. 103.
73. Kickasola, *The Films of Krzysztof Kieślowski*, p. 239.
74. Ibid., p. 240.
75. Insdorf, *Double Lives, Second Chances*, p. 124.
76. Žižek, *Fright of Real Tears*, p. 120.
77. Ibid., p. 98.
78. Ibid., p. 98.
79. Christian Metz, *Psychoanalysis and Cinema* (London: Macmillan, 1983), p. 60.
80. Kickasola, *The Films of Krzysztof Kieślowski*, p. 214.
81. Insdorf, *Double Lives, Second Chances*, p. 99.
82. Ibid., p. 101.
83. Haltof, *The Cinema of Krzysztof Kieślowski*, p. 97.
84. Ibid., p. 97.
85. Claudia Gorbman, 'Why Music? The Sound Film and its Spectator', in Kay Dickinson (ed.), *Movie Music, The Film Reader* (London: Routledge, 2003), p. 40.
86. Chion, *Audio-vision*, p. 8.
87. Iwona Sowińska, 'Preisner: post scriptum', Andrzej Gwóździa (ed.), *W Kręgu Krzysztofa Kieślowskiego* (Katowice: Instytucja Filmowa 'Silesia-Film', 2006), p. 79.
88. Colebrook, *Gilles Deleuze*, p. 31.
89. Grosz, *Nick of Time*, p. 186.
90. Kickasola, *The Films of Krzysztof Kieślowski*, p. 177.
91. Ibid., p. 175.
92. Trotter, *Cinema and Modernism*, p. 72.
93. Coates, *Lucid Dreams*, p. 101.
94. Žižek, *Fright of Real Tears*, p. 114.
95. Kickasola, *The Films of Krzysztof Kieślowski*, p. 192.
96. Coates, *Lucid Dreams*, p. 102.
97. Sean O'Sullivan, '*The Decalogue* and the Remaking of American Television' in Steven Woodward (ed.), *After Kieślowski: The Legacy of Krysztof Kieślowski* (Detroit: Wayne State University Press, 2009), p. 219.
98. Grosz, *Nick of Time*, p. 173
99. Bergson, *Matter and Memory*, p. 177.
100. Rashkin, Esther, 'Unmourned Dead, Filtered History, and the Screening of

Anti-Semitism in Kieślowski's *A Short Film About Killing*', *American Imago* 66.3 (2009), p. 322.
101. Ibid., p. 322.
102. Ibid., p. 316.
103. Garbowski, *Krzysztof Kieślowski's* Decalogue *Series*, p. 54.
104. Barthes, *Camera Lucida*, p. 96.
105. Mulvey, *Death*, p. 56.
106. Insdorf, *Double Lives, Second Chances*, p. 69.
107. Kickasola, *The Films of Krzysztof Kieślowski*, p. 187.
108. Insdorf, *Double Lives, Second Chances*, p. 84.
109. Coates, *Lucid Dreams*, pp. 105–6.
110. Ibid., p. 106.
111. Haltof, *The Cinema of Krzysztof Kieślowski* p. 99.
112. Brian Massumi, *Parables for the Virtual*, p. 23.
113. Ibid., p. 25.
114. Ibid., p. 26.
115. Sarah Cooper, 'Living On: From Kieślowski to Zanussi', Steven Woodward (ed.), *After Kieślowski*, p. 41.
116. Insdorf, *Double Lives, Second Chances*, p. 91.
117. Ibid., p. 90.
118. Trotter, *The Uses of Phobia* (Malden and Oxford: Wiley-Blackwell, 2010), p. 164.
119. Ibid., p. 165.
120. Ibid., p. 165.
121. Massumi, *Parables for the Virtual*, p. 23.
122. Ibid., p. 24.
123. Colebrook, *Gilles Deleuze*, p. 39.

Epilogue

This book has emerged partly as a response to developments in film theory that offer new ways of thinking about cinema's affective and sensory potential. Theories of embodiment and affect particularly invite us to return to films that were consistently seen as cold and distancing, such as *L'Avventura*, and to a lesser extent, the *Decalogue* series, giving us a new vocabulary which we can use to write about them. As Stern has written, affect in cinema derives its force not merely from the immediacy of touch but from the capacity of the object to elude our grasp. The movement of the image 'invests the delineation of things with a particular affectivity ... a relation obtains between temporality and affectivity'.[1] Throughout this book, I have attempted to understand cinema's affective and sensory appeal as intertwined with the thematic concerns of particular films. I have seen the relationship between affect, sense and texture, meaning, and theme as interpenetrating through duration. The concept of interpenetration was inspired by a Bergsonian view of duration as made up of variegated rhythms and in which psychical states modulate and transform, bleed into each other, rather than forming discrete units that can be neatly separated. In my analysis of each film, I have attempted to trace the gradual modulation of particular elements: movements between surface and depth in *L'Avventura*, corporeal materiality and its destabilisation in *Mirror*, and the unfolding and dissolution of meaning in the *Decalogue*.

Attending to various processes of duration enables us to see how temporality often destabilises the fixed concepts that have been configured around particular films. While many theoretical concepts may cohere and operate satisfactorily in the abstract, their formulations often seem less adequate when seen in relation to the operation of time in a specific film. As Dudley Andrew writes, the logic of theory must follow the movement and duration of the films under study, which demand rich and varied readings, and will ultimately never submit to a single overarching framework.[2] Each of the chapters has conducted a close analysis of the films in order to trace a variety of interpenetrating rhythms and inform a range of theoretical approaches. This kind of analysis is aided by the availability of the films on DVD. On the one hand, as Mulvey has made clear, using new technologies to pause a film's images allows for a moment of reflection, which is not 'lost when the film is returned to movement', but continues to inflect the process of film viewing.[3] On the other hand, however, DVD technologies can also be seen as a way of re-engaging with the abstracted fragments of a film that emerge in criticism, in the reproduction of film stills alongside critical writing, and even in memory, which tends to serialise images and abstract them from their context of temporal flow. Arguably, DVD technologies provide film theorists with a greater opportunity to consider unfoldings, fluctuations, transfigurations and the various rhythms of duration.

L'Avventura, *Mirror* and the films of the *Decalogue* series exhibit heterogeneous engagements with time's own heterogeneity. It is possible, nevertheless, to trace connections between the films. All three works are now frequently seen as films of the art cinema, although they may not have been intended for this. *L'Avventura*, for example, was released as a commercial feature. The *Decalogue* series fell somewhere between television and cinema. With many films of the art cinema, however, they share a predilection for ambiguity and open-ended narratives. The films are so densely woven with resonances, affects, and associations, that they call for multiple, attentive viewings. By seeing meaning as a fluid process, rather than as a fixed entity, I have attempted to be sensitive to the gradual unfolding and dissolution of significances that the films perform through time.

Each of the films has been associated with a mystery, with something that remains beyond our knowledge and vision. In *L'Avventura*, this is associated partly with the disappearance of a major character into unknown depths. In relation to *Mirror*, Tarkovsky himself promoted the idea that his films evoke something spiritual and transcendent, and the *Decalogue* has encouraged contemplation of religion and the metaphysical. My interest has not necessarily been to explore the spiritual possibilities of an encounter with the films, but rather to examine how each of the works forces viewers and critics to come up against a hermeneutic threshold, a certain limit beyond which the films fall forever from our attempts to understand and analyse them. Nowell-Smith has formulated this eloquently in relation to *L'Avventura*: 'even today it remains a hard film to write about. For the greatness of the film consists precisely in the fact that it takes the cinema's powers of expression beyond the point where language can follow it.'[4]

Images of stains and spillages recur across the films. In *L'Avventura*, Sandro deliberately knocks over an ink bottle on an unfinished architect's drawing; the ink spreads in a black rivulet across it. The image of black stain on white is then echoed as a stream of schoolboys, dressed in black, emerge on to a sunlit courtyard. In *Mirror*, spilled milk drips slowly onto wood, as the camera follows the direction of the spillage downwards. In the *Decalogue*, Krzysztof's spreading ink stain is echoed in Magda's spilled milk and Tomek's spilled blood, as he cuts his wrists in a basin. As Sobchack has written in relation to *Decalogue 1*, the stain made by the ink is also one of 'spreading and uncontainable signification'.[5] This interest in spillage and spreading is perhaps reflective of the images in general, which continually escape containment in rigid symbolic systems.

All of the works in some way question the integrity of present moments, their separation from past and future. In *L'Avventura*, traces of the past circulate in a temporalised space, while the staging of images in depth encourages a temporalised process of viewing. In *Mirror*, past and present are fluid categories that are continually interweaving. In the *Decalogue*, the past weighs upon the characters, while omens seem to direct us towards some future catastrophe. The films encourage us to recognise that temporal heterogeneity is also relevant for understanding film viewing. Viewers are likely to draw upon their own memories in interpreting and responding to film images. In *L'Avventura*, viewers are encouraged to search through their memories for the last glimpse of Anna. *Mirror* continually provides viewers with new contexts for its stuttering images, and the *Decalogue* films require us to continually revise what we think we know about the narratives, characters, and images.

L'Avventura, *Mirror*, and several of the *Decalogue* films show characters who are often waiting, watching, and reflecting. Claudia, Maria and Dorota are picked out by the camera to stand alone. While their motivations, thoughts and emotions frequently remain opaque, we, in part, share the temporality of their waiting, thus inviting a paradoxical sense of both closeness and distance. On the other hand, each of the cinematic works feature moments where time is shown passing indifferently to human presence, suggesting, as Deleuze writes, that 'the only subjectivity is time . . . and it is we who are internal to time, not the other way around'.[6] Time, as Grosz further writes, 'is not merely the attribute of a subject . . . it is what the universe imposes on us rather than we on it, it is what we find ourselves immersed in'.[7]

In all three cinematic works, the camera has its own focus and direction, allowing characters to leave the frame, creating moments that have been called 'dead times'. In the killings of *Decalogue 5*, pauses, elongated actions, and cutaways extend time, which passes even as human lives come to an end. I have suggested, however, that such moments are not 'dead' at all, but rather constitute a powerful engagement with temporality. They allow viewers to reflect upon the images before them, encouraging us to notice things that we ordinarily would not, and endowing the objects within the frame, and the camera movements that display them to us, with an affective force. As Agacinski writes, 'it is as *dead* time that duration becomes palpable'.[8] The 'frame of mind for letting oneself be touched' she continues, requires the viewer to open themselves up to the possibilities and potentialities of a ceaseless duration, to allow the continual process of intertwining together and separating out (of affect, aesthetic form, thematisation, and memory, for example) to occur.[9] This kind of relationship encourages the viewer not to attempt to concretise the film into specific moments of meaning, but rather to, as Agacinski wrote, 'grant things their own temporality, their own particular rhythm', to allow our responses to be changed and transformed by cinematic time.[10]

Notes

1. Lesley Stern, 'Paths', p. 321.
2. Dudley Andrew, *Film in the Aura of Art* (Princeton: Princeton University Press, 1992), p. 4.
3. Mulvey, *Death*, p. 186.
4. Nowell-Smith, *L'Avventura*, p. 12.
5. Sobchack, *Carnal Thoughts*, p. 96.
6. Deleuze, *Cinema 2*, p. 80.
7. Grosz, *Nick of Time*, p. 4.
8. Sylviane Agacinski, *Time Passing: Modernity and Nostalgia*, trans. by Jody Gladding (New York: Columbia University Press, 2003), p. 55.
9. Ibid., p. 55.
10. Ibid., p. 55.

Bibliography

Abel, Richard, *French Film Theory and Criticism: A History/Anthology 1907–1939* (Princeton: Princeton University Press, 1988).

Affron, Charles, *Cinema and Sentiment* (Chicago: University of Chicago Press, 1982).

Agacinski, Sylviane, *Time Passing: Modernity and Nostalgia*, trans. by Jody Gladding (New York: Columbia University Press, 2003).

Altman, Rick, 'Sound Space', in Rick Altman, *Sound Theory, Sound Practice* (New York: Routledge, 1992), pp. 46–64.

Andrei Rublev, film, directed by Andrei Tarkovsky. Soviet Union: Mosfilm, 1966.

Andrew, Dudley, *Film in the Aura of Art* (Princeton: Princeton University Press, 1992).

Antonioni, Michelangelo, 'Cannes Statement', in Seymour Chatman and Guido Fink (eds), *L'Avventura: Michelangelo Antonioni, Director* (New Brunswick, NJ and London: Rutgers Films in Print, 1989), pp. 177–9.

Aragon, Louis, 'On Décor' (1918), in Richard Abel (ed.), *French Film Theory and Criticism: A History/Anthology 1907–1939* (Princeton: Princeton University Press, 1988), pp. 165–8.

Arrowsmith, William, *Antonioni: The Poet of Images* (Oxford: Oxford University Press, 1995).

Attridge, Derek, 'Roland Barthes's Obtuse, Sharp Meaning and the Responsibilities of Commentary', in Jean-Michel Rabaté, *Writing the Image After Roland Barthes* (Pennsylvania: University of Pennsylvania Press, 1997), pp. 77–89.

Avventura, L', film, directed by Michelangelo Antonioni. Italy/France: Cino Del Duca, 1960.

Balázs, Béla, *Theory of Film: Character and Growth of a New Art*, trans. by Edith Bone (London: D. Dobson, 1952).

Barker, Jennifer M., 'Bodily Irruptions: The Corporeal Assault on Ethnographic Narration', *Cinema Journal*, 34.3 (1995), 57–76.

Barthes, Roland, 'Cher Antonioni', in Geoffrey Nowell-Smith, *L'Avventura* (London: BFI Publishing, 1997), pp. 63–8.

Barthes, Roland, *Image, Music, Text*, trans. by Stephen Heath (London: Fontana, 1977).
Barthes, Roland, *Camera Lucida: Reflections on Photography*, trans. by Richard Howard (London: Cape, 1982).
Barthes, Roland, 'The Metaphor of the Eye', in Georges Bataille, *Story of the Eye* (London: Penguin, 1982), pp. 119–27.
Baudry, Jean-Louis, 'Ideological Effects of the Basic Cinematographic Apparatus', in Gerald Mast, Marshall Cohen and Leo Braudy (eds), *Film Theory and Criticism* (Oxford: Oxford University Press, 1992), pp. 302–12.
Bazin, Andre, *What is Cinema?* (Berkeley, Los Angeles and London: University of California Press, 2005).
Beasley-Murray, Jon, 'Whatever Happened to Neorealism? – Bazin, Deleuze, and Tarkovsky's Long Take', *iris*, 23 (1997), pp. 37–52.
Benjamin, Walter, 'The Work of Art in the Age of Mechanical Reproduction', in Gerald Mast, Marshall Cohen and Leo Braudy (eds), *Film Theory and Criticism* (Oxford: Oxford University Press, 1992), pp. 665–81.
Bergson, Henri, *Matter and Memory* (London: George Allen & Unwin, 1962).
Bergson, Henri, 'Duration and Intuition', in J. J. C. Smart (ed.), *Problems of Space and Time* (New York: Macmillan, 1976), pp. 139–44.
Bergson, Henri, 'The Idea of Duration', in Keith Ansell Pearson and John Mullarkey (eds), *Henri Bergson: Key Writings* (New York and London: Continuum, 2005), pp. 49–77.
Bergson, Henri, *Creative Evolution* (Basingstoke and New York: Palgrave Macmillan, 2007).
Bird, Robert, *Andrei Tarkovsky: Elements of Cinema* (London: Reaktion, 2008).
Biro, Yvette, *Turbulence and Flow in Film: The Rhythmic Design* (Bloomington: Indiana University Press, 2008).
Bogue, Ronald, *Deleuze's Way: Essays in Transverse Ethics and Aesthetics* (Hampshire: Ashgate, 2007).
Bondanella, Peter, *Italian Cinema* (New York: F. Ungar Pub. Co., 1983).
Bordwell, David, *Narration in the Fiction Film* (London: Routledge, 1995).
Bordwell, David and Noël Carroll, *Post-Theory: Reconstructing Film Studies* (Madison: University of Wisconsin Press, 1996).
Brown, Tom and James Walters, *Film Moments* (London: Palgrave Macmillan, 2010).
Brunette, Peter, *The Films of Michelangelo Antonioni* (Cambridge: Cambridge University Press, 1998).
Bruno, Giuliana, *Atlas of Emotion: Journeys in Art, Architecture and Film* (New York: Verso, 2002).
Burgin, Victor, *The Remembered Film* (London: Reaktion, 2006).
Buck-Morss, Susan, 'Aesthetics and Anaesthetics: Walter Benjamin's Artwork Essay Reconsidered', *October*, 62 (1992), pp. 3–41.
Cameron, Ian, 'Michelangelo Antonioni', *Film Quarterly*, 16.1 (1962), pp. 1–58.

Canudo, Ricciotto, 'The Birth of a Sixth Art' (1911), in Richard Abel, *French Film Theory and Criticism: A History/Anthology 1907–1939* (Princeton: Princeton University Press, 1988), pp. 58–66.

Cardullo, Bert (ed.) *Michelangelo Antonioni: Interviews* (Jackson: University Press of Mississippi, 2008).

Cardwell, Sarah, 'About Time: Theorising Adaptation, Temporality, and Tense', *Literature Film Quarterly* (2003), http://www.redorbit.com/news/science/6467/about_time_theorizing_adaptation_temporality_and_tense/.

Chatman, Seymour, *Antonioni: Or, The Surface of the World* (Berkeley: University of California Press, 1985).

Chatman, Seymour and Guido Fink (eds), *L'Avventura: Michelangelo Antonioni, Director* (New Brunswick, NJ: Rutgers University Press, 1989).

Charney, Leo, *Empty Moments: Cinema, Modernity and Drift* (Durham: Duke University Press, 1998).

Chion, Michel, *Audio-Vision: Sound on Screen* (New York: Columbia University Press, 1994).

Chion, Michel, *The Voice in Cinema* (New York: Columbia University Press, 1999).

Christie, Ian, 'Introduction: Tarkovsky in his Time', in Maya Turovskaya, *Tarkovsky: Cinema as Poetry* (London: Faber and Faber, 1989), pp. ix–xxvii.

Ciment, Michel and Hubert Niogret, 'Pańskie Filmy są Rentgenogramami duszy ...', *Film na Świecie*, 3.4 (1992), p. 31.

Coates, Paul, 'The Curse of the Law: *The Decalogue*', in Paul Coates (ed.), *Lucid Dreams: The Films of Krzysztof Kieślowski* (Wiltshire: Flicks Books, 1999), pp. 94–115.

Colebrook, Claire, *Gilles Deleuze* (London: Routledge, 2002).

Comolli, Jean-Luc and Jean Narboni, 'Cinema/Ideology/Criticism', in Gerald Mast, Marshall Cohen and Leo Braudy, *Film Theory and Criticism* (Oxford: Oxford University Press, 1992), pp. 682–9.

Cooper, Sarah, 'Living On: From Kieślowski to Zanussi', in Steven Woodward (ed.), *After Kieślowski: the Legacy of Krzysztof Kieślowski* (Detroit: Wayne State University Press, 2009), pp. 34–48.

Dalle Vache, Angela, *Cinema and Painting* (London: Athlone, 1996).

Danius, Sara, *The Senses of Modernism* (Ithaca: Cornell University Press, 2002).

Decalogue, film/TV series, directed by Krzysztof Kieślowski. Poland: Zespół Filmowy Tor, 1989.

Deleuze, Gilles, *Cinema 1: The Movement Image* (London: Continuum, 2005).

Deleuze, Gilles, *Cinema 2: The Time Image* (London: Continuum, 2005).

del Río, Elena, *Deleuze and the Cinemas of Performance* (Edinburgh: Edinburgh University Press, 2008).

Deserto Rosso, Il, film, directed by Michelangelo Antonioni. Italy/France: Film Duemila, 1964.

de Valck, Marijke and Malte Hagener, 'Down with Cinephilia? Long Live

Cinephilia? And Other Videosyncratic Pleasures', in *Cinephilia: Movies, Love and Memory*, ed. by Marijke de Valck and Malte Hagener (Amsterdam: Amsterdam University Press, 2005), pp. 11–24.
Doane, Mary Ann, *The Emergence of Cinematic Time* (Cambridge: Harvard University Press, 2002).
Doane, Mary Ann, 'The Close-Up: Scale and Detail in the Cinema', *Differences*, 14.3 (2003), pp. 88–112.
Doane, Mary Ann, 'The Indexical and the Concept of Medium Specificity', *Differences*, 18.1 (2007), pp. 129–49.
Double Life of Veronique, The, film, directed by Krzysztof Kieślowski. France/Poland/Norway: Sideral Productions, Zespół Filmowy Tor, Norsk Film, 1991.
Douglass, Paul, 'Bergson and Cinema: Friends or Foes?', in John Mullarkey (ed.), *The New Bergson* (Manchester and New York: Manchester University Press, 2007), pp. 209–27.
Dufrenne, Mikel, *In the Presence of the Sensuous: Essays in Aesthetics* (Atlantic Highlands, NJ: Humanities Press International, 1987).
Dulac, Germaine, 'Aesthetics, Objects, Integral *Cinegraphie*' (1926), in Richard Abel (ed.), *French Film Theory and Criticism: A History/Anthology 1907–1939* (Princeton: Princeton University Press, 1988), pp. 389–97.
Durand, Regis, 'How to See (Photographically)', in Patrice Petro (ed.), *Fugitive Images: From Photography to Video* (Bloomington: Indiana University Press, 1995), pp. 141–51.
Durgnat, Raymond, *Films and Feelings* (London: Faber & Faber, 1967).
Eclisse, L', film, directed by Michelangelo Antonioni. Italy/France: Cineriz, 1962.
Epstein, Jean, 'Magnification and Other Writings', in Stuart Liebman (ed.), *October*, 3 (1977), pp. 9–25.
Epstein, Jean, 'The Senses I (b)' (1921), in Richard Abel (ed.), *French Film Theory and Criticism: A History/Anthology 1907–1939* (Princeton: Princeton University Press, 1988), pp. 241–6.
Faure, Élie, 'The Art of Cineplastics' (1923), in Richard Abel (ed.), *French Film Theory and Criticism: A History/Anthology 1907–1939* (Princeton: Princeton University Press, 1988), pp. 258–67.
Fisher, Jennifer, 'Relational Sense: Towards an Haptic Aesthetics', *Parachute*, 87 (1997), pp. 4–11.
Flaxman, Gregory, 'Cinema Year Zero', in Gregory Flaxman (ed.), *The Brain is the Screen: Deleuze and the Philosophy of Cinema* (Minneapolis: The University of Minnesota Press, 2000), pp. 87–108.
Ford, Hamish, 'Antonioni's *L'Avventura* and Deleuze's Time-image', *Senses of Cinema*, 28 (2003), http://www.sensesofcinema.com/contents/03/28/l_avventura_deleuze.html.
Forgacs, David, 'Antonioni: Space, Place, Sexuality', in Myrto Konstantarakos, *Spaces in European Cinema* (Exeter: Intellect, 2000), pp. 101–11.

Frampton, Daniel, *Filmosophy* (London and New York: Wallflower, 2006).
Garbowski, Christopher, *Krzysztof Kieślowski's Decalogue Series: The Problem of the Protagonists and Their Self-Transcendence* (Boulder: East European Monographs, 1996).
Gorbman, Claudia, 'Why Music? The Sound Film and its Spectator', in Kay Dickinson (ed.), *Movie Music, The Film Reader* (London: Routledge, 2003), pp. 37–47.
Green, Peter, *Andrei Tarkovsky: The Winding Quest* (Basingstoke: Macmillan, 1992).
Gregg, Melissa and Gregory J. Seigworth, 'An Inventory of Shimmers', in Melissa Gregg and Gregory J. Seigworth, *The Affect Theory Reader* (Durham and London: Duke University Press, 2010), pp. 1–25.
Gromaire, Marcel, 'A Painter's Idea's About the Cinema' (1919), in Richard Abel (ed.), *French Film Theory and Criticism: A History/Anthology 1907–1939* (Princeton: Princeton University Press, 1988), pp. 174–82.
Grosz, Elizabeth, *The Nick of Time* (Durham and London: Duke University Press, 2004).
Grosz, Elizabeth, 'Thinking the New: Of Futures Yet Unthought', in Elizabeth Grosz (ed.), *Becomings: Explorations in Time, Memory and Futures* (Ithaca and London: Cornell University Press, 1999), pp. 15–28.
Groves, Tim, 'Cinema/Affect/Writing', *Senses of Cinema*, 25 (2003), http://www.sensesofcinema.com/contents/03/25/writing_cinema_affect.html.
Groves, Tim, 'Entranced: Affective Mimesis and Cinematic Identification', *Screening the Past*, 20 (2006), http://www.latrobe.edu.au/screeningthepast/20/entranced.html.
Guerlac, Suzanne, *Thinking in Time: An Introduction to Henri Bergson* (Ithaca and London: Cornell University Press, 2006).
Haltof, Marek, *The Cinema of Krzysztof Kieślowski: Variations of Destiny and Chance* (London and New York: Wallflower Press, 2004).
Hansen, Miriam Bratu, 'Benjamin, Cinema and Experience: 'The Blue Flower in the Land of Technology', *New German Critique*, 40 (1987), pp. 179–224.
Herzog, Amy, 'Images of Thought and Acts of Creation: Deleuze, Bergson, and the Question of Cinema', *Invisible Culture* (2000), http://www.rochester.edu/in_visible_culture/issue3/herzog.htm.
Huyssen, Andreas, *Twilight Memories: Marking Time in a Culture of Amnesia* (New York and London: Routledge, 1995).
Insdorf, Annette, *Double Lives, Second Chances: The Cinema of Krzysztof Kieślowski* (New York: Hyperion, 1999).
Johnson, Vida T. and Graham Petrie, *The Films of Andrei Tarkovsky: A Visual Fugue* (Bloomington: Indiana University Press, 1994).
Kawin, Bruce F., *Mindscreen: Bergman, Godard, and First-Person Film* (Princeton: Princeton University Press, 1978).
Keathley, Christian, *Cinephilia and History* (Bloomington: Indiana University Press, 2006).

Kickasola, Joseph G., *The Films of Krzysztof Kieślowski: the Liminal Image* (New York and London: Continuum, 2006).
Klinger, Barbara, 'The Art Film, Affect, and the Female Viewer: *The Piano* Revisited', *Screen*, 47.1 (2006), pp. 19–41.
Kral, Peter, 'Tarkovsky, or the burning house', *Screening the Past* (2001), http://www.latrobe.edu.au/screeningthepast/classics/cl0301/pkcl12.htm.
Krauss, Rosalind and Yve-Alain Bois, *Formless: A User's Guide* (New York: Zone, 1997).
Kozloff, Sarah, *Overhearing Film Dialogue* (Berkeley: University of California Press, 2000).
Le Fanu, Mark, *Cinema of Andrei Tarkovsky* (London: BFI, 1987).
Leger, Fernand, '*La Roue*: Its Plastic Quality' (1922), in Richard Abel (ed.), *French Film Theory and Criticism: A History/Anthology 1907–1939* (Princeton: Princeton University Press, 1988), pp. 271–91.
L'Herbier, Marcel, 'Hermes and Silence', in Richard Abel (ed.), *French Film Theory and Criticism: A History/Anthology 1907–1939* (Princeton: Princeton University Press, 1988), pp. 147–53.
Lim, Bliss Cua, *Translating Time: Cinema, the Fantastic, and Temporal Critique* (Durham and London: Duke University Press, 2009).
Lomax, Yve, 'Thinking Stillness', in David Green and Joanna Lowry (ed.), *Stillness and Time: Photography and the Moving Image* (Brighton: Photoworks, 2006), pp. 55–63.
Lubelski, Tadeusz, 'Dekalog', in Marek Lis and Adam Garbicz (eds), *Światowa Encyklopedia Filmu Religijnego* (Kraków: Biały Kruk, 2007), pp. 101–3.
Małatyńska, Maria, 'Dekalog, Kieślowski', *Życie Literackie* 19 November 1989.
Marks, Laura U., *The Skin of the Film* (Durham: Duke University Press, 2000).
Martin, Jean-Clet, 'Of Images and Worlds: Toward A Geology of the Cinema', in Gregory Flaxman (ed.), *The Brain is the Screen: Deleuze and the Philosophy of Cinema* (Minneapolis: The University of Minnesota Press, 2000), pp. 61–85.
Massumi, Brian, *Parables for the Virtual: Movement, Affect, Sensation* (Durham: Duke University Press, 2002).
Metz, Christian, *Psychoanalysis and Cinema* (London: Macmillan, 1983).
Mirror [*Zerkalo*], film, directed by Andrei Tarkovsky. Soviet Union: Mosfilm, 1975.
Moore, Rachel, *Savage Theory: Cinema As Modern Magic* (Durham: Duke University Press, 2000).
Mullarkey, John, *Bergson and Philosophy* (Notre Dame: University of Notre Dame Press, 2000).
Mullarkey, John, *Philosophy and the Moving Image: Refractions of Reality* (Basingstoke: Palgrave Macmillan, 2010).
Mulvey, Laura, 'Visual Pleasure and Narrative Cinema', in Robert Stam and Tony Miller (eds), *Film and Theory: An Anthology* (Malden and Oxford: Blackwell, 2000), pp. 483–94.

Mulvey, Laura, *Death 24x a Second* (London: Reaktion, 2006).
Norton, Glen, 'Antonioni's Modernist Language' [no date], http://www.geocities.com/Hollywood/3781/antonioni.html.
Notte, La, film, directed by Michelangelo Antonioni. Italy/France: Nepifilm, 1961.
Nowell-Smith, Geoffrey, *L'Avventura* (London: BFI Publishing, 1997).
Nowotny, Helga, *Time: The Modern and Postmodern Experience* (Cambridge: Polity Press, 1994).
Odin, Roger, 'For a Semio-Pragmatics of Film', in Robert Stam and Tony Miller (eds), *Film and Theory: An Anthology* (Malden and Oxford: Blackwell, 2000), pp. 54–66.
Olkowski, Dorothea, *Gilles Deleuze and the Ruin of Representation* (Berkeley: University of California Press, 1999).
Orban, Clara, 'Antonioni's Women, Lost in the City', *Modern Language Studies*, 31.2 (2001), pp. 11–27.
O'Sullivan, Sean, 'The Decalogue and the Remaking of American Television', in Steven Woodward (ed.), *After Kieślowski: The Legacy of Krysztof Kieślowski* (Detroit: Wayne State University Press, 2009), pp. 202–25.
O'Sullivan, Simon, *Art Encounters Deleuze and Guattari* (New York: Palgrave Macmillan, 2006).
Owens, Craig, *Beyond Recognition: Representation, Power, and Culture* (Berkeley: University of California Press, 1992).
Pearson, Keith Ansell, *Philosophy and the Adventure of the Virtual* (London: Routledge, 2002).
Perez, Gilberto, *The Material Ghost: Films and Their Medium* (Baltimore: Johns Hopkins University Press, 1998).
Perry, Ted, 'Introduction', in *Antonioni: The Poet of Images*, William Arrowsmith (Oxford: Oxford University Press, 1995), pp. 3–19.
Petric, Vlada, 'Tarkovsky's Dream Imagery', *Film Quarterly*, 43.2 (1989), pp. 28–34.
Peucker, Brigitte, *Incorporating Images: Film and the Rival Arts* (Princeton: Princeton University Press, 1995).
Rashkin, Esther, 'Unmourned Dead, Filtered History, and the Screening of Anti-Semitism in Kieślowski's A Short Film About Killing', *American Imago*, 66.3 (2009), pp. 311–42.
Restivo, Angelo, *The Cinema of Economic Miracles* (Durham: Duke University Press, 2002).
Richardson, Dorothy, 'Narcissus', in James Donald, Anne Friedberg and Laura Marcus (eds), *Close Up 1927–1933: Cinema and Modernism* (Princeton: Princeton University Press, 1999), pp. 201–2.
Rifkin, Ned, *Antonioni's Visual Language* (Michigan: UMI Research Press, 1982), p. 14.
Rodowick, D. N., *Gilles Deleuze's Time Machine* (Durham: Duke University Press, 1997).

Rohdie, Sam, *Antonioni* (London: BFI Publishing, 1990).
Rosen, Philip, 'History of Image, Image of History: Subject and Ontology in Bazin', in Ivone Marguiles (ed.), *Rites of Realism: Essays in Corporeal Cinema* (Durham: Duke University Press, 2003), pp. 42–79.
Rosenbaum, Jonathan, *Placing Movies* (Berkeley: University of California Press, 1995).
Rutherford, Anne, 'Cinema and Embodied Affect', *Senses of Cinema* (2002) http://www.sensesofcinema.com/contents/03/25/embodied_affect.html.
Rutherford, Anne, 'Precarious Boundaries: Affect, Mise-en-scene and the Senses in Angelopoulos' Balkans Epic', *Senses of Cinema* (2002), http://www.sensesofcinema.com/contents/04/31/angelopoulos_balkan_epic.html.
Sacrifice, The [Offret], film, directed by Andrei Tarkovsky. Sweden/France/UK: Svenskafilminstitutet, 1986.
Scar, The, film, directed by Krzysztof Kieślowski. Poland, Zespół Filmowy 'Tor', 1976.
Schliesser, John, 'Antonioni's Heideggerian Swerve', *Literature Film Quarterly*, 26.4 (1998), pp. 278–87.
Schrader, Paul, *Transcendental Style in Film: Ozu, Bresson, Dreyer* (Berkeley: University of California Press, 1972).
Schwarzer, Mitchell, 'The Consuming Landscape: Architecture in the Films of Michelangelo Antonioni', in Mark Lamster (ed.), *Architecture and Film* (New York: Princeton Architectural Press, 2000), pp. 197–215.
Shaviro, Steven, *The Cinematic Body* (Minneapolis: University of Minnesota Press, 1993)
Short Film About Killing, A, film, directed by Krzysztof Kieślowski. Poland: Zespół Filmowy 'Tor', 1988.
Short Film About Love, A, film, directed by Krzysztof Kieślowski. Poland: Zespół Filmowy 'Tor', 1988.
Sobchack, Vivian, *The Address of the Eye: A Phenomenology of the Film Experience* (Princeton: Princeton University Press, 1992).
Sobchack, Vivian, *Carnal Thoughts* (Berkeley: University of California Press, 2004).
Sontag, Susan, *Against Interpretation* (London: Eyre & Spottiswoode, 1967).
Sorlin, Pierre, *European Cinemas, European Societies 1939–1990* (London: Routledge, 1991).
Sowińska, Iwona, 'Preisner: Post Scriptum', in Andrzej Gwóździa (ed.), *W Kręgu Krzysztofa Kieślowskiego* (Katowice: Instytucja Filmowa 'Silesia-Film', 2006), pp. 74–85.
Stam, Robert, *Film Theory: An Introduction* (Malden: Blackwell, 2000).
Stern, Lesley, 'I Think, Sebastian, Therefore... I Somersault', *Paradoxa*, 3 (1997), http://www.lib.latrobe.edu.au/AHR/archive/Issue-November-1997/stern2.html.
Stern, Lesley, 'Paths That Wind Through the Thicket of Things', *Critical Inquiry*, 28.1 (2001), pp. 317–54.

Stern, Lesley and Kouvaros, George, 'Descriptive Acts: Introduction', in Lesley Stern and George Kouvaros (eds), *Falling For You: Essays on Cinema and Performance* (Sydney: Power Publications, 1999), pp. 1–35.

Stok, Danusia, *Kieślowski on Kieślowski* (London and Boston: Faber & Faber, 1993).

Stoller, James, 'Antonioni's *La Notte*: Dissolution of Love', in Pierre Leprohon (ed.), *Michelangelo Antonioni: An Introduction* (New York: Simon and Schuster, 1963).

Synessios, Natasha, *Mirror* (London: I. B. Tauris, 2001).

Taussig, Michael, 'Tactility and Distraction', *Cultural Anthropology*, 6.2 (1991), pp. 147–53.

Tarkovsky, Andrei, *Sculpting in Time* (London: The Bodley Head, 1986).

Thompson, Kristin, *Eisenstein's* Ivan the Terrible: *A Neoformalist Analysis* (Princeton: Princeton University Press, 1981) p. 273.

Timm, Mikael, 'Przykazania Jako Gra', *Film na Świecie*, 3.4 (1992), pp. 59–71.

Totaro, Donato, 'Time, Bergson, and the Cinematographical Mechanism', *Offscreen* (11 January 2001), http://www.horschamp.qc.ca/new_offscreen/Bergson_film.html.

Totaro, Donato, 'Muriel: Thinking With Cinema About Cinema', *Offscreen* (July 2002), www.horschamp.qc.ca/new_offscreen/muriel.html.

Trotter, David, *Cinema and Modernism* (Malden and Oxford: Blackwell, 2007).

Trotter, David, *The Uses of Phobia* (Malden and Oxford: Wiley-Blackwell, 2010).

Truppin, Andrea, 'And Then There Was Sound: The Films of Andrei Tarkovsky', in Rick Altman (ed.), *Sound Theory, Sound Practice* (New York: Routledge), pp. 235–48.

Turovskaya, Maya, *Tarkovsky: Cinema as Poetry* (London: Faber & Faber, 1989).

Turvey, Malcolm, 'Jean Epstein's Cinema of Immanence: The Rehabilitation of the Corporeal Eye', *October*, 83 (1998), pp. 25–50.

Willemen, Paul, *Looks and Frictions: Essays in Cultural Studies and Film Theory* (Bloomington: Indiana University Press, 1994).

Wilson, Emma, *Memory and Survival: The French Cinema of Krzysztof Kieślowski* (London: Legenda, 2000).

Wilson, Emma, *Cinema's Missing Children* (London and New York: Wallflower Press, 2003).

Woodward, Steven, 'Introduction', in Steven Woodward (ed.), *After Kieślowski: the Legacy of Krzysztof Kieślowski* (Detroit: Wayne State University Press, 2009), pp. 1–16.

Youngblood, Gene, Criterion Collection DVD Audio Commentary, *L'Avventura*, directed by Michelangelo Antonioni. Italy/France: Cino Del Duca, 1960.

Žižek, Slavoj, *Looking Awry* (Boston: The MIT Press, 1997).

Žižek, Slavoj, *The Fright of Real Tears: Krzysztof Kieślowski Between Theory and Post-Theory* (London: BFI, 2001).

Index

affect, 5–7, 21, 32, 33–4, 37, 52, 65, 66–7, 116, 149, 177–9, 183, 188
alienation, 51, 53, 76, 80, 121
anamorphosis, 68–9
Andrei Rublev, 120
aura, 69

Balázs, Béla, 20
Barthes, Roland, 21–2, 52, 98, 122, 145, 174–5
Bataille, Georges, 145–6
Bazin, André, 73, 93
Benjamin, Walter, 15–16, 21, 69, 96
Bergson, Henri, 2–4, 8, 14, 20, 31–2, 35, 36–7, 38–9, 40–1, 72–3, 75, 77, 173
Bordwell, David, 23–4

cinephilia, 19–20, 61, 123
close-up, 16–17, 20, 56–7, 58, 59, 60
cognitivism, 23–4
Colebrook, Claire, 5–6, 32–3, 64–5, 95–6, 183
crystal-image, 126–7, 128

dead time, 9, 49, 77–9, 190–1
Deleuze, Gilles, 6, 20, 21, 33, 37–8, 58, 65, 69, 70, 73–4, 76, 92–3, 94, 99, 100, 104, 122, 126–7, 128, 190
depth, 53–5, 56, 57, 60, 73, 74
Doane, Mary-Ann, 2, 13–15, 17–19, 56, 57, 60, 96, 97, 98
Double Life of Veronique, The, 138
duration, 2–4, 9, 10, 32, 34, 35–7, 39, 40–1, 72, 75, 77, 78, 82, 91, 93, 95–6, 98, 99, 120, 128, 144, 168, 182, 188, 191
DVD, 2, 61, 62, 189

Eclisse, L', 74–5
Epstein, Jean, 16–17, 19

Grosz, Elizabeth, 1, 3, 35, 36, 39, 77, 173, 190

identification, 63–4, 69
imaging, 7, 9, 62, 65, 67, 69, 116, 118, 119, 123
indexicality, 15, 97–8
informe, 146

kinaesthesia, 39, 40, 93, 109

Lacan, Jacques, 157–8
long-take, 90, 91, 92, 93–5, 99

Marks, Laura, 7–8, 25, 26, 29, 31–2, 57, 69, 109, 111, 128
Massumi, Brian, 5, 6, 33–4, 177, 178–9, 183
meaning, 5, 6, 10, 21, 22, 51–2, 107–8, 115, 138, 141–2, 146, 147, 161, 168, 174, 183, 189
memory, 2, 31–2, 60–2, 73–6, 90, 99–101, 110, 111, 128–9, 158, 190
Metz, Christian, 20, 21, 26, 28, 163
mimesis, 28, 39
moments, 1, 2, 10, 14, 15, 17, 19, 25, 29, 34–5, 61
montage, 92
movement-image, 37, 92
Mullarkey, John, 1, 9, 10, 39, 40–1
Mulvey, Laura, 22–3, 61, 83, 98, 107, 120, 175, 189

music, 3, 20, 81–2, 123, 124–5, 156, 159, 165–7, 175

neo-realism, 50, 76

pace, 50, 56, 76–8, 79, 80–1, 82, 95
painting, 15, 19, 52, 53–4, 59, 60, 101, 117–18
photogénie, 13, 17–19, 20
photography, 19, 22, 23, 52, 54, 98, 174–5
psychoanalysis, 20, 26, 126, 161

resonance, 5, 68, 148
rhythm, 3, 9, 36, 39, 76–82, 90, 95, 96–7, 115, 125
Rutherford, Anne, 24, 25, 28, 30–1, 32, 40

Sacrifice, The, 115, 131
semiotics, 21
senses, 7–8, 16, 25, 27–8, 30, 31, 32, 33, 34, 108–10, 111
 touch, 8, 28, 29, 30, 32, 58
Shaviro, Steven, 26, 28, 29

Sobchack, Vivian, 7, 24–6, 27–30, 31, 32, 33, 35, 104–5, 109, 110, 126, 142, 147, 151, 157–8
Sontag, Susan, 26, 61, 121
sound, 81, 100, 106, 114, 121–4, 129, 157, 165–8, 171, 173, 178, 179–80
Stalker, 117
Stern, Lesley, 8, 13, 25, 32, 39–40, 58, 120, 188
symbolism, 70, 107–8, 111–13, 138, 144–6, 147–8, 153–4, 155, 160, 168–9, 190

temps morte see dead time
texture, 8, 55, 57, 58, 107, 109, 110, 111, 116, 118, 119, 120
threshold, 55, 102, 122
time-image, 37, 92–3, 94, 100, 104
Trotter, David, 4–5, 138, 148, 182–3

uchronia, 97, 99

Žižek, Slavoj, 68–9, 140, 141, 144, 145, 147, 153, 161, 170

EU representative:
Easy Access System Europe
Mustamäe tee 50, 10621 Tallinn, Estonia
Gpsr.requests@easproject.com